FUTURE EVENTS

A Prophecy of Coming Times

Michael H. Brown

Spirit Daily Publishing
11 Walter Place
Palm Coast, Florida, 32164
www.spiritdaily.com

The publisher recognizes and accepts that the final authority regarding the apparitions in the Catholic Church rests with the Holy See of Rome, whose judgment we willingly submit.

Future Events: A Prophecy of Coming Times by Michael Harold Brown

For additional copies, write:
Spirit Daily Publishing
11 Walter Place
Palm Coast, FL 32164
or contact: www.spiritdaily.com

ISBN: 979-8-218-30262-7 (softcover)
ISBN: 979-8-218-31638-9 (eBook)

Cover and Interior Design/Formatting by Vickie Swisher, Studio 20|20

To God the Father, in the Name of Jesus

Chapter 1

THE REPORTS COME FROM ALL OVER. There are strange rumblings, heard around the world. There are what seem like subterranean booms, or tectonic grinding. In other cases, the sounds—trumpet-like—seem to be coming from the sky. There are strange, eerie lights in the sky, sometimes near the ground, sometimes in the clouds. There are unexplained flashes of light, at times the backdrop for holy figures who, it's alleged, come to warn.

The "veil" is parting. There are supernatural phenomena. Miracles. Angels. Saints. The Virgin Mary. Above all, Christ. There are reports of weeping statues. There are those who continue to hear the "voices" of Heaven with admonitions—and warnings—for mankind.

There is also a rising tide of strangeness: Rarely if ever—in part due to the internet and social media, in part simply a product of our moment—have so many hauntings, occult crimes, unearthly creatures (see *Wisdom* 11: 15-19), and instances of demonism been reported. As a pope, Leo XIII, foresaw a century and a half ago—and now reaching a crescendo—a vault that once restrained hell had been unlatched. Any exorcist will tell you that. It has been unleashed at all levels of society. If it's not Satanists, seeking to establish an after-school club, or another classroom massacre, there are war crimes, threats of nuclear annihilation, Christians

1

slain in Africa and the Middle East, war in Israel, or felonies the likes of which history has not known; so many serial killers that one loses count; so many mass shootings that names blur, as do locations. At the same time, we're confronted by those who have decided to be a gender other than what they are—what God designated—or mutilate their bodies with bizarre piercings. Some actually try to morph (with implanted horns) into replicas of the demonic. In politics are great rancor and the threat in various nations—in Europe, North and South America, in Russia—of civil conflict. Around the globe were what the Pope, just before the attack on Israel by Hamas, called "the winds of war."

And so come prophecies from deep Africa to Italy, from South America to the American West.

"Dear children!" says the Virgin Mary at the famous apparition site of Medjugorje (October 25, 2022). *"The Most High permits me to be with you, and to be joy for you and the way in hope, because mankind has decided for death.*

"That is why He sent me to keep instructing you that without God you do not have a future. Little children, be instruments of love for all those who have not come to know the God of love. Witness joyfully your faith and do not lose hope in a change of the human heart. I am with you and am blessing you with my motherly blessing. Thank you for having responded to my call."

Lesser known seers make like pronouncements—some of them suspicious, perhaps products of the subconscious, or deceptive spirits (in this era of Great Deception), but others emanating the gravity of authenticity.

"Several civil wars raged in almost all countries," recalls a seer in Germany of her alleged visions and apparitions. "In addition, there were severe natural disasters because man misused God's Creation. The earth trembled. I saw the whole world tremble. It was the result of that sin. Heavy storms hit the earth and something fell to earth from heaven. The world briefly became Babylon—but on a grand scale. The power of mammon (devil) supported the rulers. A wave of violence swept around the globe."

"Things are going to happen fast," says another, this one in Louisiana. "It's coming. It's coming." Says a mysterious stranger encountered in New York, *"Soon the world will not be the world you know. The very artifice of your societies is false and against the accordance of God's Will. This artifice shall not last. There is going to be a major disruption in a region of the world that will affect everyone. The event to come will surprise all who have offered a prognostication, and show even recalcitrant scientists, though not all, that there is fundamental alarm in Heaven over their arrogant and wayward course. The angels have their instructions from east to west, and now a time-table has been set in motion. When the huge light is seen, I will act in a way I have not acted before."*

Many foresee an even more intense darkness on its way—spiritual *and* physical—though splitting it are Jesus and Mary, in brilliant yet soothing light. More powerful than the sun yet seen without squinting the eyes does Heaven send its messengers—Michael, mysterious strangers, angels—and their prophetic indications are as hopeful as they are alarming.

Heaven exists. God exists. There is intervention, and still time.

But what was once called a "final hour" is now less than that.

A time-table has been set in motion.

Angels have taken their positions, while God, in His ineffable mercy, waits until the last moment.

"Only those in union with God will be able to see in the darkness which so many expected and that already is upon the earth," says a "word of knowledge." *"In union with God*

comes all protection, as the dark spirits are now allowed to materialize in full due to the pretense and aspirations of man. It is a final battle. Not until the initial event will the curtain be drawn that reveals the entirety of the plan, and even then, it will be parted only slowly, in the woes of purification."

Whether Catholic or Protestant, denominational or non-denominational, even believer or not, the prophecies, the expectations, of major events are at a fever pitch and have been accompanied by natural disasters that tick upward: earthquakes, floods, "bomb" cyclones, wildfires, volcanoes, warfare, and a pandemic unlike any seen since 1918. Tellingly, that plague occurred just after famous secrets were given at that hallowed place in Portugal called Fátima where Mary appeared to the three children and gave them secrets, one of which has yet to unfold.

Barely recovering from coronavirus, humankind quickly was deafened as bombs shocked Ukraine—which one major visionary, now deceased, a man who'd spent decades in the Soviet gulag, warned is an "apocalyptic nation."

We're in the midst of historic upheaval that is only now truly beginning and will display itself in ways that at turns are startling. Yet it is important—crucial—to keep one thing in mind: if we live our lives, our *own* lives, in accordance with Jesus, in the end we will be in a place of fantastic glory. It's true: we live forever. And with strict adherence to the Faith, we avoid the netherworld and unpleasant transitional realms of the afterlife as well as calamities here on earth. *You will be conscious—and indescribably loved* —forever. After this place of trial will come realms where there's no time, no death, no final chapter. The past and future will meld into the present. Everything will be here and now. In light of that reality—and it *is* a reality—no one could be frightened, no matter what comes on earth, and no matter how "apocalyptic," for one thing we know for certain is that the world *will* end, upon death, for every one of us. When it does, all questions will be answered, the instant we even think of one. On earth, we are confounded by just about everything. We are confused by contradictions in science and government, in religion. We're not sure what foods are good for us. We can't fathom illness. We see bizarre rulings in the legal system—which in large measure has collapsed—and bizarre stories on the internet of UFOs.

Strangeness surrounds us.

In the final analysis, are UFOs true or not? What about this or that claim of the miraculous? And was Einstein really correct in all he stated? Did he have any real idea, and do astronomers, of final mysteries? What *is* the universe—the stars, the galaxies above us? Is it all mechanical, as astronomers insist, or might it be part of a spiritual dimension through which one day, upon our passing, we will traverse?

Why did God make humans? Why did He make snakes? Why is there suffering? Why is there evil?

Upon death—upon transition into eternity—everything will make sense.

"Oh, now I understand!" we will think or shout with joy about the mysteries that have most perplexed, troubled, and haunted us.

The questions are endless.

So is God's protection.

So are His patient warnings.

In that once-primitive village of Medjugorje in the holy terrain of Hercegovina—land once under control of Soviet Communists, who may once again be eyeing it (now a little city) —the Virgin Mary continues to speak. *"For years, Satan has been fighting for war,"* she says. *"That is why God sent me among you to guide you on the way of holiness, because humanity is at a crossroads. I am calling you to return to God and to God's Commandments that it may be good for you on earth, and that you may come out of this crisis into which you have entered because you are not listening to God who loves you and desires to save you and lead you to a new life* (3/25/22). *I am looking at you and I see that you are lost. I am calling all of you: return to God, return to prayer"* (4/25/22). *Your mother tonight wants to warn you that Satan is active in a special way these days. Don't allow emptiness inside of you; fill this emptiness with prayer* (February 19, 1990). *Dear children, Satan is very strong and, therefore, I ask you to dedicate your prayers to me, so that those who are under his influence may be saved* (February 25, 1988).

"Pray, pray! Do not be discouraged. Be in peace because God gives you the grace to defeat Satan (9/16/83).

"I am with you even when you think there is no way out and [when it seems] that Satan is in control (July 25, 1988). *I beseech you: withdraw in silence. Your obligation is not so much to do, but to adore God, to stay with Him* (6/24/86). *Satan is strong and with all his force wants to bring as many people as possible closer to himself and to sin."* (5/ 25/95). *In this time [he] wishes to act through small, small things, dear children. Therefore, pray!* (10/ 2/92)." A chastisement—a series of them—was coming, she said. *"It is the upheaval of a region of the world,"* Mary intoned in August of 1985, after showing a visionary that seer's first secret.

"Those who say, 'I do not believe in God': How difficult it will be for them when they will approach the Throne of God and hear the Voice: 'Enter into hell' (September 1985).

We're in a pitched, historic battle that has surprised and will *continue* to. In Eurasia, civilians are slaughtered, raped with no mercy; in Florida, Disney makes a turn toward sinful sexuality; in New York, pedestrians are brutally attacked for no reason; in Washington, D.C., politicians approve of murder in the fourth degree (some call it abortion) and Bible-toting riorters smash into the nation's Capitol; all the while, the Church travels to Golgotha. (As you will see, amazing is at least one prophecy about that!)

Whether liberal or conservative, atheist or born-again, agnostic or devotee of the Rosary (put me in that category), war is at our doorstep; the devil is trying to destroy nature. He is at war on and also with this planet—with every soul who has not signed on with him. "The combat has commenced," a famous abbot, Prosper Guéranger, said in a sermon. "The miseries of this present life are the test to which God puts His soldiers; He passes judgment upon them, and classifies them, according to the degree of courage they have shown. Therefore is it, that we all have our share of suffering. God is looking on, watching how each of us conducts himself."

It must be a time of reality. It must be a time of reconciliation. The horrible division of recent years has to end—or humankind will greatly suffer. There is never an excuse to hate. Our true enemy is the devil. His "evil" spells "live" backwards and his darkness fills the minds of those who don't read the Bible nor partake of Church charisms.

Fantastic is the degree of current evil.

Our Lady succinctly put it on September 25, 1991, just before the war in Bosnia-Hercegovina, when she said that *"now as never before Satan wants to show the world his shameful face by which he wants to seduce as many people as possible."*

Let that be our screaming headline—*true* news—a headline more important than those you see on television, internet, and in social media, The devil is no longer hiding in shadows and the extent of his manifestations can't be synopsized. Euthanasia. Witchcraft. Who would have prophesied clergy abuse, serial killers, the extreme greed of Wall Street (and Main Street, and Silicon Valley), the robotic inhumanity of algorithms and robots programmed for actual sex? Who knew that a great deception was afoot to convince humans that their true "gods" were aliens?

No coincidence was it that the destruction of New York's tallest skyscrapers came with demonic faces—visible via news photos—in the fiery smoke.

This, and far more, is what we struggle against. It is sand dwindling in the hourglass. It is a final countdown. It is the clock passing midnight. It's not something you hear from most pulpits.

TikTok—that clock.

Instead of hiddenness, Facebook.

Instead of obedience, blogs attacking the Church.

Instead of Catholicism, bishops hankering to ordain women. Schism in the ranks?

Instead of sermons that soar, YouTube rants that sink the spirit.

You will see that we have much ground to cover.

As famed Seer Maria Lucia de Jesus dos Santos of Fátima once wrote (to a priest), "Father, the devil is in the mood for engaging in a decisive battle against the Blessed Virgin. And the devil knows what it is that most offends God and which in a short space of time will gain for him the greatest number of souls. Thus the devil does everything to overcome souls consecrated to God, because in this way the devil will succeed in leaving the souls of the faithful abandoned by their leaders, thereby the more easily will he seize them."

That was said in 1957. She said the world was in the throes of a great "diabolical disorientation."

Can anyone doubt that we have seen the materialization of Sister Lucia's words in the past couple decades—and now a crystallization of it that is more intense by the day? Did this seer not point to specific Bible passages (chapters 8 and 13 of *Revelation*) that as you will see should give us all great pause? Yet said Lucia, "Father... my mission is not to indicate to the world the material punishments which are certain to come if the world does not pray and do penance beforehand. No! My mission is to indicate to everyone the imminent danger we are in of losing our souls for all eternity if we remain obstinate in sin."

This seer left us an incredible prophecy unknown to even many who have followed Mary's secrets.

There is Heaven. There is hell. There are points in-between. This should be our main preoccupation. This must be the great warning to the world.

But before it is so, we will see tremendous events, events sent by our Good God Who looks down and calls us all back in an urgent tone to His safe embrace.

Chapter 2

ALONE, IN HER CONVENT CELL, the famous Fátima seer was a tortured soul. No solace: her prayers seemed to bounce off Heaven. She was torn. Her quandary was whether to obey the Blessed Mother, who had not yet directed her to release the third part of a prophecy she'd been given, or an archbishop who was ordering the novitiate to promptly write it down and send it to him.

This was in 1944, toward the end of World War Two. Along with cousins Francisco and Jacinta Marto, Lucia had witnessed at least six apparitions of the Blessed Madonna from May to October, 1917, when they had been entrusted with those "secrets." The other two were known; they had announced the end of World War Two but a new, graver one if mankind did not reform. The end of the first one indeed took place a year after. But a second war? It would be announced, according to the secrets, by a "great sign," which, two decades later, Lucia took to be an unusual eruption of northern lights in 1938, auroras that from November into 1939 enflamed the sky from England to northern Africa, the Alps to the Rockies, seen by pilots as curtains of fire in the midst of Hitler's annexation of Austria, the first act in what became the second war.

In those first two parts—dauntingly—had been another true prophecy. Mary foretold the rise of atheistic Communism in Russia, which took place the very same year as her appearances, with Lenin's revolution of 1917, and true to her words it began to spread what Our Lady warned would be "errors" around the world.

But what was in that third part?

For the time being in the Order of Saint Dorothy (as she waited to enter the Carmelites), Lucia had received subsequent apparitions of both Mary and Jesus as the Infant, and had come to learn, from there, that the tantalizing third part should remain sequestered until 1960, when, she was told, it would become clearer (*"mas claro"*). That directive had occurred not at Cova da Iria, where the historic events had taken place, but in two Spanish cities, Pontevedra and nearby Tuy, while Lucia had bided her time (from 1925 to 1946), waiting for a return to the Serra de Aire in her beloved Portugal, the border of which she could virtually see when she stared yearningly to the horizon.

There was the almost primitive, stone-walled courtyard, overlooking equally-old tiled roofs—where the Child appeared to Lucia near a wood-latched door and small grotto rail—and her cell, austere quarters where both Our Lady and the Child materialized, from time to time, in brilliant luminance. Tuy, where she went a mere year later, was twenty-six miles away and similar, with a sanctuary calling to mind the chapel of the Miraculous Medal in Paris, the altar cloth exquisitely laced, statues striking the right balance between sanctity and entrancement, Mary looking skyward, hands immortalized in prayer (as depicted at Lourdes), Jesus subtly indicating His Sacred Heart.

Lucia's cell: indifferent white walls, the requisite chest of drawers (with just a picture of Mary on it), a dorm-issue bed, and a small, spartan desk where, in obedience to the Bishop of Leiria, Sister Lucia, who during this time was suffering a high, unexplained fever, tried to write down the secret (this was 1943), but, due to physical and emotional duress, was unable to.

The bishop insisted, fearing the fledgling nun, now in her thirties and begging to join the Carmelites, might die without ever putting it on paper. It seemed like some kind of pleurisy, the tissue of her chest walls inflamed and causing acute pain with each inhalation.

Breathing was penance enough, coughing torture. At times, mere movement of her upper body shot pain to Lucia's shoulders and like a shiv down her back. A fungus? Virus?

Not far from her mind, and the minds of those around her, was how Lucia's fellow seers—her *cousins*—had succumbed to an historic influenza that infected half a billion in 1919 and 1920, killing at least fifty million (ten times covid) and causing the afflicted basically to drown in their own fluids.

Was synchronicity playing out, with something similar and sinister now menacing the sole surviving seer?

The bishop, José Alves Correia da Silva—relentless in his quest for what became famous as the Third Secret—went to Tuy and spoke at length to Lucia, who, when he asked her to record the message, had pleadingly replied, "Reverend Bishop, I cannot do it!"

Bishop Da Silva would hear none of it. "But then, did not Our Lady tell you to follow the path I have indicated to you?" he asked, as bishop who oversaw Fátima.

"Yes," the nun had acknowledged.

"So now this is it," Da Silva said. "I ask for the glory of God and Our Lady. She does not get angry. If she is disappointed, it will be with me (*Se ela estiver decepcionada, será comigo*). She will bless your humility and obedience."

Sister Lucia had tried to visit with two priests, one of them the bishop's nephew, accompanying Da Silva, but was desperate for the seclusion of her cell.

The nun was known to often do this: seek solitude, even during Fátima celebrations. Her apprehension about granting him the secret remained for a simple, insurmountable reason: She had not received orders from Heaven to do so. Da Silva was not to return with the secret. "This created a dilemma in her conscience," according to Carmel nuns who soon after lived with her. "Whom to obey? For now, she was not obliged to do this work due to her state of health, which would continue for some time."

If, like a tortured pendulum, between improvements and high temperatures, the pleurisy were not bad enough, there was also the painful infection in her leg due to an injection.

When the seer's doctor told her they would have to excise the pus, Lucia insisted she not be placed under general anesthesia, afraid her subconscious would mutter something confidential.

The fever lasted several months. "If only my strength allowed me to, I wanted to write what the bishop had ordered me but I cannot explain what was happening to me as my hand shook and I could not form the words," she recounted. "This may have been caused by my impression that I had to write something against the orders of Our Lady, but still by obedience, I attempted several times without getting any results. Because of this conflict, I wrote to the Bishop of Lieria, telling him what was happening to me. His Excellency replied by renewing the order he had already given me, perhaps in more expressive terms, in a letter dated October 16, 1943. After receiving this letter, I wanted to write again, but I did not succeed. The Good Lord gave me orders not to tell anyone. His representative [the bishop] told me to write it. A real struggle raged within me and this is why I wanted advice and direction before writing it."

Yet God seemed silent. On December 19, Lucia wrote Bishop Da Silva, again explaining her block: how she had "tried five times and I was not able. I do not know what it is, but every time I place the pen on the paper my hand trembles and I am not able to write a letter. I think it is an unnatural nervousness because at the same time I write something different, I have a steady hand. It also seems to me that it is not any moral fear, because I have formed my conscience according to faith, believing that it is God through His Excellency who orders me. So, I do not know what to do. But in fact this caused such an impression on me that it seems I am afraid to pick up the pen for that purpose."

Back and forth was Lucia to the chapel, or on her knees next to her small bed, shedding tears. "Who knows," she wrote. "It may be the devil who wants to prevent me from this act of obedience. But I want to obey. I do not want to displease Our Lord and therefore I wait to see if He wants to give me the grace for this one day."

Outside convent walls, world war raged. The Nazis had occupied Hungary and, ominously, were exporting Jews. But America was now in the conflict, Russia had liberated Majdanek, and inmates at Auschwitz rose up against their captors at three p.m. on October 7—Feast of the Rosary—blowing up a crematorium.

Yes, there were still "death marches." There was liquidation of the Krakow ghetto.

But help was on the way.

By January 3, 1944, help was also on the way for Sister Lucia.

"I knelt beside the bed which sometimes served as a writing table, and again I experienced the same without success," recalled the nun. "I then asked Our Lady to let me know if it was the Will of God. I went to the chapel at four p.m. in the afternoon, the hour that I always made a visit to the Blessed

Sacrament because I was ordinarily alone.

"Then I knelt in the middle, next to the rung of the Communion rail, and asked Jesus to make known to me what was His Will. Accustomed as I was to believe that the order of the Superiors was the expression of the Will of God, I couldn't believe that this wasn't. Feeling puzzled and half absorbed under the weight of the dark cloud that seemed to hang over me, with my face in my hands, I hoped, without knowing how, for a response. I then felt a friendly, affectionate, and motherly hand touch me on the shoulder and I looked up and saw the beloved Mother from Heaven."

Said Mary to the nun, *"Do not be afraid. God wanted to prove your obedience, faith, and humility. Be at peace and write what they order you, but do not give your opinion of the meaning. After writing it, place it in an envelope, close and seal it, and write on the outside that this can only be opened in 1960 by the Cardinal Patriarch of Lisbon or the Bishop of Leiria."*

Loosed from her fetters, the seer was now free—indeed, compelled—to write. This she did, a letter to Bishop José that, recounting the vision comprising the Third Secret, said, "I write in obedience to you, my God, Who commands me to do so through his Excellency the Bishop of Leiria and through your Most Holy Mother and mine.

"After the two parts [of the prophecy] which I have already explained, at the left of Our Lady and a little above, we saw an Angel with a flaming sword in his left hand; flashing, it gave out flames that looked as though they would set the world on fire; but they died out in contact with the splendor that Our Lady radiated towards him from her right hand: pointing to the earth with his right hand, the Angel cried out in a loud voice: 'Penance, Penance, Penance!' And we saw in an immense light that is God: 'something similar to how people appear in a mirror when they pass in front of it' a Bishop dressed in White 'we had the impression that it was the Holy Father.' Other Bishops, Priests, men and women Religious going up a steep mountain, at the top of which there was a big Cross of rough-hewn trunks as of a cork-tree with the bark; before reaching there the Holy Father passed through a big city half in ruins and half trembling with halting step, afflicted with pain and sorrow, he prayed for the souls of the corpses he met on his way; having reached the top of the mountain, on his knees at the foot of the big Cross he was killed by a group of soldiers who fired bullets and arrows at him, and in the same way there died one after another the other Bishops, Priests, men and women Religious, and various lay people of different ranks and positions. Beneath the two arms of the Cross there were two Angels each with a crystal aspersorium in his hand, in which they gathered up the blood of the Martyrs and with it sprinkled the souls that were making their way to God."

There he—the Church—had it: If the first two secrets were spoken words, prophesying the war and rise of atheism, the third, it turned out, was solely visual.

Commenting on the secret, Cardinal Josef Ratzinger was later to claim the image represented Church persecution—culminating, after a century of torture in places like the Soviet Union, with the shooting of John Paul II. He was the "bishop in white." And though he had not been killed, glaring was the fact that the attempt on his life had occurred on May 13, 1981—anniversary of the first 1917 apparitions. Moreover, it was said the bullet penetrating Saint John Paul II's abdomen had taken a remarkable route, narrowly missing vital organs and vessels, and that a mysterious nun may have bumped the shooting hand of the Communist-sent gunman, who had fired four times. Likewise were the assertions that at the critical moment, the great pontiff had slightly bent to better see a medallion of Mary worn by a pilgrim. If nothing else, his survival seemed related to the image in the secret of Mary, overcoming the actions of a punitive angel, set to torch the world. Certainly, a gun while firing is "flashing."

But was that the whole of it? Didn't a "flaming sword," with flames that looked like "they would set the world on fire," seem to indicate something beyond a shooting, even if a Pope?

If Sister Lucia harbored those questions, she was to be further "enlightened" by a new revelation that seemed to imply, as did the original image, an event or events that related to global calamity.

For at that Communion rail in Tuy, in front of the tabernacle, kneeling before Jesus and His mother in 1944, Lucia had "felt my spirit flooded by a mystery light that is God and in Him" and according to a remembrance by her fellow nuns, *A Pathway Under the Gaze of Mary*, heard these startling words:

"The tip of the spear as a flame unlatches and touches the axis of the earth. It shudders. Mountains, cities, towns, and villages with their inhabitants are buried. The sea, the rivers, and the clouds emerge from their limits, overflowing and bringing with them in a whirlwind houses and people in numbers that are not possible to count. It is the purification of the world by sin as it plunges. Hatred and ambition cause the destructive war!'"

This was not an assassination and it did not seem to pertain, at least not solely, to World War Two. Yes, the war had not formally ended, and in fact Hiroshima and Nagasaki—involving smoke, involving clouds, and fire—occurred the following year.

But cities, towns, and villages "buried"? The sea, the rivers, emerging from their limits?

This remained in mankind's future.

17

And in some ways, it was more dramatic than the Third Secret.

Lucia recalled the rapid beating of her heart; and in her thoughts, her internal dialogue, she heard the "echo of a gentle voice" saying, *"In time, one faith, one baptism, one Church, Holy, Catholic, and Apostolic. In eternity, Heaven!"* The word "Heaven," she said, "filled my soul with peace and happiness, so that almost without realizing it, I was repeating for a long time: 'The Heaven, the Heaven!' The greatest supernatural strength passed and I wrote and did it without difficulty on January 3, 1944, on my knees, resting on the bed that served me as a table."

It was extraordinary. It told a story never previously told. It brought Fátima forth in an entirely new light. Potentially, even probably, it served as a roadmap to the future.

For years, since the release of the third secret in June of 2000, it had been believed that the last and most famous prophecy from 1917 was a wordless image, perhaps a "video-tape," that mainly portrayed persecution.

Did this "enlightenment" not seem like more than that?

While no one could be sure if the "bishop in white" portrayed in the Third Secret as being killed alluded to John Paul II or a future one, it was obvious that it aptly characterized the incredible martyrdom of bishops, priests, and the religious, along with lay believers, would face in Soviet republics as well as Eastern Europe and elsewhere. *Millions* died in prison camps, or by way of Stalin fiendishly starving Ukraine. Many more died at the hands of Nazis, who were steeped in the occult and set to construct their own "Vatican" at a mysterious old castle known as Wewelsburg. When I wrote a book with Ukrainian mystic Josyp Terelya—who had spent about twenty years in the gulag for his faith—he told me of cases whereby faithful were slaughtered as if penned animals and priests even nailed to the wall. He had spent months in solitary confinement, at times in a "freeze cell" where they tried to kill him (but for an intervention of Mary, who came to him also), and in a prison yard during winter—north of Moscow— buckets of water had been poured over his head, the water thickening to ice as Soviet guards, testing him, demanded he remove religious items from his neck (he refused).

So, there had been the "Maximilian Kolbes" in concentration camps. There had been wholesale destruction of churches across Soviet-controlled Eurasia. As during the French Revolution, church structures allowed to stand were turned into temples or museums of atheism or used as crop warehouses. Church bells were melted into bullets. and yes, many had labored like Christ at Golgotha up to a metaphoric *"big Cross of rough-hewn trunks as of a cork-tree with the bark."*

These were simple facts. They *happened.*

And the shooting of the heroic John Paul was almost certainly related to Communism, for the plot was suspected as having its origins with the Bulgarian KGB, which was under the direction of Soviet spies. The shooting occurred just before the short reign of a furtive-looking Soviet Leader, Yuri Andropov, who had been a lifer in the KGB and openly detested Rome, stating that "the Pope is our enemy"—as if in homage to Stalin, who likewise despised Rome and mocked it when he famously said: "The Pope—how many divisions has the Pope?"

Soviet leadership believed the very selection of Karol Wojtyla—coming as he did from Poland—had been an American plot to precipitate the collapse of Communism.

That was the persecution part of the secret.

Most electrifying in the secret were those words: *"After the two parts which I have already explained, at the left of Our Lady and a little above, we saw an Angel with a flaming sword in his left hand; flashing, it gave out flames that looked as though they would set the world on fire."*

Initially, the interpretation of it seemed obvious: The "sword" was a warhead, the "fire" a nuclear exchange. After all, this was an apparition that focused largely on armed conflict, Communism, and Russia—which was soon to amass the world's greatest cache of atomic weapons (albeit not as sophisticated and efficient, some might argue, as those in the nearly equally voluminous American stockpile). The secrets had warned of Russia spreading its errors and causing the *"annihilation of nations."* That had been in the first two parts of the Fátima prophecy, and did not a nuclear explosion ignite torrents of incredible fire (and "clouds"), with the potential, in all-out conflict, to literally destroy entire countries? Could not Russia wipe out all of Britain and hardly notice any warheads missing from its stockpile?

Beyond that were the coincidences. Right after John Paul II, attempting to fulfill the Fátima request to consecrate Russia, had dedicated the entire world to her Immaculate Heart (with allusions to, but not specific mention of, Russia), an explosion had destroyed two-thirds of missiles stockpiled for the Northern Fleet at the Soviets' Severomorsk Naval Base. The blast killed hundreds of technicians and took out workshops needed to maintain the missiles. Western military experts called it the worst Soviet naval disaster since the Second World War, and it was followed, was that "coincidence," in December of the same year, by the sudden, mysterious death of a belligerent Soviet defense minister and soon the rise of a pacifist named Mikhail Gorbachev who hinted at an affinity for Christianity and had been a prime catalyst for the collapse of Communism: first in Eastern Europe (starting with the Pope's homeland of Poland) and then Soviet republics themselves, including Ukraine and most stunningly, Russia itself.

Chapter 3

NO ONE EVER THOUGHT THEY'D LIVE TO SEE THIS. No expert on "Meet the Press" dared such far-fetched notions. No foreign minister, no analyst at the U.S. State Department, no history prof—not at Harvard, Princeton, nor at Oxford—had projected the fall of Communism. Truly a bolt from beyond, it could only have been orchestrated by God, Who chose to do so through an emissary named Mary.

Later, in 1993, Sister Lucia would tell visiting Filipino Cardinal Ricardo Vidal (and a retinue of eight others) that not only had the Consecration brought down Communism, but that *"the Consecration of 1984 prevented an atomic war that would have occurred in 1985."*

That was dramatic: a direct quote from Lucia, recorded by a translator, that seemed to confirm the secret's image: Our Lady halting the "flaming" angelic sword from unleashing a nuclear horror.

But now, in 1944, with Lucia's Enlightenment, it was obvious more was in store for mankind.

Without massive repentance, indicated the elucidation, planet earth would find itself with an apocalypse, unimagined upheaval, and it seemed the "Pope of the Secret," John Paul II, knew about it in 1980, when, asked outside the Cathedral of Fulda in Germany about the as yet unreleased Third

Secret, he had said, "We must be prepared to undergo great trials in the not-too-distant future; trials that will require us to be ready to give up even our lives, and a total gift of self to Christ and for Christ. Through your prayers and mine, it is possible to alleviate this tribulation, but it is no longer possible to avert it.

"Given the gravity of its contents, so as not to encourage the worldwide power of Communism to take certain steps, my predecessors in the chair of Peter preferred, out of diplomacy, to delay its publication," he reportedly added. "On the other hand, all Christians must be content with this: if it is a question of a message where it is said that the *oceans will entirely flood certain parts of the earth, that from moment to moment millions will die*, hearing this, people should not long for the rest of the secret [my italics]. Many people desire to know only out of curiosity and a taste for the sensational, but they forget that to know implies a responsibility for them. It is dangerous to want only to satisfy one's curiosity, if one is not at the same time prepared to do something, or if one is convinced that we can do nothing to prevent the misfortune predicted."

The future saint's mention of oceans flooding was not something he would have drawn from the Third Secret itself, which he read while recovering at Gemelli Hospital from the shooting months previously. It *was* something that could have come from the later 1944 addendum.

Next John Paul II, dressed in customary white, had taken out a rosary, holding it up for his questioners. "Here is the remedy against evil," he reportedly said. "Pray, pray, and nothing more! Entrust all to the Mother of God." According to *Stimme Des Glaubens*, the Pope told the small assembly that the Catholic Church was prepared for personal trials, even martyrdom—an ironic statement, coming as it did just months before an assassin shot him. That suffering was necessary, he said, "to give ourselves completely to Christ, and for Christ!" Through prayer, he reportedly added, it is "still possible to diminish this great trial, but it is no longer possible to avert it, because only in this manner can the Church be effectively renewed." When it released the third secret in 2000, the Vatican said John Paul II "asked for the envelope containing the third part of the 'secret' following the assassination attempt" and explained that on 18 July 1981, Cardinal Franjo Šeper, Prefect of the Congregation for the Doctrine of the Faith, had conveyed the secret via an archbishop serving in the Vatican's Secretariat of State. It consisted of two envelopes, one white (Sister Lucia's original text, in Portuguese), the other orange, with the Italian translation of the secret. The following August, the archbishop returned the envelopes to the Archives of the Holy Office.

The Church had often been renewed with blood, he said. It wouldn't be otherwise now. "Be strong! Be prepared! We must trust ourselves to Christ and His mother, pray often, and say the Rosary. Then, although we have done little, we have done everything."

Also privy to the Enlightenment of 1944 apparently was *Neues Europa*, a small publication that on October 15, 1963, published what it said was an excerpt of the third secret. The mysterious prophecy had been obtained from diplomatic sources in Washington, London, and Moscow after Pope Paul VI had sent it to John Kennedy and Nikita Khrushchev, in hopes it would startle them into slowing the nuclear arms race. And, indeed, soon after, pointed out the publication, an atomic test ban treaty was announced. What *Neues Europa* claimed was that a great punishment was coming to mankind in the second half of the twentieth century and that the punishment would involve a "big, big war" and that "fire and smoke will fall from the sky and the waters of the oceans will be turned to steam—hurling their foam towards the sky, and all that is standing will be overthrown. Millions and more millions of men will lose their lives from one hour to the next, and those who remain living at that moment will envy those who are dead. There will be tribulation wherever the eye can see and misery over the earth and desolation in all countries." There would be, it said, claiming to quote from the secret, "the hardest trials for the Church. Cardinals will be against cardinals, and bishops against bishops. Satan will put himself in their midst. In Rome, there will be big changes. What is rotten will fall, and what will fall must not be maintained. The Church will be darkened and the world plunged into confusion... The time of times is coming and the end of all ends, if mankind is not converted and if this conversion does not come from above, from the directors of the world and the directors of the Church. But woe, woe if this conversion does not come about and if all remains as it is, nay, if all becomes even worse."

Chapter 4

WHILE GETTING TIME-FRAMES WRONG (obvious-
ly, it didn't occur in the second part of the last century), and
while not what Lucia said was in the secret itself, it too somehow got the gist of the Enlightenment and bore stunning resemblance to a message that was "received" ten years after,
in 1973, to Sister Agnes Katsuko Sasagawa, a deaf nun in the
remote outskirts of Akita, Japan, who belonged to the Hand-
maids of the Holy Eucharist and quoted Mary—who spoke to
her from a weeping statue—as saying, *"As I told you, if men
do not repent and better themselves, the Father will inflict a
terrible punishment on all humanity. It will be a punishment
greater than the deluge, such as one will never have seen before. Fire will fall from the sky and will wipe out a great part of
humanity, the good as well as the bad, sparing neither priests
nor faithful. The survivors will find themselves so desolate that
they will envy the dead. The only arms which will remain for
you will be the Rosary and the Sign left by My Son."* As for the
Church, according to Sasagawa there indeed would be *"cardinals opposing cardinals, bishops against bishops"*—highly
similar, nearly verbatim, of course, to *Neues Europa*.

Did the cloistered nun somehow see the obscure German
publication? Did she receive it independently? Were she and
Neues Europa clued in, by different means (one natural, one
through grace) to the secret?

When the secret was finally released, in 2000, Cardinal

Ratzinger wrote in the official Vatican document, "And so we come to the final question: What is the meaning of the 'secret' of Fátima as a whole (in its three parts)? What does it say to us? First of all we must affirm with [Vatican Secretary of State] Cardinal Angelo Sodano: 'the events to which the third part of the 'secret' of Fátima refers now seem part of the past.' Insofar as individual events are described, they belong to the past. Those who expected exciting apocalyptic revelations about the end of the world or the future course of history are bound to be disappointed. Fátima does not satisfy our curiosity in this way, just as Christian faith, in general, cannot be reduced to an object of mere curiosity. What remains was already evident when we began our reflections on the text of the 'secret': the exhortation to prayer as the path of 'salvation for souls' and, likewise, the summons to penance and conversion." Likewise, before the release, many priests and Fátima experts had speculated, as did Father Joaquin Maria Alonso, that "the content of the unpublished part of the secret did not refer to new wars or political upheavals, but happenings of a religious and intra-Church character, which of their nature are still more grave." The final Fátima message, said Leiria Bishop Alberto Cosme do Amaral, "speaks neither of atomic bombs nor nuclear warheads, nor Pershing Missiles nor SS-20s. Its content concerns only our faith. To identify the secret with catastrophic announcements or with a nuclear holocaust is to deform the meaning of the message. The loss of faith of a continent is worse than the annihilation of a nation; and it is true that faith is continually diminishing in Europe."

That was certainly accurate. If he could have seen the future state of that continent—England, Germany, the quickly declining faith in Ireland—he would have been astounded. But in dismissing the notion of monumental calamities—natural and military—those who framed it as a Church matter missed the bullseye. It had to do with all religions, the world at large, all of humanity. And it *was* calamitous. It did pertain to physical peril. There were elements that were apocalyptic and seemed too specific to dismiss as metaphors. Was it mankind's—the earth's—sure destiny, etched in stone?

It was surely much of that, and a summons, absolutely, to prayer. In fact, Lucia no doubt had dedicated many prayers to the safety of the Holy Father—perhaps preventing those bullets from hitting a vital vein, a crucial artery. Prophecies in this way were conditional. They were not just to frighten or warn. They were to orchestrate prayers.

Lucia's surprising Enlightenment was Heaven *itself* explaining the 1917 vision (or part of it, the angel and flaming sword). And the picture did not seem solely of war. Nor did it seem to be entirely in the past. Most pertinent was that one key element that transcended a nuclear scenario: the angel touching—"unlatching"—the "axis of the earth." At the least, this indicated the possibility of one or more fantastic natural calamities and was more in line with what *Neues Europa* claimed and what would be prophesied at reputed apparitions in various parts of the world in subsequent decades.

Could warheads touch the axis of the earth and cause it to "shudder"?

Metaphorically, yes. Also, in a metaphoric sense, could such explosives bury "cities, towns, and villages." Oh, yes. But level mountains? Cause the "sea, the rivers, and the clouds" to "emerge from their limits"?

This was more difficult to visualize. It was true that a nuclear device, launched from a submarine and exploded near a coast, could cause the sea to exceed its limits (a tsunami), but the largest bombs possess a detonation force of about 10^{17} Joules, or several tens of megatons, whereas the earth's rotational energy, at around 10^{29} Joules, is exponentially greater. To get technical for another moment, if all the power of a nuclear explosion was focused so to push the earth in a particular direction (or try to), the energy would be less than a *trillionth* that of the rotational energy (as a science site noted, "like trying to divert a speeding car with the energy of a flying mosquito"). For purposes of comparison, the quake behind the great Asian Tsunami in 2004—a magnitude-9.3 (at more than 10^{22} Joules, roughly 100,000 times that of the largest bomb)—had shifted the North Pole by a mere inch and shortened the day by just a few millionths of a second. Thus, any effects of a nuclear blast on earth's rotation would be far below what is measurable, and even hundreds of blasts would not have a noticeable impact. The largest nuclear detonation ever recorded caused a seismic pulse of magnitude-five—exponentially less intensity than even moderate quakes.

But if hundreds, if thousands, were unleashed (Russia had 4,477 at last count, the U.S. 3,708)?

There would, of course, be no one left to record the results; even a limited exchange, perhaps ten weapons ignited by each side, would kill not just those at or near ground zero, obliterating a hundred times the area of Hiroshima, but many millions of others as clouds of radioactivity spanned great distances and fall-out tainted the rivers and oceans, calling forth *Revelation* 8:11: *"The name of the star is called Wormwood; and a third of the waters became wormwood, and many men died from the waters, because they were made bitter."* (Remarkably, the word for "wormwood" in Ukrainian was "chernobyl.")

A "whirlwind" encompassing mankind?

This a nuclear blast could cause: There were test explosions four thousand times as powerful as the one in 1945 at Hiroshima, which caused its own sort of whirlwind and occurred the year after Lucia's revelation.

Military conflict clearly was part of the 1944 revelation, and placement of that sentence (*"Hatred and ambition cause the destructive war!"*) immediately followed the events that involved rivers, clouds, and seas. If nothing else, soil and dust would be kicked up, during nuclear combat, diminishing or blotting out sunlight for years, which would radically alter the climate. There would be maddening dryness in some regions during a "nuclear winter"—desiccation—and relentless unprecedented precipitation in others, causing rivers and clouds to burst at their seams. Unmentioned was famine that would ensue as photosynthesis ground to a standstill.

But again, what about leveling mountains? Could the greatest of blasts do that?

Perhaps lesser mountains, far smaller than Everest, but so impenetrable were many that the United States and Canada had embedded military control centers (see Cheyenne Mountain at Colorado Springs) inside of them.

Could a nuclear weapon vaporize a sea, as *Neues Europa* had it?

Probably not even Lake George in New York.

Thus did it appear at least two catastrophic scenarios were described by the Enlightenment, including a natural event or series of them.

Most mysterious was the word "unlatch," which called to mind a door or hatch: the entrance to a subterranean construct. Forces below would be jarred and unloosed. *"Nature is asking for vengeance because of man, and she trembles with dread at what must happen to the earth stained with crime,"* Mary intriguingly had prophesied in 1846 at LaSalette. *"Tremble, earth, and you who proclaim yourselves as serving Jesus Christ and who, on the inside only adore yourselves, tremble, for God will hand you over to His enemy, because the holy places are in a state of corruption...*

"The seasons will be altered, the earth will produce nothing but bad fruit, the stars will lose their regular motion, the moon will reflect only a faint reddish glow. Water and fire will give the earth's globe convulsions and terrible earthquakes which will swallow up mountains, cities."

Chapter 5

NO QUESTION, THERE WERE DOUBTS about that version of an alleged LaSalette secret. Penned by seer Mélanie Calvat, it apparently had been presented in 1851 to Pope Pius IX, who—despite push-back by certain bishops—accepted and believed Mélanie's secret, telling one aide he was "terrified" by its contents. In addition to the global convulsions, a version of what Mélanie allegedly was told said, *"The Pope will be persecuted from all sides, they will shoot at him, they will want to put him to death, but no one will be able to do it, the Vicar of God will triumph again this time"*—a prediction one could see as fulfilled by the survival of Saint Pope John Paul II despite the attempt by Mehmet Ali Agca on May 13, 1981.

A more detailed version of the secret circulated in 1879. Among other things, it said, *"Woe to the inhabitants of the earth! There will be bloody wars and famines, plagues and infectious diseases. It will rain with a fearful hail of animals. There will be thunderstorms which will shake cities, earthquakes which will swallow up countries.*

"Now is the time, the abyss is opening. Here is the king of kings of darkness, here is the Beast with his subjects, calling himself the Savior of the world. He will rise proudly in the air to go to Heaven. He will be smothered by the breath of the Archangel Saint Michael. He will fall, and the earth, which will have been in a continual series of evolutions for three

days, will open up its fiery bowels; and he will be plunged for
eternity with all his followers into the everlasting chasms of
hell. And then water and fire will purge the earth and con-
sume all the works of men's pride and all will be renewed. God
will be served and glorified."

However doubtful, to many, that version seemed, one
had to step back and ask if *"thunderstorms which will shake*
cities, earthquakes which will swallow up countries," not to
mention a *"purge"* due to sin, did not ring a bell with Lucia's
Enlightenment (*"It is the purification of the world by sin as it*
plunges").

Fátima spoke of the "annihilation" of nations. It did not
necessarily mean something nuclear.

Had there not been entire civilizations in Turkey, the
Middle East, and South America that in ancient times had
vanished from what scholars conjectured had been floods
and drought (*"altered seasons"*) and seismicity? Mélanie had
directly said "earthquakes," and her mention of a yawning
"abyss": although probably referring to hell, it pried forth the
notion of a hatch.

And *"fiery bowels"*?

This vaguely recalled that *"tip of the spear as a flame"* in
the 1944 Enlightenment.

Who told Lucia this: Mary, an angel, Jesus?

What we know, getting back to LaSalette, is that a few
short years after the controversial version of Mélanie's La-
Salette secret began to circulate, another pontiff, Leo XIII,
had his own famous enlightenment, of the devil unloosed
with minions from the bowels of hell to test the Church, as indeed the Church—through persecutions and later scandal—
was to be sorely tested and would be again in the future, if the
past was prologue, if the past was a blueprint, if prophecies,
past and present, were correct.

Yes, Satan had been unleashed—as if from a hatch—but always one was drawn back to geophysics. In Rwanda I was introduced to Anathalie Mukamazimpaka, a visionary from the Church-approved site of Kibeho who, when asked what she had been shown about the future, said Mary warned that due to sins of impurity and materialism the world is headed for an "abyss" (there was that word again).

The seer then went further. "I saw mountains crashing into each other," she told me. "Stones coming out of the earth, nearly as if they were angry. I saw storms crashing against each other and fire coming from them. I don't know what this means. I was told that people are causing this and that it is coming."

It did not seem simply symbolic when she described it. It *did* seem like the fiery bowels of the earth, like something had touched the axis, like what is below, once more, had been unlatched.

For now, Anathalie like Lucia said before chastising the earth, the Lord was exhausting all His remedies in an hour of mercy.

A minute to Him was an eternity for us. And an hour—even a final one—was by His clock, which could be the duration of what seemed like a split second or an "hour" wrought in the glacial grind of geologic time.

Woe! (Also: *whoa.*)

Just as the predictions at Fátima—war, natural disturbances, sickness—were to parallel prophecies in current days, so too did developments and events, the very context surrounding the apparitions, bear similarities to our own time.

There had been World War One, which at the time of the 1917 Fátima apparitions was still in full swing, ironically the year Ukraine declared its independence.

Just as there had been Vladimir Lenin who rose to power in Russia that same year of 1917—immediately after the Fátima warning—so in our own time was a revanchivist named Vladimir, surname Putin, seeking to reclaim former Russian territories.

And:

Just as a devastating tornado struck the town of Mattoon, Illinois, in 1917, so were tornadoes in our day causing massive destruction, in a swerving climate, as "Tornado Alley" expanded south and eastward.

Just as there had been plague right after the Fátima appearances, killing millions, as sort of a prelude to the next conflict, World War Two, so was there plague now.

And just as fateful events surrounded the granting of secrets at Cova da Iria, so now were there the secrets of Medjugorje, which John Paul II called "the fulfillment of Fátima."

Tellingly, as if linking the two, a statue at Pontevedra, where Lucia had seen the Christ Child, and where the request had been made to consecrate Russia, was the same as a statue (reportedly one of special graces) at the altar of St. James Church in Medjugorje.

If the secrets of Fátima were now all revealed, none at Medjugorje had yet been made public, but they drew closer by the hour. Did they relate to what Lucia heard in the Enlightenment? So many questions. The seas and rivers emerging beyond limits was easy to envision—steadily rising seas, floods, tsunamis—and if one insisted on viewing her revelation as solely to do with nuclear warfare, it was possible to see bombs, aimed at strategic dams, causing catastrophic inundation.

But what could cause those geologic effects? And what was meant by clouds emerging from *their* boundaries?

It was the picture of a world in turmoil, a taste of which was granted with covid, and in another coincidence, it was to be recalled that the beginning of World War One was the same year as major apparitions in the hamlet of Hrushiw, Ukraine.

Hrushiw was less than a day's drive from Lviv, and during that appearance— near a miraculous, historic well in 1914— Mary sadly and stunningly had informed twenty-two peasants that they faced eighty years of war, famine, and persecution. It was a prophecy that indeed materialized with eight decades of horrible suppression until Ukraine broke free of the "evil empire" (as Ronald Reagan called the Soviet Union).

Four years before, Mary had returned to Hrushiw, witnessed in some cases by *hundreds* in a towering glow above the modest wood church on April 26, 1987—first anniversary of the horrible Chernobyl nuclear accident.

This was a hamlet more primitive than Medjugorje in its early days, with telephones, radios, and cars rare commodities. The main seer at Hrushiw, Maria Kizyn, lived, I found, upon visiting, in a primitive hovel with one room dedicated to sheltering livestock on nights that were brutally cold. Not even highway patrolmen had cars (they hid behind trees, flagging down speeders), but now they were waking from a terrible nightmare, and the Blessed Mother was there to announce it. She was observed not just in Hrushiw but a dozen or more other places: like a living tableaux at St. Paraskovey's in Pidkamin; in flaming light at a monastery in Pochaiv (Ternopil Oblast); as a radiant woman in Hoshiw (where during World War Two a 3,000-pound bell had been melted into Nazi bullets).

Near Buchach, where manifestations of Mary occurred at the end of both world wars (once more bookending Fátima), she now was seen carrying the infant Christ in a light above Trinity Orthodox Church.

At Zarvanytsya, near another miraculous well (encircled by barbed wire during the Communist years), a number of peasants testified to extraordinary sights. "One day on my way to cut wheat, I stopped to see why there was a crowd around the well," Chornij Zenovia, a saintly woman who had spent years at a Russian concentration camp in Siberia, told me. "The people said they were seeing the Holy Mother. I knelt and started praying very hard and suddenly instead of the well I saw a big glow, like a mountain, and in it I saw a lady holding a baby in her arms. The lady was in blue clothes with a white sash, and a barefooted baby was in her arms. The light was like silver. I saw this for about half an hour. On her head Mary had a white shawl. The glow was seen very often for two or three weeks in 1987, I think the autumn. The Holy Mother warned us to return to the Church and love one another."

Although the KGB moved in—unleashing attack dogs and clubbing pilgrims to the point where a number required hospital care—the apparitions continued at least through 1988, I learned from Mykola Krushelnyckyi, a factory worker who was walking up a dirt road in the evening when he spotted something in the sky over the vicinity of the well.

"I was going to the next village, approaching the river, and I saw above the forest a huge glow," he told me. "In the middle was a round picture that from the waist up looked like the Virgin Mary holding Jesus in her arms, with silver clothes. On her head was a golden crown. I returned home because I was scared. I had a feeling when she was holding the Baby in her arms that she was moving her head, bowing or looking toward the Baby. I didn't hear any sound. The light around her was like the moon. There was a cross hanging from her neck and a heart. She was rather sad. She was looking toward the sky and making this head movement."

The glowing mass, at least twice the height of a tall tree, moved north over the woods and meadows before fading behind a mountain like an ephemeral cloud.

Chapter 6

MANY WERE THE MYSTERIES IN UKRAINE. Many were the mysteries of Russia.

"I see fire," Mary allegedly told one witness to the apparition at Hrushiw. *"The villages are burning. Water is burning. The very air is on fire. Everything is in flames. If people do not convert to Christ, there will be war. There shall be conflagration."*

Was this what later occurred during the Russian invasion—or was it something yet to arrive, something nuclear?

"My daughter Ukraine," she had said, *"I have come to you because you have remained faithful to me amidst this desolation."*

Despite horrendous atrocities, Ukraine maintained faith, as too did the peasants at Medjugorje, where Communists had tried to stop the apparitions to six young seers who were to be given ten secrets. These pertained to events that would come as "warnings" to the world, a great miracle that would mystify all who came and encountered it, a "great sign" (the same verbiage as at Fátima, though these isolated, Communist-repressed peasant kids had never heard of Sister Lucy), events in the Church and at Medjugorje itself, and finally a series of global "chastisements" that seemed as massive as they were tantalizing and daunting. Not in the secrets but a forerunner was a terrible civil war all around Medjugorje, a conflict that tore Yugoslavia apart (but despite attempts at bombing the village, never touching it), leaving Medjugorje within a new set of boundaries known as Hercegovina. In these early years of apparitions, which began in 1981, and like Fátima were immediately preceded by a house-rattling storm, came however some good news: a nuclear war, it was said, had been averted due to prayer. This was stated in an unofficial message at Medjugorje in the early 1980s, when a second message reportedly had said a terrible event in a secret given seers (each destined for ten) had been eliminated or substantially reduced due to prayer.

Was the secret—or at least the nuclear exchange that had supposedly been averted—related to the "atomic war" Lucia mentioned that had been scheduled for 1985?

What was it about this part of the globe?

Why was so much at stake here?

Was it a coincidence that Ukrainians were called "white Croatians"?

And was it not noteworthy that Russia's invasion of Ukraine in 2022 would stand not only as the first such European conflict since the world wars mentioned in the Fátima secrets, but also inspire Pope Francis to consecrate Russia and Ukraine to the Immaculate Heart of Mary—precisely as had been outlined by Mary to Lucia in Tuy, specifying Russia by name, which previous consecrations had not?

Prayed the Pope (in concert with the world's bishops): "Therefore, Mother of God and our Mother, to your Immaculate Heart we solemnly entrust and consecrate ourselves, the Church and all humanity, especially Russia and Ukraine. Accept this act that we carry out with confidence and love. Grant that war may end and peace spread throughout the world. The 'Fiat' that arose from your heart opened the doors of history to the Prince of Peace. We trust that, through your heart, peace will dawn once more. To you we consecrate the future of the whole human family, the needs and expectations of every people, the anxieties and hopes of the world."

That same day, March 25, 2022, the monthly message at Medjugorje to seer Marija Pavlović-Lunetti seemed like a direct response to the action of Pope Francis. *"Dear children!"* said Mary, to repeat what I quoted previously. *"I am listening to your cry and prayers for peace. For years, Satan has been fighting for war. That is why God sent me among you to guide you on the way of holiness, because humanity is at a crossroads. I am calling you to return to God and to God's Commandments that it may be good for you on earth, and that you may come out of this crisis into which you have entered because you are not listening to God who loves you and desires to save you and lead you to a new life."* In his Consecration the Pope implored the Blessed Mother to bring peace, saying, "Now with shame we cry out: Forgive us, Lord!" In her message that same day, Mary said, *"I am listening to your cry and prayers* for peace." In the Consecration prayer, Pope Francis mentioned "the mystery of iniquity that is evil and war." In her message at Medjugorje, Mary said, *"For years, Satan has been fighting for war."* During his consecration, Francis said the prayer was coming "at this dark hour," bringing to memory the early Medjugorje messages, especially one mentioning *"the hour of the power of darkness."*

Just as the Pope named the sinfulness of mankind as leading to the war, Mary said she was inviting humanity *"to be good on earth and overcome the crisis you fell into because you did not listen to God."*

The prayer of Consecration implored Mary under several titles, including "Queen of Peace"—the title by which she is known at Medjugorje. When asked afterward about this message, Marija seemed caught off guard when the interviewer, a priest, asked if she thought "there is a danger of a nuclear world war" (or whether it was "just the devil's way of frightening"). Replied the visionary haltingly, "I don't want to go into the secrets."

Thus, if Fátima had to do with the potential for atomic or nuclear war—as it did—so, it seems, does Medjugorje.

And if Fátima left the door open too for great natural events, this could also be inferred at Medjugorje and the secrets to do with warnings and chastisements, though one had been lessened, or even lifted, due to prayer (causing one to reflect on how similar it was to the image in the third-secret, when, at least for a duration, Mary's illumination overcame the flaming tip of the angel's spear).

But other events were said to be inevitable. Save for sacrifice and prayer—*"penance, penance, penance"*—humans could do nothing; governments were incapable of stopping this. Were geophysical events held in the secrets of Medjugorje? We knew only that tremors were common to the village, with one in 2022 jolting the region more than usual, spurring fear and casting back to an old-time local sage named Maté Sego (born 1901) who was said to have predicted the events of Medjugorje, including throngs of foreigners who would radically alter the village. "Listen to me, my children!" Sego said. "Medjugorje will be very important! People will come here by the thousands from all corners of the world, people of all colors. They'll come here to pray. The church will no longer be this little church I grew up with. There will be a new one, much bigger, and it will be full. It will not even be able to contain all the people who come! Some day they will dynamite the church of my childhood, and that will be the day I die."

According to Sister Emmanuel, a French woman stationed there, that's exactly what occurred after damage from a natural event—a tremor—collapsed the steeple of the old church, which had been razed to make way for the current larger new one.

Tradition has it this—three years before the appearances of Mary—indeed was when Sego had died.

Our Lady ("Gospa") was going to come, Sego reputedly insisted, adding—and here is the relevant point: "Listen, listen to me, my children! There will be a spring right around here. A spring with lots of water! So much water that it will make a lake and our folks will own boats that they will tie to a big rock." Elsewhere Sego, a bit differently—in relating this geophysical event, which might be a great sign—was quoted as saying, "You know, I had a dream. I dreamed that I was on the Podbrdo and that from a small hole in the rocks came a small source of water. The water ran down the hill making its way between the earth and the stones until you get to the shops at the entrance of the Podbrdo that slowly began to flood. So many pilgrims together with the inhabitants of Medjugorje began to dig to divert the water from the shops but more water came out of the source to become a real stream. The heaps of earth dug by the people diverted the water on the road that leads to the mountain and the water passed the road and headed towards the plain leading to the church, and at the edges there was a crowd of pilgrims along the way. Along the water dug the bed of the stream that ended up flowing into the stream that passes behind the church of San Giacomo [St. James]: Everyone was shouting at the sign and everyone was praying at the edge of the new little river." When seers allude to the secrets (in their brilliantly elliptical way), they say a "permanent sign" will be left at Medjugorje and seen at or on Podbrdo, site of the *Gospa's* first appearances and the hill of

Sego's reputed vision.

Only a great geological shift could cause this parched landscape to suddenly bear a lake.

Any geological disturbance served as metaphor for the fissures and rockiness in current society. Lucia had said it well when, in 1970, writing to a friend, she called it a "diabolic disorientation" that was "sweeping" the world.

On all sides, vitriol. On all sides, confusion—befuddlement. Balance was a thing of the past.

At Medjugorje, Mary in May of 2022 called it an "*unclean spirit of division.* Where was the love and kindness that time and again, in various places—from Hercegovina to Venezuela, Africa to Ireland, from Argentina to Ukraine—the Blessed Mother said could forestall or even vanquish some of the "chastisements"?"

Rancor had entered the sanctuary. While Lucia was disturbed by liberal attempts to distort doctrine—profoundly concerned—at the same time the seer, speaking on March 3, 1998, with Cardinal Anthony Padiyara of India and Cardinal Ricardo Vidal of the Philippines, had said, "He who is not with the Pope is not with God; and he who wants to be with God has to be with the Pope."

A worldly approach to Catholicism had compromised the Faith. The Church was under attack on all sides, by various wolves, many sanctimonious, in sheep's clothing.

Others blatantly sinned, rejecting notions of punishment.

Yet Sister Lucia's words were very clear: "Hell is a reality," she said. "It is a supernatural fire and not physical. It cannot be compared to fire that burns wood or charcoal. Continue preaching about hell because Our Lord Himself spoke about hell, and it is in Sacred Scripture. God does not condemn anyone to hell. God gave men the liberty to choose, and God

respects this human liberty." Tellingly, the seer had added:
"Atheism is a greater instrument utilized by the devil in our
days. It is a grave sin against God that rejects His own existence and allows the practice of a variety of diabolic acts like
abortion. Communism ended, but materialism continues...
People should desire more the things of God instead of first
desiring the material things.'"

Clever was Satan, instigating celebrities such that a "reality"-show star was to parade around the Vatican in a high-
cut skirt and low-cut shirt, skintight, while her sister, another
such celebrity, traipsed up a church aisle during her wedding in what amounted to a bikini with see-through veil and
a large image of Mary halfway down its lace.

There were occult toys. Ouija was all the rage. A luxury
fashion company advertised its ware with children posed
suggestively, in one case a young girl with a blank stare holding a teddy bear strapped with sado-masochistic regalia.
Could anyone fault those who pondered a worldwide "elite,"
an underground of pedophiles, in the wake of Jeffrey Epstein
and, in the U.K., Jimmy Savile, a mega-celebrity broadcaster
and friend to royalty who, it turned out, ran a massive pedo-
phile ring?

Oh, the language. Oh the lust! The "f-word" was now more
common than "darn." Far worse was the blasphemy—God's
Name—spat freely on airwaves, ignorant, as most were, that
in 1846 at LaSalette the Blessed Virgin had warned use of her
Son's Name in swearing would lead to crop failure, famine,
and disease—which began less than a year later with the great
French-Irish potato famine (failure of the *"pommes de terre"*).

Curse words were nothing, back then, like they are now.

Would history repeat itself? And would disasters increase
proportionately, which meant exponentially? *"God will strike
in an unprecedented way,"* had said Melanie's secret. *"Woe to*

the inhabitants of the earth! God will exhaust His wrath upon them, and no one will be able to escape so many afflictions together. The chiefs, the leaders of the people of God have neglected prayer and penance, and the devil has bedimmed their intelligence."

Who didn't see the great moral dumbing-down of shepherds and their flocks?

It was a treacherous time.

In Canada a fashion company promoted the video of a woman about to commit suicide (through legal euthanasia, now available even for kids), extolling its "natural," softer way to die.

Such was the disorientation.

Lucia herself had declared, back in 1957, her mission was not to indicate physical punishments, which were sure to come if the world did not repent, but more importantly to indicate "the imminent danger we are in of losing our souls for all eternity if we remain obstinate in sin." In Belgium, just 2.5 percent of Catholics were attending church, and thousands had recently applied for formal "de-Baptism" (which the Church does not grant).

Meanwhile, vandalism against churches had skyrocketed, just as it had in Rwanda before the genocide and, hinting at its supernatural nature, three images of Mary burst into flames in Spain in incidents that didn't involve vandals around Holy Week 2023. During apparitions at San Nicolás, Argentina, Mary said that *"it is your duty to teach the Almighty's justice, and blessed is he who learns it. You must be warned, children, the plague is big. At these moments all humanity is hanging by a thread. My children, the senseless person is dead, even if alive, because he does not fear the justice of God, nor fears not fulfilling of His commandments. He wants to ignore the fact that the Lord's day and His judgment will arrive. Blessed are those who fear God's judgment."*

And at Kibeho?

"You must prepare," the Virgin allegedly said, *"while you still have time!"*

An earthquake was one thing. Massive temblors have occurred on fault lines arching from Chile to Alaska, and threats of major rocking loom over the Midwest: In 1811 and 1812, epic shaking along the Mississippi may have reached magnitude-eight and were this to recur, but farther east (say near Charlottesville, West Virginia, where rock underlay could better telegraph the seismic pulse), it would devastate Baltimore, Washington D.C., and towns betwixt, causing major damage also to Philadelphia and New York City. More than five hundred miles from the epicenter—in Boston—would be the collapse of many brick structures.

And what if bigger?

For sure, a seismic event like that causing the Asian tsunami, which flooded the coasts of at least six countries, could be described as the sea, bays, and rivers *"emerging from their limits."* When it hit, it brought a whirlwind of houses. Also, hotels. Offices. Hospitals. No question: if a similar wave hit America's East Coast—or, Lord forbid, a quake yet more intense—it would kill *"in numbers that are not possible to count."* The Asian quake-tsunami, which occurred at Christmastime (catastrophes sometimes taunted holy days; a great quake in 1964 in Alaska took place on Good Friday, and a historic quake on the day of All Saints in 1755 destroyed much of Lisbon), seemed like a sneak preview—perhaps a microcosm—of what could come. Such an event (or plural, "events") would indeed seem to jar the *"axis of the earth"* to *"shudder."*

47

And the catastrophe in Lucia's locution did not seem solely related to one region. It mentioned *"mountains, cities, towns, and villages with their inhabitants"* being "buried").

No, something was coming that would involve the whole planet (*"It is the purification of the world...!"*).

Mention of the earth's "axis" always drew alarm, for if not a metaphor, it implied a catastrophe different from what can be caused even by the fury of a nuclear exchange. Not just the surface of earth but its interior seemed involved, and while war remained a viable component of the prophesied events, and while, with Russia and China flexing muscles, the threat of such a holocaust has hardly vanished, the Enlightenment of 1944, revealed by Sister Lucia's fellow nuns, raised the prospect of both war *and* extraordinary natural disasters.

How much did such experts really know?

And what about asteroids? Could they cause the globe to "shudder"?

The earth's axis is defined by its tilt and is what determines seasons. Any change in it would alter climate. To alter it meant to somehow push it from a narrow range. Only a comet four times the size of the moon and striking a glancing blow at the equator could change the earth's rotation (according to one expert, who added there is no known asteroid that size). Emphasize the word *"known."* A fiery sword that would be! For such is the mass of earth that even a chunk of space rock as large as what some believe led to the extinction of dinosaurs would hardly budge it, tweaking the length of a day by a mere .004 seconds.

Was there such a comet or planetoid in the outer regions of our solar system? If not, might something like it wing our way from another star system or galaxy, or be out there roaming the endless darkness of space? One force right in our so-lar system that could shake the planet is the sun itself, which is 333,000 times the mass of earth with a gravitational force hard to fathom. A twitch of it could knock our planet out of *orbit*, never mind jolt the axis. If not the sun, what about a planet straying from its path, or an unknown wave of ener-gy from the cosmos? We had been lulled into complacency, thinking we knew more about space than we did—when in reality we don't really know what space *is*. During near-death experiences, many described moving not through a classic "tunnel" but instead into space, past planets and stars and toward light that would sound to an astronomer like star clus-ters and to others like mystical cities of God (levels or king-doms of Heaven). The very luminosity of nebulae seemed like they could spark life. Photos taken through telescopes showed formations with uncanny resemblances to spirits. Cosmic "clouds" formed silhouettes. Faces took shape. Rays of light formed "wings." In other cases, the traces of space looked diabolical.

Was the vastness mostly "space"—empty—or did it har-bor other dimensions? There were clusters of galaxies—hun-dreds or thousands—that wandered "like lost souls, emitting a ghostly haze of light," said one science site. "A recent infra-red survey by the Hubble Space Telescope suggests that these stars have been wandering around for billions of years."

Translation: anything could happen.

We are not even sure how large the solar system is. For there are comets and asteroids—millions of them, some as large as Pluto—beyond the known planets and exerting un-told effects. The closest star was calculated as twenty-five tril-lion miles distant.

We really had little idea of much. We didn't fully under-stand our own bodies—not by a long shot. New life forms on

49

earth were still being discovered. No one knew what all was on the ocean floor. We were still dissecting cells. We were baffled by the common cold—viruses, bacteria. Could not an unseen undiscovered force wreak havoc with the earth's axis?

Chapter 7

BUT WE KNOW THIS: Parts of ocean floor we *have* explored harbor entire mountain ranges, some taller than any on our surface, higher than Everest.

And some of those are of volcanic origin—with a recent study cataloging 19,325 small new ones.

All of earth—oceans, continents—sits on tectonic plates in constant grinding movement, responsible for land masses separating or joining each other, as South America may once have been joined to Africa and North America to Eurasia. There were seven such "plates": the Eurasian one carrying two continents. Just as we had (at best) vague knowledge of the cosmos, so too were we in the deep when it came to potential tectonic events. We did know this: a major tectonic event could "touch" or "unlatch" the tilt of earth.

And of late the interior of the earth was showing signs of unsettlement, which Anathalie at Kibeho saw as colliding boulders, great sparks as mountains "crashed into each other."

Most feared: the tectonic boundary known as the "Ring of Fire" that runs from Australia and the Philippines up through Japan and finally Alaska, swooping down the coasts of Canada and California to Mexico and the volatile western coast of South America, most notably Chile. On that ring had been born many classic pagan cults: aboriginal ones in Australia, Oriental beliefs in Japan, the dragon in China (breathing flames), the rituals of Eskimos, the Indian-paganism-turned-New Age that plagued the coast from the state of Washington to southern California, the sacrificial rites of Indians in South America. Many of the most momentous quakes and volcanic eruptions had occurred along the "ring": seventy-five percent of the 450 *known* volcanic eruptions and ninety percent of significant earthquakes.

So it was plain: shaking of the earth and the fall of fire—cosmic inflammation—could be connected. A second seer at Kibeho had reported Mary, referring to coming events, had once said, *"Where will you go when the fire is everywhere?"*

And then there was the great saint, Padre Pio, who, questioned about the future, said: "Can't you see the world catching on fire?"

These then were possibilities that could be drawn from what Lucia had dramatically revealed to fellow nuns who made it public in their largely unknown biography of her. That excellent book, with somewhat quick mention of the Enlightenment, raised this question: Why had there been so much hype around the Third Secret and so little around this supernatural explanation of it?

Had the media nothing to say?

The Vatican?

Did no one see it?

Did it seem too unnerving: "apocalyptic"?

Or was it simply the disregard for mysticism held by a world and Church that had plunged into scientism, veering from what Paul (*2 Corinthians* 11:3) called "the simplicity and purity of devotion to Christ."

Chapter 8

THIS MEANT THE GARDEN OF EDEN was not just sexual purity; it wasn't just an allusion to occult knowledge and disobedience; it had to do with scientism, the mindset and intellectuality, whether secular or theological, that discounted supernaturality—what Paul VI called the "smoke" entering the Church.

In that mindset, anything prophetic was "end-times" fabulism, melodramatic, the stuff of superstition, and yet it was difficult to read the Fátima Enlightenment and not ponder, even only at a scientific level, if something inside of the earth—the theoretical "molten" core—was shifting in a way that would tilt the earth or affect its rotation, at the same time shaking loose volcanoes and causing tremendous quakes. It was the great mystic Maria Esperanza who'd once said, "The earth's core, it is not in balance."

The upshot: we had no idea what the most dramatic effects could be. Scientists weren't even sure what the core was like.

But earth changes?

The history of geology was full of those, and it was scientists themselves who theorized a time when Antarctica was at the equator and the Western hemisphere was welded to Euro-Africa. Magnetic effects, including from the sun, could cause the crust to liquefy, jolting and shifting the surface. Some believe that massive crustal shifts occur every six to twelve thousand years, placing it in line with the biblical reckoning of when the "world" (as we now know it) was formed. However old the earth, the key question is whether the earth's molten core and crust are on the move again. If so, this would not only affect the geographical poles—causing the planet to tilt more one way than another—but, depending on the extent, also cause massive seaquakes, volcanic disruptions, profound, even radical changes in weather patterns ("the clouds emerge from their limits"), or even reshape coastlines and continents, altering the surface of the earth.

Some believe movements in the molten iron or other parts of the earth's innards would cause loud explosions, and whether or not it's related, loud, unexplained "rumblings" or "booms" have been reported in recent years around the world. These sounds, in such places as Idaho, South Carolina, Nevada, New Mexico, Texas, South Dakota, and New Jersey, are often eerie, with investigators at a loss to determine if the origin is subterranean or atmospheric. At the same time, Eskimos in Canada have observed changes in where the stars are now seen and the position of the sun as it rises. That has been accompanied by higher temperatures and melting of permafrost—the ground they stand on—which has caused the destruction of ancestral ice cellars and telephone poles to collapse.

Something was underway. Unusual gamma radiation was hitting the earth—perhaps from the collision of two stars—and in 2022 an angel allegedly told a prophet "that some energy fields of the earth are beginning to shift and said this is one of the reasons there is such a change in the climate. He said soon there will be a change that causes a drastic increase in earthquakes. In this time there will be a major significant war that will come to India, and a sign of it will be a major earthquake in India before that. He also said that China will continue to advance its plans to attack Taiwan, but they will not stop there. Right before he left, he said, 'Tell the Lord's people their prayers are not in vain."

Accompanying the geophysical effects were sociological ones. A spirit of disruption, much of it caused by the pandemic, was afoot far above the molten core. There was a sense of unsettlement, bitterness. A spirit of division. People wanted to turn over every table they saw. If there was a bronze bull near Wall Street, there was also one plowing through the American psyche. Respect for scientists, professors, judges, politicians, media, banks, and public officials plummeted and disdain was reaching a boiling point. As was prophesied during a charismatic event at the Vatican (way back in 1975), institutions were crumbling. Said one charismatic priest connected to the meeting: "Days of darkness are coming on the world, days of tribulation... Buildings that are now standing will not be standing. Supports that are there for my people will not be there."

Few listened. There was no reality but the reality concocted by "rationalists" who (in reality) were irrational. Only information amenable to one's notions was tolerated—everyone was in a cyber bubble—with roaring denunciations of contrary opinion. Bricks were thrown through storefronts in Manhattan, while protesters swarmed the U.S. Capitol.

The great storms—societal as well as meteorological—were arriving. Since Hurricane Andrew, which once seemed like the ultimate, a number of cyclones rolled ashore with yet more violence, hitting one after another.

Year after year, there were historic fires. Drought. Followed by record rain. Year after year, more homes slid into the Pacific.

In Europe, rivers were shriveling in Italy, Germany,

France, revealing boats sunk centuries or even millennia before. The Danube. The Rhine. In China, the Yangtze. The same was occurring in Israel to the Dead Sea and River Jordan where Jesus had been baptized.

The extremes reflected a society that had let a famous football star get away with murder, that had six-year-olds learning about sex toys, that had governments quick to pay for men to become women and women to become men or no gender at all.

When Cardinal Carlo Caffarra was commissioned by John Paul II to establish a pontifical institute for marriage and family, he'd written Sister Lucia through her bishop. Neither he nor anyone was allowed to do so directly. "Inexplicably, since I did not expect a reply, seeing as I had only asked for her prayers, I received a long letter with her signature, which is now in the archives of the Institute," the cardinal later recalled. "In that letter we find written: 'Father, a time will come when the decisive battle between the kingdom of Christ and Satan will be over marriage and the family. And those who will work for the good of the family will experience persecution and tribulation. But do not be afraid, because Our Lady has already crushed his head.'"

Victory was etched into destiny. Nothing and no one—no force—could alter that. God always wins. If He stood as the Empire Building—or all the skyscrapers in Manhattan, or in the world, one stacked upon another, from Dubai to Beijing—Satan was in comparison less than a grain of sand.

But as yet, this was not apparent. And by all indications, that observation was substantially in the future—perhaps not until major events, an angel unlatching the axis.

The assaults on marriage, children, and heterosexuality were relentless. No longer had He created purity. No longer had He created gender! There was now the threat of prosecution-persecution for "anti-gay" morality, which meant one could no longer fully practice Christianity, Judaism, or Islam, for that matter. Around us sprung folks who, like dark ritualists, had covered their bodies and faces with piercings, tattoos, and implants (in several cases, horns to resemble Satan), and it was no accident that satanists and witches championed abortion as a sacrament and gender confusion as a tenet. Unabashed devil worshippers held conferences, established after-school clubs, and formulated city council prayers. When a fashion firm—catering to the rich and famous—ran ads of kids in provocative pose, with tributes to Baal and teddy-bear-like stuffed animals strapped with the accouterments of sado-masochism, one was forgiven for believing it couldn't get worse, though, by all reckonings, it would and was. Scientists labored to create artificial wombs for homosexual parents while in some quarters there were moves to encode three-member marriage. *Leave It To Beaver* was to these folks what a Crucifix was to a vampire. It was hard to envision a more fundamental assault, save for outright outlawing the traditional family. All of this was a backdrop for the most heinous sin since abortion: euthanasia. In Canada, a doctor prescribed a lethal drug for a sixty-five-year-old who was suffering *depression*. In Belgium, new rules allowed euthanasia for kids older than one. Satan would not win, but it was a time for glee. Once sex was detached from pregnancy, women's liberation could construct "its own ethics on the ash-heap of puritan morality," promised Lawrence Lader, a found of the pro-abortion movement. Ultimately, said Lader, the "most radical feminists" wanted "an even more sweeping revolt—the end of the nuclear family."

Who, in 1917, foresaw the day when, through medical procedure, a man could carry a child to term or a surrogate nurture a "designer" embryo modified to suit the tastes of "parents"? Who foresaw a famous actress announcing that she was both mother and father? Who'd predicted a male cabinet secretary in the United States who, with "husband," was raising twins? Or a sordid trial starring a revered "superstar" who was best friends with an actual satanic "priest" (see: Johnny Depp and Marilyn Manson)? Who thought Christians would become disoriented to the point of putting politics above religion, guns above plowshares, cultural causes above Christianity? Oh, how proud would be Herod!

Who saw kids gunning down classmates or an erstwhile young man slaying shoppers at a supermarket with an automatic weapon?

Who imagined the horror of Mariupol and the Donbas in Ukraine and the gall of an Orthodox Russian patriarch who pronounced the slaughters as a Christian cause?

Who envisioned that church after Catholic church would be defaced, with statues of Christ and His Blessed Mother decapitated?

(Oh, a warning was this, for precisely that occurred in Rwanda shortly before a historic genocide!)

Who saw physicians coaching those who wanted to die via remote computer chat?

Suicides were being live-streamed. In some cases, so were shootings. How wonderfully open was our culture. How tolerant!

By the Grace of God, Lucia had been able to pass from this life in 2005, before it got *really* bizarre. If clinics of abortion were closing (praise God), were we prepared for the killer pills that would take their place (via mail) and perhaps one day Amazon (which already sold witchcraft supply kits and at one point an actual human finger)?

No. We had not been ready.

Who had foreseen talk of bionic humans or a hybrid that was part human, part chimpanzee?

Chapter 9

AND SO THERE WOULD BE THE SPEAR OF THE ANGEL, the unlocking of a hatch. And so there would be bursting clouds, rollicking seas.

And so, there would be fire.

That had also been indicated at Akita, Japan, where, to repeat, the nun heard a tearing statue of Mary warn that *"if men do not repent and better themselves, the Father will inflict a terrible punishment on all humanity. It will be a punishment greater than the deluge, such as one will never have seen before. Fire will fall from the sky and will wipe out a great part of humanity, the good as well as the bad, sparing neither priests nor faithful. The survivors will find themselves so desolate that they will envy the dead."*

They were not serious words. If true, they were *terrifying* ones. Not with Noah? Not at Sodom, or in the time of Moses, not at Pompeii, not with the Black Death, nor Germany, with Hitler, not Nagasaki, nor with the Asian Tsunami? A punishment never seen before?

To find oneself "desolate" meant to find oneself in a place that was bleakly "empty and bare"—the exact dictionary definition. Synonyms? "Unpeopled." "Barren." Would there be entire regions devoid of life forms above those of viruses, bacteria, insects?

Fire from the sky most brought readily to mind nuclear conflict, a comet, or a mega-volcano, with the nuclear possibility paramount when one considered where Akita was located (Japan.) Vladimir Putin and Kim Jong-un had openly threatened this. *"Know that men will drink the poison prepared by their own hands,"* a seer in Brazil quoted Mary as prophesying. In the Italian city of Civitavecchia, a statue of Mary brought from Medjugorje shed tears of oil and blood and those who owned it claimed to have messages that among other things said, *"Humanity is facing a looming tragedy. He doesn't realize he's about to get into a world war"* and *"My children, the darkness of Satan now darkens the entire world and also darkens the Church of God. Prepare yourselves to live what I had revealed to my little children of Fátima."*

War was the major threat, though certainly not the only potential for globally devastating pyrotechnics. Few realize the famous mega-volcano at Yellowstone once erupted with a force that covered what are now nine American states with more than six feet of ash, heavily dusting the rest of the continent and shutting off sunlight globally, thus bringing photosynthesis—plant life—to a grinding halt: perhaps for decades. In a full-scale eruption, ash would be an inch thick from Los Angeles to Chicago, from the Dakotas to Arizona, and several *feet* deep in large swaths of Colorado, Wyoming, Montana, Idaho, and Utah. Moreover, odds were great that the supervolcanoes most feared (such as Yellowstone) wouldn't be the ones to blow, and if they did, would be smaller eructations.

Those were the odds. The best bet was to expect the unexpected. The best prediction was in prayer. There had been only forty-seven supervolcanic explosions known to history. The last (if we believed dating methods) were in New Zealand around 24,000 B.C. and the lurch of tectonic plates that caused a larger detonation in Indonesia, fifty thousand years before that, leading to a "global winter" that almost erased the nascent human population (or so history told us). Not many knew there'd been eruption of a much smaller volcano in 1815 that with its atmospheric effects damaged crops worldwide, leading in America's Northeast to the "year without summer;" nor that in 1883, the year before Pope Leo's famous vision of hellfire, and three decades before Fátima, there'd been another in the same Indonesia.

Volcanoes, especially on the ocean floor, were a major possibility, perhaps a series set off at the same time by a jolt to the planet's axis.

Were there other forms of fire that could "fall"—perhaps a flare from the solar orb or some other astronomical phenomenon? Another question: might falling "fire" be a metaphor for a comet or meteorite storm, or—man-made—an electromagnetic attack?

There was also the Church in crisis. Catholicism faced one challenge after another, in pews, in the pulpits, in episcopates. To repeat, the Akita message had foreseen *"bishops against bishops,"* and nowhere was this crystallized as in Germany, where prelates, meeting in a "synod," had all but created a schism, one threatening to become a literal, expanding one. In essence many bishops there were declaring that despite its 2,000-year history, the Church should suddenly conform to societal whims, especially the "rights" of gay betrothal and transgenderism. They also fancied the idea of female priests and sought to weaken the authority of bishops, handing more power, even sacramental authority, to laity.

In effect, there was an attempt at turning Catholicism protestant ("synod" was a Presbyterian term) in the same country that had produced Martin Luther.

How many knew that as a seminarian, poor Luther had suffered diabolical seizures? How many realized he'd been tormented by the devil on his deathbed? How many knew that he had posted his 95 Theses on Halloween (October 31, 1517)?

While Rome stood firmly against the German attempt, the Vatican was burdened by arcane bureaucratic formality, overwrought tolerance, and polysyllabic lingo that muddied the water. Some legalese was understandable: situations could be complex. But the Church's vertiginous approach since the "Age of Enlightenment" (fashioning of seminaries after secular colleges) was summed up by titles of scheduled events such as the "First Session of the Synod on Synodality for a Synodal Church (in October 2023)."

A tongue twister. A brain teaser. There were endless examples.

This much was beyond debate: the Church was not speaking with the simplicity of Christ.

The Vatican was ground zero for controversies evoked by both liberals who sought radical change and conservatives who ignored precepts in the Bible, attacking the Magisterium as if it were a political party. That was problematic not only from the standpoint of Scripture ("Obedience is more important than sacrifice," said *1 Samuel* 15:22), but, for the legal-minded, of canon law.

Yet in the political circus of current times, Popes were viewed as fair targets, even accusations of heresy (which was confusing in that it was the Magisterium that owned authority for making such declarations).

There was that, the rancor. Some Vatican wounds were "friendly fire," self-inflicted. There was little question that at times Pope Francis, due in part to Argentinean flair, had difficulties communicating, with impromptu remarks that could seem contradictory because they were not quite brought to completion. So it was, on the return from papal trips, speaking to the press aboard the Vatican plane, that major controversies erupted. When asked if he'd allow a repentant homosexual into a seminary, the Holy Father had infamously answered the question with another ("Who am I to judge?"), and while on more than one occasion he had admonished seminaries *not* to admit men who had homosexual proclivities, his attempts at compassion, free-wheeling, sometimes awkward, were taken out of context and misrepresented as support for sodomy.

It was a difficult way to start a papacy, and on other trips the Pope seemingly besmirched Medjugorje or at least those seers still claiming regular messages (cracking more than once that Mary was "not a postman)"—while at the same time accepting and lauding the final report by a Vatican Commission, following years of intensive investigation, that declared the first week of apparitions on that hillside in Hercegovina to have been real. Official verdict: Mary had appeared there.

In all that were seven Church-authenticated apparitions, one more than the six accepted by the Vatican at Fátima.

He was a complicated pontiff, was Francis, on the one hand friends with a notoriously liberal Jesuit priest, conferring the red hat on liberal U.S. clergy; open to allowing divorced to receive Communion; perhaps open also to a limited number of married priests in the Amazon, where clerics were in desperately short supply; and placing restrictions on Latin Mass everywhere. Yet he was close to Pope Benedict, whom he called Benedict a "saint" (and to whose side he rushed when the emeritus pontiff died), and while the Pope was widely denounced for allowing a pagan idol Pachamama when Amazonians (who revere it as an earth-mother) brought it on a trip to the Vatican (he replaced a planned prayer with an *Our Father—"deliver us from evil"*—instead of ordering the idol out), Francis constantly urged Catholics to be vigilant when it came to the devil. No pontiff in recent memory had warned about evil spirits more frequently (for demons sought to "ruin everything," said Francis, and came in "well-mannered" disguise).

Indeed.

The greatest challenge to the Church at this point was external: the steep rise of secularism. By the droves young people were forsaking the Christianity of their baptism and when asked their affiliation, proudly and loudly chose "none."

They were "spiritual" but not "religious," was the rationale. Others made no pretense—outright declaring themselves atheists, or at best agnostic, which again hearkened to Lucia: In 1998, during the reign of the great John Paul II, in a final message to visiting cardinals, she warned, to repeat, that "atheism is a greater instrument utilized by the devil in our days. It is a grave sin against God that rejects His own existence and allows the practice of a variety of diabolic acts like abortion."

Chapter 10

IN THE CONFUSION, IN THE MAELSTROM, in a small town called Sievernich, in Westphalia, in Germany, was a seer who brought the Church crisis into sharp relief during dramatic visits from the Virgin Mary, the Archangel Michael, and, allegedly, the Lord.

Tacitly approved by her local parish, under the watchful eyes of the current bishop, she received her apparitions on church grounds, a pleasant, peasant woman who still lived on her parents' farm (with husband and son, technically a hamlet called Düren), and was of particular interest because she'd met in Rome with Benedict XVI when he was Cardinal Josef Ratzinger (prefect of the powerful Sacred Congregation for the Doctrine of the Faith, which, among other issues, oversaw mystical claims) and during the 2004 visit mentioned a secret she allegedly had been given.

Immediately after, Manuela was summoned by Ratzinger's office to return and present her secret the next day to Saint John Paul II himself (February 11, feast day of Lourdes).

More than fifteen years later, on October 30, 2021, Manuela was told she could make the secret public and did so immediately, revealing intriguing words. Some had to do precisely with the Church, others with prayer. Much involved coming world events. She started with a description of how it all came about.

"In the parish garden [at Sievernich], I was supposed to wait for the Blessed Mother, Mary the Immaculate," recalled Manuela. "I waited for her in prayer. We were standing directly behind the vicarage in that garden when three bright flashes appeared at intervals in the sky above.

"I was afraid those lightning bolts would hit me. I saw a bright oval light in it. From this light emerged Mary, the Immaculate, who floated down to me on a cloud. I saw Our Lady descending towards us on a golden ray. She then stood to the left of the altar, wearing a light blue cloak and a white dress underneath. The cloak featured gold trimmings at the hem. In her hands was a golden rosary. She had folded them in prayer. She was standing on a cloud and had a golden rose on her left foot. Now she looked at us.

"I felt different than normal, as if electrified. Something extraordinary was happening to my body. Mary beamed and smiled at me sweetly, greeting and blessing me and coming very close. I saw that she wore three keys on a gold ring.

"She took the first key from this ring and put it in my right hand. It was red. Now she went back a bit and opened her coat. With the first key I saw something like a movie flash by very quickly, but somehow I was involved; I can't describe it any other way.

"I saw hell now, and it was abysmal: very dark and cold and almost empty. I only saw its master [Satan] and the darkness. Then I saw the earth. I saw Islamist groups in different places, organized and carrying out several attacks and atrocities in all parts of the world.

"A terrible persecution of Christians by Islam began. I saw the Christians of the Middle East and their martyrdom. Muslims asserted their claim to power, and for a short time, it looked like they were going to win. [In the vision] the Church of Christ suffered materially and many priests and Christians, religious, were killed because they loved and truly followed

Jesus. An Islamist was elected to the head of government in Germany. The Catholic Church was in dire straits because many priests no longer followed Jesus.

"The Church stood before decay—its own destruction. Upheaval followed upheaval. There was a short time of terror—a brief reign of terror. Sin reigned. What was in hell was released in all its forms on earth. Several civil wars raged in almost all countries," went on the visionary. "In addition, there were severe natural disasters because man misused God's Creation. I saw the whole world tremble. It was the result of that sin. Heavy storms hit and something fell to earth from heaven. The world briefly became Babylon, but on a grand scale, and the power of mammon (devil) supported the rulers. A wave of violence swept around the globe."

During the secret, claimed Manuela, a map materialized and Mary dropped a rose ("as willed by God") on three nations displayed in it: Germany, Argentina, and Italy. Manuela took the first rose as an indication of a Pope who would be from Germany (as it turned out, Cardinal Ratzinger himself); the second a prediction of Pope Francis (Argentina). But what, precisely, I wondered, did the third place—*Rome* mean?

"I don't know," Manuela answered. "I think it might also be for the Church—maybe the next Pope will be Italian, from Rome—or something there."

"The cloud on which the Mother of God stood had now become a [revolving] globe," she said in her previous recounting. "The boot of Italy was approaching. I saw the city of Rome and the Vatican. Then I saw a meeting room where many cardinals were sitting, debating. The discussion was about standardizing the celebration of Mass without the Eucharist. Only one loaf of bread is to be broken, together with the congregation, since many do not believe in the Eucharist."

The apparition went on for months. Then, in 2005, Our Lady bid farewell, according to her translator, Dr. Michael

Hesemann, a respected scholar and on occasion papal advisor from Düsseldorf. According to Hesemann, it was on October 30, 2021, twenty years after she'd received it, that Heaven freed Manuela to release the secret. "She said, *'Dear children, even if you are also being tempted, especially in this earthly time, do not stop praying. I am with you. I can't tell you often enough: Call me children if you need help! I'm here for you, children!'* said Dr. Hesemann. "That appearance of the Infant, it turns out, was a harbinger. For thirteen years, there was no public apparition—until November 2018, when the Holy Infant of Prague recommenced alleged appearances. *'A severe time will come, harder than ever before,'* Jesus said. *'Many souls will err and lose their faith. I come to convert the sinners. I am the king of Mercy.'*"

On December 2, 2019, the Lord allegedly announced "three difficult years," and indeed it was weeks before the onset of Covid-19.

While the pandemic, masks, vaccines, and lockdowns (and Manhattan a ghost town) dominated headlines, other events occurred. One, in Westphalia, July of 2021, Manuela predicted a day before: extreme rainfall that beat down on Germany, Switzerland, the Netherlands, and Luxembourg (but not Sievernich, which, though near the epicenter of flooding, was miraculously spared).

Raging rivers. Creeks bursting their banks. Mudslides down hillsides.

Some of the regions affected had not seen rainfall of this magnitude, it was estimated, in a thousand years.

Nor was Europe alone. Cyclones blasted India, typhoons in the Philippines, and landslides in Asia. As for voodoo-drenched Haiti: a quake killing two thousand was followed by a tropical storm; in the U.S. a tornado touched down in Kentucky, sweeping into six states the same year as Hurricane Ida, a category-five, slammed Louisiana (no stranger either to voodoo).

In California, like clockwork, wildfire, and soon also, Hawaii.

On April 25, 2021, Manuela had a vision of the Holy Infant sprinkling several countries with His Precious Blood.

"Many do not understand me," the German housewife heard Him say. *"Worried about their lives, they do not see how Satan tries to lead them into a war. This spark of the adversary could inflame the entire world. This is why I am asking you for an act of reparation. This spark of evil can become a scourge for the whole earth. Pray, sacrifice, do acts of reparation."*

"As the priest raised the chalice of the Precious Blood of Christ, I saw the Infant Jesus floating over the chalice," recounted the seer. "He plunged His scepter into the chalice like an Aspergill and sprinkled some of the lands of the earth which I now saw arranged around the chalice. It was Russia, Ukraine, America, Europe. He sprinkled each land three times with an intent expression on His face. I worshiped the Lord. When I received the Holy Host, it beat like a heart three times in my mouth. Then I saw the Infant Jesus standing in front of me.

"Now He wore a simple but brilliant white robe embroidered with small red lilies and golden borders. Around His Head I again saw the halo with three overlapping rings in it. He shone beautifully golden. The Infant Jesus comforted me and put His hand on my shoulder. She claimed the Lord then placed "a white, rectangular stone at my feet."

An "aspergill" is a synonym for "aspersorium"—bringing to mind the Third Secret of Fátima, which depicted that vision of *"two arms of the Cross"* and beneath it: *"two Angels each with a crystal aspersorium in his hand, in which they gathered up the blood of the Martyrs and with it sprinkled the souls that were making their way to God."*

In 2019 the Lord told this visionary, *"I have given you the standard of My Precious Blood, which has 'The children of God, the apostles of the end times' as a sign. Where this banner of My Precious Blood flies, the commandment of the Eternal Father reigns and is preserved in love. My little apostles may also bear this mark in the tribulation. The time of the apostles of the end times has come. Come, rest on My Heart and refresh yourself for a moment and taste what it will be like in My Kingdom."*

In August 2021 came one more message, this saying: *"Russia may become the scourge for your people."*

"When the winter comes, Jeremiah will sing his lamentations again."

Chapter 11

THIS IT DID, and the use of an atheist nation as a scourge, specifically Russia, had been a central theme of the Fátima secrets as happened with Lenin and Stalin and now another scourge came as an awful Russian invasion took place during 2022.

This was led by another Vladimir, surname Putin, and while many had lauded him as standing against the undeniable disintegration of Western moral values, seeing him as a strongman-savior—reputedly, a devout Orthodox close to the patriarch, even bathing in frigid waters on the Epiphany as per Eastern custom and lighting candles to Marian icons—it could not be forgotten he was also a former agent of the KGB whose specialty of propaganda (including posing with various props and generating "fake news," which he would later marshal into social media) and assassination: Political opponents met very suspicious deaths, dozens, begging the question of how an authentic Christian could so audaciously flaunt the Fifth Commandment. Goebbels in Germany had been right: the bigger the lie, the more people would believe it. America was finding that out. There was great demonic power in prevarication. A charisma of pretense had assumed a life of its own. Only in the new climate of virtual reality could a "Christian" mow down and pulverize civilians.

In the early days of Medjugorje, Mary had been asked about Russia and supposedly had said: *"It is the people where*

God will be most glorified. The West has made civilization progress, but without God, as if they were their own creators."
And so that might turn out to be the case.

But for now, the word "supposedly" was key, and there was not just Putin but the distressing fact that Russia led the world in its rate of abortions, and, despite hype, church attendance was far lower than in North America.

Too, in Ukraine, was a war that saw unimaginable suffering, death wrought not just against opposing military personnel—conscripts—but elderly, women, and children.

Such was not the work of a Christian nation.

The U.S. had its war sins. The photograph of a naked little Vietnamese girl screaming as she ran during a napalm attack, the chemical scalding her, had become an iconic poster against war. Although the Viet Cong who had started it, it was American companies that manufactured napalm as well as Agent Orange, which caused thousands of birth defects among civilians and during manufacture or use as a herbicide contaminated America's own land with dioxin, one of the most lethal compounds ever synthesized.

There were other examples: America's consumerism, financial charades, and obsession with luxury, sex, and entertainment. These and other transgressions had spiraled out of control.

But neither America nor any nation in the West had so ruthlessly and massively, methodically, murdered civilians.

The world was aghast. The Pope called it the "third world War." And his warnings on the devil continued into Christmas of 2022, when he urged watch for "refined" and "well-mannered demons." This was in fact the way Satan was reforging his ranks: as cultured players both in daily life and on the world stage. Good had become evil and evil good. Hatred was suddenly tolerated by Christians, and Christ's Name was so widely and constantly used in vain as to defy calculation. Yet, God knew the tally.

Now, warnings were again rising. Every year, new alarms rang. *"Nature is asking for vengeance,"* she had said at La-Salette. And it certainly seemed that way. So great was a howling, paralyzing blizzard that at one point, every fire truck in Buffalo was stranded.

Cutting off heat, the storm had been part of a system the Associated Press said was "nearly unprecedented, stretching from the Great Lakes near Canada to the Rio Grande along the border with Mexico. About sixty percent of the U.S. population faced some sort of winter weather advisory or warning, and temperatures plummeted drastically below normal from east of the Rocky Mountains to the Appalachians."

Another news source noted that "Some major cities in the Southeast, Midwest and East Coast recorded their coldest Christmas in decades. In Florida, it will be the coldest December 25 since 1983 for Miami, Tampa, Orlando and West Palm Beach. New York City also saw record cold temperatures on Christmas Eve at several locations, including its JFK and LaGuardia airports. The high at Central Park was 15 degrees, marking it the second-coldest December 24 in at least 150 years."

This was all in a year that also saw near-record *heat.*

Indeed, globally, eight years including 2022 had been the warmest on record and clearly the extremes were signs of the times. In 2023, just about every record seemed broken. It was climbing up to 128 degrees at Death Valley. Might a weather system paralyze not just Upstate New York and the Midwest but the continent soon? Could the entire electrical grid collapse? In short, were smaller warnings leading up, as prophesied at Medjugorje and the site in Spain, to a major warning?

73

On October 7, 2019, according to Dr. Hesemann, the Lord had announced to Manuela that there would be a warning (some called it "The Warning") for a future day when *they change My word.*" Saint Michael likewise appeared, Manuela claimed, and cited passages from Scripture, including *2 Timothy*: "There will be terrible times in the last days. People will be lovers of themselves, lovers of money, boastful, proud, abusive, disobedient to their parents, ungrateful, unholy, without love, unforgiving, slanderous, without self-control, brutal, not lovers of the good, treacherous, rash, conceited, lovers of pleasure rather than lovers of God—having a form of godliness but denying its power. Have nothing to do with such people."

Was anyone—were Christians—listening?

While a singular, massive event commanding world focus had not yet occurred, the two decades since Manuela received her secret had seen her homeland of Germany become the epicenter of ecclesial mayhem. Those who subscribed to the Spanish site of Garabandal (where four seers saw Mary in the 1960s) wondered about the prophecy there of a Church event that would precede calamity in one of their secrets.

A synod?

The Church was being weakened from the outside and inside, especially through attacks on the Magisterium itself.

Some was understandable.

Some was diabolic.

In 1973, when, despite her deafness, Sister Sasagawa heard Mary speak at the convent in northern Japan, the Virgin had said through the weeping statue that *"the demon will be especially implacable against souls consecrated to God"*—as had LaSalette, where Mary had forewarned that many priests would be entrapped in *"cesspools of impurity"* and nuns leave religious life or become devotees of Asmodeus (a prince of demons).

Among the religious who stayed were some who (entangled by the New Age) beat drums in circle prayers, played with enneagrams, or were reiki masters.

We went to the place in the afterlife that matched the "robes" we wore, robes that, given upon death, reflected the state of the soul—the brightness or blotchiness, grayness, the smudges, perhaps blackness—and did so with unyielding truth.

There was no balderdash past the pearly gates, no traipsing with sin onto endless verdure pastures by living waters that fell like cataracts or pooled into crystalline lakes a soul could bathe in, cleansing from those trials of life. Healing. Endless scenes of beauty and color and song and aromas permeate the place to which all humans must aspire.

In Heaven, the soul inhaled water and drank music and touched colors—of so many kinds that there isn't a place on earth, not off the coasts of New Zealand, not at Rotorua (and not in an artist's palette), that could approach even the least of Heaven's hues.

Variety? So much we needed eternity to explore them. God wasn't as great as we imagined. He was infinitely greater than we *could* imagine.

And so getting there—Heaven—took purity. It took faith. It required kindness. There was no hidden thing. It wasn't enough just to confess: Yes, that "saved" the soul from nether regions. But to enter Heaven one had to repent—wash the robe, which meant permanent change. One had to purify through love—which defeated all darkness.

Instead, there was rancor. There were "cardinals opposing cardinals, bishops against other bishops." The *Neues Europe* "secret" predicted "a time of hardest trials for the Church" when Satan would put himself in the midst of priests, bishops, and cardinals (*"What is rotten will fall."*). And even if this wasn't literally what the Vatican released as the actual secret in 2000, nor precisely the 1944 Enlightenment, it turned out to be a true prophecy, describing with chilling inerrancy what was occurring (oh, the sexual abuse!) in seminaries, rectories, and sanctuaries—sometimes in confessional booths themselves.

The *Neues Europa* "secret" had been so similar to Sister Sasagawa's prophecy that another question about them arose: Was there something in those two descriptions that was never released by either the Vatican or Sister Lucia—the part detailing Church scandal—or had Sister Sasagawa read about the *Neues Europa* "secret" and mimicked it?

Was this something in her subconscious?

Though no fraud, a final answer was not resolved. Few things in the realm of mysticism could be "proven." And yes, it did seem that what was in *Neues Europa* may also have been on the mind of John Paul II when he spoke to that small clutch of pilgrims in Fulda and in reply to a question about the secret, had said it was enough to know of the possibility that oceans would "entirely flood certain parts of the earth, that from moment to moment millions will die."

Compare that to the *Neues Europa* version of the third secret, which declared that "fire and smoke will fall from the sky and the waters of the earth will be turned to steam—hurling their foam towards the sky, and all that is standing will be overthrown. Millions and more millions of men will lose their lives from one hour to the next."

"From one hour to the next" (Neues Europa).

"From moment to moment" (the Pope at Fulda).

As for Sister Sasagawa (whose prophecy had so dramatically declared that "fire will fall from the sky"), this brought to mind that portion of the *Neues Europe* article which in 1963 (a decade before Akita) had said, almost verbatim, "fire and smoke will fall from the sky."

Fire and smoke. Volcanoes. A comet. A warhead. A detonation of the latter in the upper atmosphere could take out our electronics like wind blasting the feathery gray globe of a dandelion.

The same could happen with a flare from the sun (or elsewhere).

Might such an event or events—asteroids, volcanoes—have played a part in the Fall of Rome, which was devastated by bad weather, floods, and plague, in addition to war?

When Pope Gregory the Great led a procession around the stricken city, it was no small coincidence that upon conclusion, and announcing an end to what the Pope himself called a "chastisement," the apparition of an angel taken to be Michael materialized atop what became Castel Sant'Angelo, returning a sword to its scabbard.

Was Michael likewise the angel depicted by Lucia? And was it the same sword?

Something big—larger than the fall of Rome—was in store. At Medjugorje it was indicated that after the events, a peasant lifestyle—simplicity—would replace our artificial reality.

Haunting words:

"Region of the world."

"Great part of humanity."

In miniature, we already were seeing war and geological events.

Had the Enlightenment meant it literally—both natural and military upsets—or was it mixing metaphors?

On October 5, 2020, in Germany, at Sievernich, sixty witnessed the miracle of the sun while praying with Manuela. *"When I admonish the world,"* the Lord told her, *"it will be for you as if the time would stand still. And so you will look at your own soul."*

Dr. Hesemann reported that Jesus used the word *aviso* ("warning," in Portuguese), the exact word quoted at Garabandal, of which Manuela—who knew neither Portuguese nor Spanish—was unaware.

In an interview with a periodical dedicated to the events, one of the Garabandal visionaries, Mari Loli Mazón, repeated the claim that during the *aviso*, everyone would see their souls.

There would be an "illumination of conscience."

There would be terror.

Q. Reportedly, you have said that when the Warning occurs everything will stand still, even planes in the sky. Is this true?

A. Yes, but just for a few moments.

Q. You mean that everything will stop at a given moment and at that moment the Warning will occur?

A. Yes.

Q. Do you know how long the "Warning" will last?

A. Just a few minutes.

As for the chastisement that would follow, it was "very, very great, in keeping with all that we deserve," in the words of a second seer, Conchita Gonzáles, who claimed to have witnessed previews of it, more fearful "than anything we can imagine," "something never seen on earth before."

It would be worse, she claimed, "than if we were enveloped in fire. Worse than if we had fire above us, and fire beneath."

There was that notion, again, of "fire." What conceivably would cause flames from above as well as below? A wildfire like the historic one that encompassed hundreds of square miles in Wisconsin in 1871, burning even the roots of trees (after an apparition of Mary near Green Bay warned of chastisement)?

Unlike the irrevocable "warning," the Chastisement, she said, was conditional. It could be lessened by prayer, repentance, adoration of the Blessed Sacrament, and the Rosary. This too was stated at Medjugorje (though "warnings" was used in the plural in at least three secrets).

At Garabandal such was shown on what seers called the "night of the screams." Conchita explained that "in spite of continuing to see the Virgin, we saw a great multitude of people who were suffering intensely and screaming in terror. The Blessed Virgin explained to us that this great tribulation, which was not even the Chastisement, would come because a time would arrive when the Church would appear to be on the point of perishing. It would pass through a terrible trial. We asked the Virgin what this great trial was called, and she told us it was Communism.

"Then she showed us how the great Chastisement for all mankind would come, and explained that it would come directly from God.

"At a certain moment, not a single motor or machine would function; a terrible heat wave will strike the earth and men will begin to feel a great thirst. In desperation they will seek water, but this will evaporate from the heat. Then almost everyone will despair and they will seek to kill one another. But they will lose their strength and fall to the ground. Then it will be understood that it is God alone Who has permitted this.

"We saw a crowd in the midst of flames. The people ran to hurl themselves into lakes and seas. But the water seemed to boil, and instead of putting out flames, it seemed to enkindle them even more. It was so horrible that I asked the Blessed Virgin to take all the young with her before all this happened. But the Virgin told us that by the time it came, they would all be adults."

Chapter 12

THIS IS WHAT WAS CLAIMED, and caution was critical. So too was analysis.

What could cause motors, engines, turbines to halt instantly, and at the same time, fire everywhere?

That paralysis of machines was a stumbling block. A comet, volcano, or wildfire could cause massive destruction. But stop engines, turbines, and all things mechanical and electronic worldwide? If one chose to take the prophecy literally, the cause had to be something else. Did it have to do with gravity, electromagnetism, some undiscovered cosmic force?

As was increasingly likely in the era of North Korea and Iran with nuclear capability, not to mention Russia and China, an electromagnetic pulse at the behest of a high-altitude nuclear blast could "fry" the electrical infrastructure of a nation or cluster of them. When I asked a physicist named Ernie Hildner, at the time director of the Space Weather office (in Boulder, Colorado), if it was possible for such a pulse from the sun or bomb (or other military weapon) to cause disruption of power—a catastrophic one—in the United States, his simple unqualified answer had been, "Yes." Though recent technology lessened the possibilities of a complete "meltdown" by a single burst, the consequences if it happened were clear: total paralysis in food, fuel, medical, informational, financial, and transportation systems.

And more interesting still, it took us straight back to Cova da Iria, where a "great sign" had been prophesied and as mentioned took place subsequently (in 1938) when a solar storm interacted with the magnetic field of earth, emitting luminosity that caused an extraordinary display of the aurora borealis, which was seen on the Eastern Seaboard from the Carolinas out to Bermuda and from southern California to the far north of Canada while in Europe it awed observers from northern Norway and Eastern Austria to Sicily and the Rock of Gibraltar.

So strong was its red illumination that countless millions thought it was due to a *fire from the sky.*

In England, the King's Guards summoned the fire department, and many peering from their windows thought the end of the world was nigh, the phenomenon striking wonderment in some areas, terror in others, as far south as southern Australia. "Britons Thought Windsor Castle Ablaze—Scotts See Ill Omen—Snow-Clad Alps Glow," said the subhead under a *New York Times* article.

In Tuy, Spain, where she was cloistered—where she would soon receive her momentous, if still largely unknown, word of knowledge—Lucia observed the aurora from her lonely convent window and remembered the words spoken to her twenty-one years before. *"When you see a night illumined by an unknown light, know that this is the great sign given you by God that He is about to punish the world for its crimes, by means of war, famine, and persecutions of the Church."*

In 2001 great displays of the aurora were photographed not long after 9/11 and just before the onset of wars in Afghanistan and Iraq.

One of them, taken on September 23, 2001, near Jyväskylä, Finland, looked like a towering angel ready to sound a shofar, or trumpet.

At times hissing, groans, a hum, trumpet blasts, crackling, or a rumbling noise seemed associated with such lights, and similar sounds indeed have been known to accompany geomagnetic disturbance. From whatever source, recent years had recorded them worldwide and often with what seemed like omens.

Was the sun heading for a period of extremes as in the Middle Ages, when solar activity altered earth's climate, a simple massive electromagnetic event?

No refrigeration. No heat. No air conditioning. No internet. No banking. No television. No chargers.

In a total regional outage—not to mention a national or international one—soon there also would be little to drink, for facilities depend on electricity to draw, treat, and pump water.

And cars?

Service stations need power to pump gas.

It was former Congressman Newt Gingrich, husband of a former ambassador to the Vatican, who warned that in a total blackout, "millions would die in the first week alone."

Days of darkness.

The best prevention: prayer.

For if it went on beyond a few weeks, marauding gangs would scour neighborhoods, even heading to farmland in search of plunder. Uninhibited by police, who would be immobilized by the shortage of fuel, outlaws could form their own checkpoints, stripping anyone who approached of what gang members wanted.

I recall the vision of Dr. Howard Storm, a former atheist who, during a near-death experience, saw future scenarios in which people were shooting each other over a "cup of gasoline."

A massive coronal discharge might not take out the entire grid, but a nuclear bomb?

"In theory, a relatively small device over Omaha would knock out about half the electricity generated in the United States," fretted Gingrich. "Without adequate preparation, we would basically lose our civilization in a matter of seconds." Intelligence sources issued a report to the effect that China now possessed "super-electromagnetic-pulse" weapons, knew how to protect itself against a reciprocal EMP attack, and had developed a program that would allow it to conduct a first-strike.

"Fire will fall."
That had been said in 1973, and had not yet occurred.
Heaven was spelling it out.
But prayer could stop anything.
Perhaps prayer already had.
But China now possessed those super-EMP weapons.
"Everything is happening as my Divine Son Jesus wishes," an alleged message in 2003 from Sievernich said. *"Remain calm. I recommend to you my gown, the scapular of Mount Carmel. Wearing it constitutes the most profound consecration to my Immaculate Heart."*

On October 7, 2002, Manuela herself had received three "keys"—secrets handed to John Paul II in 2004 regarding "the future of the world and the Church," according to Dr. Hesemann.

"Remain silent about this, remain silent!" Our Lady said on October 7, 2002. *"The keys will serve you as a weapon against all darkness. You now know what will happen... Only your Holy Father in Rome, my beloved Shepherd* [the Pope], *will receive these keys from me. Please remain silent, you will not be believed, yet everything will come to pass in this way."*

Hesemann was certain of one thing: the devil was getting "more active than ever before." He was "infiltrating the Church, seducing theologians and even bishops to question the teachings of the Church," warned the theologian, "to drag all of us into sin and into an apocalyptic Third World War."

"Regarding the future," Dr. Hesemann told me, "Manuela saw a persecution of the Church, Islamic terrorism, civil wars in several countries, earthquakes, hurricanes, and a meteor or asteroid impact, the Warning and, if mankind does not convert, a chastisement. The most important word is 'if'— *if* man continues to sin and offend God, terrible things will happen. If man converts, if we follow Heaven's call for prayer, conversion, and acts of reparation, we will find peace."

Chapter 13

ALL THIS HAD IMMEDIATELY PRECEDED A PAN-DEMIC that killed more than six million. Entire neighborhoods, cities, and countries masked up and locked down. More than the virus itself was the threat, the uncertainty. Images of New York as a ghost town: it became an icon of the Great Contagion, and once more a prophetic forerunner. Soon, the virus would wipe out entire floors at nursing homes in that city and across New York State, which always had been a locus for whatever trend, a harbinger.

Soon, refrigerated trucks would serve as morgues.

In Central Park, a tent hospital materialized.

Bars, restaurants, offices: closed or barely in business.

For the Church, foretastes of future times were also displayed. Mass was altered: no more Precious Blood, no more Holy Water, at a time when we needed them like seldom before, or liturgies were entirely halted. The suspension of all but remote Mass led to many lukewarm deciding not to return.

It was the greatest pandemic in a century (rumors swirled of a laboratory origin), followed immediately by the truly epic war, one that reminded us of Blessed Elena Aiello—a mystic from Italy who in 1960 said, "If the people do not recognize in these scourges (of nature), the warnings of Divine Mercy, and do not return to God with truly Christian living, another terrible war will come from the east to the west. Russia with her secret armies will battle America; will overrun Europe. The river Rhine will be overflowing with corpses and blood. Italy, also, will be harassed by a great revolution, and the Pope will suffer terribly."

Would the war in Ukraine truly end, or would it simmer into battles of attrition, only for a greater one to later erupt? Would Serbia (which had sought during a war with Croatia to destroy Medjugorje) once more enter the fray? Were the clouds Lucia saw (emerging from their limits) the billowing smoke of bombs?

Fátima had focused on Russia. Would it spread its "errors" again? Would it blow up dams (causing rivers to overrun their banks, as Lucia was shown)? or explode a device in the Arctic, near the "axis" of the earth, near those Eskimos?

Around that same time as Aiello, back in 1958, Sister Lucia had said to a priest named Augustine Fuentes: "Father, Our Lady is very displeased because no one has heeded her message of 1917. Neither the good nor the bad paid any attention to it. The good ones go their way unconcerned and heeding not the celestial directives; the bad, pursuing the broad way of perdition, completely ignoring the threatened punishment.

"Father," she reportedly added, "please tell everyone what Our Lady has repeatedly told me: *'Many nations are going to disappear from the face of the earth,'* Godless nations will be picked by God as His scourge to punish the human race, if through prayers and sacraments we do not bring about their conversion."

Whether for Church or world, the predictions were to be heeded. In Kibeho, Rwanda, the Blessed Mother warned in the 1980s that if Hutus and Tutsis continued with sin, *"a river of blood"* would course through that nation.

Soon after, Rwanda witnessed one of the most horrific genocides in all of history: more than 800,000 Tutsis slain, usually by machete, in less than a year. Years later I stood at the site of revelations and looked to a church less than half a mile away where a massacre had occurred inside.

Fulfillment of the prophecy had taken place within sight of the apparitions.

Bones still poked from the soil in the fields surrounding it.

Blood ran in rivulets down the center aisle of one church where several thousand were massacred, and corpses clogged the nation's key waterway, the River Kagera.

Yet that would not be the end of it.

"Where will you hide when the fire comes?" the Virgin had asked—referring to the whole world.

In this maelstrom, in the panic of madness, was the consolation—but also constant admonitions—of Mary. No one knew how many times Lucia experienced apparitions after 1917. But during them, she apparently had expanded on her general warnings. In a letter to Cardinal Carlo Caffarra that "the final battle between the Lord and the reign of Satan will be about marriage and the family."

He was not to fear, she added; he would be helped in what she labeled the "decisive issue."

In further solace, she noted, about the devil, that "Our Lady has already crushed its head."

But for now? The battle had intensified—enormously. And New York was the epicenter: it had been in Greenwich Village that the homosexual rights movement had been jump-started (with what was known as the "Stonewall Riots"), and nowhere, save for San Francisco, would display a more flagrant gay presence. It was also New York where the transgender trend had seen its early manifestations, with men dressed as women ("drag queens") in the 1960s in Times Square. It was hard to imagine, Sister Lucia seeing that. Indeed, the annual Halloween parade in New York was replete with transvestites, often in the skimpiest attire. Only San Francisco and New Orleans had parades as lascivious, lesbians dressed as nuns and gays as priests, the Virgin presented in blasphemous fashion.

It was a template for the future, though soon, by the 1980s, transvestites were to be upstaged by transsexuals— now known as "transgenders."

This was pioneered at Johns Hopkins Hospital in Baltimore by a surgeon, John Hoopes, who later renounced his own work, lamenting that those who had their genders altered had been "hysterical," "freakish," and "artificial," and were far more prone to suicide.

Now, by embracing this, were entire nations likewise killing themselves? Was there not an apocalyptic element? Shortly before his retirement, Pope Benedict had warned the Curia that "the very notion of being—of what being human really means—is being called into question" and that gender is "no longer a given element of nature, that man has to accept and personally make sense of: it is a social role that we choose for ourselves, while in the past it was chosen for us by society. The profound falsehood of this theory and of the anthropological revolution contained within it is obvious. People dispute the idea that they have a nature, given by their bodily identity, that serves as a defining element of the human being. They deny their nature and decide that it is not something previously given to them, but that they make it for themselves. According to the biblical Creation account, being created by God as male and female pertains to the essence of the human creature. This duality is an essential aspect of what being human is all about, as ordained by God. This very duality as something previously given is what is now disputed. The words of the creation account: 'male and female He created them' (*Genesis* 1:27) no longer apply. No, what applies now is this: it was not God who created them male and female—hitherto society did this, now we decide for ourselves.

"When the freedom to be creative becomes the freedom to create oneself, then necessarily the Maker himself is denied and ultimately man too is stripped of his dignity as a creature of God, as the image of God at the core of his being. The defense of the family is about man himself. And it becomes clear that when God is denied, human dignity also disappears. Whoever defends God is defending man."

"The next great challenge the Church is going to face," Benedict told a moral theologian, "is gender ideology, and it will be the ultimate rebellion against God the Creator."

Not abortion, not euthanasia, but perhaps this was the last straw?

In the Garden had been the snake, the *Mysterium Iniquitatis*, trying to strangle what *Genesis* says: "Let Us make man in Our image, according to Our likeness."

It clearly is God Who decides male and female, both made in the *Imago Dei*. Anything subverting that came from antichrist. Was it any wonder in the age of transgenderism that there was the parallel—if on the surface, unrelated—rebellion of satanism?

When, in 2023, there was a conference of satanists in Boston (followed weeks later by a "debaptizing" service), among those of prevalence were gays and transgenders.

It was anti-natural. God created nature, not unnature. There was the devil's reticulation again.

Scientists were hard at work. Soon, homosexual men would be able to have a baby. That was again reshaping Creation and seeking the Throne—humans usurping God's authority (the high sin of Lucifer).

So many good-hearted people were homosexual (certainly to be respected and loved); but sodomy was putting asunder what God had joined together, and transgenderism was a blatant affront to the Lord.

Was it really the furthest Satan could go?

Or was transgenderism a forerunner of what might actually be the "ultimate" rebellion: designer babies, artificial wombs, and computer technology integrated into the actual human body?

Transhumanism.

Part man, part machine.

Lucia's phrase "reign of Satan": it meant the devil had been allowed an upper hand due to our sin, the energy of invitation, and was now on a rampage. At Medjugorje Mary had said the same when in messages during the early days she told seers that *"darkness reigns over the whole world"; "a great struggle is about to unfold, a struggle between my Son and Satan"; "many live in darkness"; "the present hour is the hour of Satan"; "the hour has come when the demon is authorized to act with all his force and power."*

But only half of marriages in the United States were now surviving, and while the divorce rate was trending down from a peak around 1980, there were many more living together without matrimony and at the same time, gay marriage was booming as was adoption of children by homosexual couples who were celebrated with rainbow banners at Disney World and elsewhere, even with a flag at America's Vatican embassy.

And dangerously, it became a crime to disagree with acts of sodomy—acts that contravened the Bible and nature itself.

From the time of Eve and Adam, God had established marriage and two genders, not the four or five now listed on marriage and drivers' licenses. It was not just wrong but insane. Today some institutions no longer use "him" or "her."

As prince of darkness, Satan was casting shadows. He was blinding us. He was bedimming our intelligence.

This was compounded by a great loss of Church credibility due largely to homosexuality and the abuse by priests of young males.

A final battle: In such a conflict, Lucia had noted, one side loses and one wins. "Father," she'd told Fuentes, "the Most Holy Virgin did not tell me that we are in the last times of the world but she made me understand this for three reasons. The first reason is because she told me that the devil is in the mood for engaging in a final battle where one side will be victorious and the other side will suffer defeat. Hence from now on we must choose sides. Either we are for God or we are for the devil. There is no other possibility. The second reason is because she said to my cousins as well as to me that God is giving two last remedies to the world. These are the Holy Rosary and Devotion of the Immaculate Heart of Mary. These are the last two remedies, which signify that there will be no others. The third reason is because in the plans of Divine Providence, God always before He is about to chastise the world exhausts all other remedies."

Obviously, the Lord was holding off because some—a cohort, the remnant—were following Heaven's prescriptions.

Still, too few even among the devout fasted and thus many have lost the ability of discernment. Fasting was critical. It removed blinders. "It is easy to recognize the ruse of the devil and his followers, who want to lead souls away from God by leading them away from prayer," Lucia wrote. "The devil is very clever and looks for our weak points so as to attack us. If we are not diligent and attentive in obtaining strength from God, we will fall, for our times are very evil and we are very weak."

Chapter 14

HOW MANY LISTENED? How many in the Catholic flock—the Sunday crowd, or those who at least made trips to the altar on Christmas and Easter—knew that the Virgin had said the devil especially hated the Rosary because, after the liturgy, it was the sharpest rapier, a real sword, against him?

And worldliness? One had to avoid the "world," Mary implored; there could be no compromise. The Good Book said, "Do not love the world or the things in the world. If anyone loves the world, the love of the Father is not in him. For all that is in the world—the desires of the flesh and the desires of the eyes and pride in possessions—is not from the Father but is from the world. And the world is passing away along with its desires, but whoever does the will of God abides forever" (*1 John* 2:15-17).

"Set your minds on things that are above, not on things that are on earth" (*Colossians* 3:2).

"If you were of the world, the world would love its own; but because you are not of the world, but I chose you out of the world, because of this the world hates you" (*John* 15:19).

"You adulterous people! Do you not know that friendship with the world is enmity with God? Therefore whoever wishes to be a friend of the world makes himself an enemy of God" (*James* 4:4).

No wonder that way back in the 1960s, when Sister Lucia was writing some of her letters, a rock-'n'-roll album bore the title *Their Satanic Majesties Requests.*

Largely, the devil, prince of this world (*John* 12:31), had gotten what he requested.

This was a society that was no longer heading off the rails but had left the tracks already.

Here was a metaphor: a cottage on Loch Ness once inhabited by Aleister "The Beast" Crowley (who in 1900 had pronounced the age of Christ over, replaced by that of Horus) was being rebuilt (having burned down years ago). This wasn't just the pop zeitgeist. This was a connection—and a real one—with sheol. Did anyone really think that "superstars" like singer Madonna were not energized (and made famous) by dark entities?

The evil spirit was good at doling out charisma and fame. But it was exactly as Sister Lucia said: a time of "diabolic disorientation."

Quite a cottage, Crowley's: said to have been the site of a church that likewise burned, trapping congregants inside, and connected via tunnel to a graveyard—so haunted that a subsequent owner, rock star Jimmy Page ("Stairway To Heaven"), moved away. (Crowley, whose image was included on the cover of "Sergeant Pepper," was an inspiration to countless musicians, hipsters, and drug users, with the credo, "Do what thou wilt," which was on a Led Zeppelin cover. "The Beast," his mother's nickname for him, was also a mastermind behind L. Ron Hubbard, founder of Scientology. Didn't folks wonder why so many rock stars died young (many, for some odd reason, at the age of 27, including the "godfather" of blues and rock-n'roll, Robert Johnson)? Jim Morrison, Janis Joplin, Jimi Hendrix, Kurt Cobain. Did fans of Bob Dylan know he had made a trek to the same rural crossroads in Mississippi (at highways 61 and 49) where Johnson, who became an iconic blues guitarist, was said to have conversed with a devil and instantly was transformed (or so said the legend) from a poor-to-mediocre musician to a man whose style would inspire stars who also went to the "crossroads" such as Keith Richards of the Rolling Stones and John Fogerty?

Mephistopheles, it seems, was a splendid musical instructor. The list of musicians was long. Elvis was born in a house at the instant a strange light hovered above, causing the poltergeist-like rattling of shelves (according to his father). At the same time, luminosity of the same color suffused the house, and a twin brother died. No wonder the mega-star favored blue and had a lifelong fascination with UFOs and psychic phenomena (including a massive collection of occult books). UFOs also played into the lives of John Lennon, Jerry Garcia, and Mick Jagger (who wrote the hit song *Sympathy for the Devil*).

A tricky stratosphere overarched the realm of entertainment. Though innocent it seemed, "I Love Lucy" often featured Desi Arnaz singing a song, *Babalu Ayé*, a Santería demigod who, warned one former satanist, "ushered the devil into our houses."

Kyrie Eleison. God, our Lord, King of ages, All-powerful and Almighty, You Who made everything and Who transforms everything simply by Your will. You Who in Babylon changed into dew the flames of the 'seven-times hotter' furnace and protected and saved the three holy children. You are the doctor and the physician of our souls. You are the salvation of those who turn to You. We beseech You to make powerless, banish, and drive out every diabolic power, presence, and machination; every evil influence, malefice, or evil eye and all evil actions aimed against us...

That was the weapon—prayer—in this war.

Was the diabolic tsunami that during the Sixties towered on the horizon not part of the cause for an angel in the Secret raising a torch to the world?

Sister Lucia at least once made reference to *Revelation* where in Chapter 8 is mentioned an angel "who had a golden censer" and "came and stood at the altar.

"He was given much incense to offer, with the prayers of all God's people, on the golden altar in front of the throne. The smoke of the incense, together with the prayers of God's people, went up before God from the angel's hand.

"Then the angel took the censer, filled it with fire from the altar, and hurled it on the earth; and there came peals of thunder, rumblings, flashes of lightning and an earthquake."

This was pointedly similar to that part of the Third Secret whereby "two Angels each with a crystal aspersorium in his hand" gathered up "the blood of the Martyrs and with it sprinkled the souls that were making their way to God." It also hearkened to the Enlightenment (storms, clouds, the earth shuddering).

And Chapter 13? "I stood upon the sand of the sea, and saw a beast rise up out of the sea, having seven heads and ten horns, and upon his horns ten crowns, and upon his heads the name of blasphemy," wrote John. "There was the beast, empowered by the dragon."

There was mention of "666."

That set of numbers was on a Led Zeppelin cover.

It was also to be noted that the Church of Satan was founded in 1966.

In the U.S., a highway with those numbers, replete with UFO sightings, phantom trucks, hellhounds, and horrid accidents, was known as Devil's Highway (and in 2003 its numbers changed to 491).

Chapter 15

SOCIETY HAD PLANTED ITSELF IN THE TOMBS OF GADARENES. How many chances had God given us to turn back? How many admonitions, now through Mary, had to be spoken? Truly, were there any chances left?

"Wars are nothing but punishments for the sins of the world," Jacinta Marto, the precious *pastorinho* of Fátima, had said. "It is necessary to do penance. Our Lady can no longer hold back the arm of her beloved Son from the world. If people change their ways, Our Lord will still avail the world; but if they do not, the chastisement will come." Added Jacinta, who died in 1919: "If men do not change their ways, Our Lady will send the world a punishment the like of which has never been seen. It will fall first . . . upon Spain."

Was the Fátima seer, just ten at her death, referring to the pandemic of 1918-1920, which would become known as the Spanish flu? Did that fit the bill as punishment the likes of which had not been seen?

Or was it something else?

While the shooting of John Paul II may have fulfilled part of the Fátima Secret—the felling of a *"bishop in white"*—there was that other part saying *"before reaching there the Holy Father passed through a big city half in ruins and half trembling with halting step, afflicted with pain and sorrow, he prayed for the souls of the corpses he met on his way."*

Unless it referred to Dresden or Hiroshima, that had not happened—not yet.

And the angel with the censer, causing thunder and quakes: as yet nothing up to now quite fit that bill.

Were answers to be found at a mountainside hamlet in Slovakia called Litmanová where apparitions as witnessed by two girls started in August 1990?

Like LaSalette, like Fátima, like Guadalupe, like Lourdes, like Medjugorje, once again it involved peasants, Katka Ceselkova and Ivetka Korcakova, and once again was at a hillside.

Recalled the girls in a statement about the first apparition, which included a third girl, and started with loud, startling sounds: "We went up to the hillside—Katka, Ivetka, and Mikulas Ceselka. It was morning about seven o'clock. On the hill we played games all day long. We made a fire and we roasted some bacon and sang. The Liturgy was celebrated in the church at 5:00 p.m., but we did not want to go home to attend, so we stayed up on the hill a little longer."

That's when sounds like someone throwing wood issued from the top of the mountain and grew louder.

Afraid, the girls had sought refuge in a hut.

"We were sorry for our sins and at this moment there was a glow but we did not pay attention to this because we thought that it was from the sun," said their joint recollection. "We did not say anything—because we thought it was something from our imagination, or out of fear. We made ourselves a pledge that during this week we would go to church every day! At this moment our fear left. We were sitting on the bed and suddenly a glow appeared in the middle of the room and we saw the Blessed Mother. We tried to see whether this was really her! She sat on the bench and was listening to us. We were staring at the bench and Katka said 'I see the Blessed Mother.' 'I see her too,' said Ivetka. We all ran out of the room, left the place in a hurry—we did not even lock the door—only ran home. The Blessed Mother followed us on the way, about two steps behind us. When we turned around, we saw her behind us. She accompanied us to the roadside Cross. There, she knelt down and prayed. Then, she went behind us and then she started to gradually disappear."

On the way home, the girls, still afraid, turned to look, spotting the Blessed Mother in front of Ivetka's uncle's house.

"She did not speak to us at the time," said their written testimony. "She was dressed in white dress, had on a blue cloak, a blue transparent veil, and on her head she wore a crown and in her hand she held a rosary.

"We returned home frightened. Ivetka told her mother about everything, but her mother did not believe her and so they went to Katka's house to ask her whether it was true.

"When Katka's mother went to work the next day, she prayed, 'Blessed Mother, give me some visible sign that the girls are not lying.' That very evening she had a dream. 'I saw the Blessed Mother with a green garland,' she said. 'I asked her why she had a green garland. She replied, *"Because I am a Virgin and I have a pure heart."* Next I asked her whether it was true what the girls had said. The Blessed Mother replied, *'Yes, do not doubt anything, but believe it all.'"*

At the end of August Ivetka, Katka, Mitko, and Ivetka's parents ventured to the hill again, and when they arrived at the hut, only Ivetka, Katka, and Mitko went into the room. "We asked our parents to leave us alone. We prayed *Our Father* and *Hail Mary* three times, the 'Golden Our Father' three times, and after that, 'O Mary, our Mother, protect us under your mantle' three times and sat on the bed. In a moment we saw a mist and in it began to distinguish the outline of the Blessed Mother. She was hardly visible and did not speak to us, did not leave any message. She then disappeared into the fog and we ran out to tell our parents what we had seen, that it was really the Blessed Mother! Mitko did not see the

Blessed Mother, only the two of us—Katka and Ivetka."

Soon as at Fátima, as at Medjugorje, as elsewhere, crowds gathered. That November, Mary allegedly appeared barefoot, with Jesus, Who was wrapped in a white cloth. "Jesus was weeping," the seers testified. "She gave us a message. She said that there are very few people that sacrifice, that Jesus made Himself a sacrifice for all nations. She gave us a proposal: *'Why don't men make sacrifices as Jesus did so many years ago?'* She told us that people have many material things, they have everything they want and yet they would even kill each other for it. They only want to get more possessions. Jesus Himself taught us that we should love one another, that we should forgive one another."

On November 25, 1990, a newly built Cross was consecrated at Litmanová, and then, on land deemed a place of prayer by the diocese, solar miracles occurred. "After the prayer of the Rosary, during Consecration, all present saw on the sun peculiar supernatural phenomena which brings to mind the sun miracle from Fátima," reported a website. "The sun, which was possible to look into, was rotating, emitting concentrated circles in various colors of the rainbow. It also turned black and then light again, shivering and changing position. A ring of small 'satellite' suns was created around the main sun. These phenomena were observed by 2,000 to 3,000 people, including the mayor Vislocky and the local priest, today`s vicar-general Jan Zavacky. Phenomena were recorded also by the cameras."

And so it went.

In 2006 construction was planned for new liturgical accommodations in service to the large numbers of pilgrims.

And in August 2008 the first building was finished. There was also a small, holy spring.

"During 1991 another revelation was offered, at that time approximately five thousand people were on pilgrimage to the Holy Mountain Zvir," related another source. "On January 13th the children reported that the Blessed Mother stated, *'I bless the entire mountain.'* Then the revelations came only the Sunday following the First Friday of the month." Mary explained, it seems, that the youngsters were to avail themselves of Confession on the first Friday because, in that state, she told the children—with contrite heart and absolution—they could more deeply contemplate the words they were hearing. Many revelations were given to the children, including a 'secret' on Sunday, April 7."

"God's visit is already close and therefore, search for love," said Mary on September 8, adding on October 6, *"I want to live in you and you in me"* and on November 3, *"I did all my life what God wanted."* On January 8, 1995, the Blessed Virgin Mary instructed the children to have pilgrims recite a prayer to the effect of: *"Lord God, I give my whole past and future to Thee and thank You for today, which is Yours also. I thank You, for Thou art with me. I rejoice, knowing You will never leave me."'*

The last apparition of the Blessed Virgin Mary occurred August 6, 1995, on the mountain called Zvir (or "Holy Mountain"), the Blessed Virgin stating, a bit ominously: *"For this time you need to repent! Please, please! You need to be more vigilant and simple; there is a time coming which is already approaching. You must have faith as a child and accept God's Will for you."*

I interviewed Katka, who had married and moved to the U.S. (Staten Island), learning that her apparitions had ended in 1995.

Q: What do you think was her most important message for us all?

"I think the most important thing that she asked for is to forgive and love each other, and prayer," said Katka. "She also asked that we would fast on Wednesdays and Fridays. In one revelation she told me this prayer: *I love and therefore I repent, I love and therefore I forgive, I love and that is my peace.*

Q: She seemed focused on purity.

"At the beginning of the revelations, we would ask Saint Mary what her name was and where she came from. She would respond, *'My name is the Immaculate Purity and I come from Heaven.'* That is why she would always urge us to have pure hearts and to protect ourselves from sin. It is not always easy, but we try to be better, and so we ask God for help, and we repent and walk on the right path."

Q: How do you think she feels about our current times— with all that is transpiring in the world and has been for several decades?

"I don't know exactly what to think," said Katka. "She did not come to judge us, but to help us. But when she came to us on this earth, she was not content with us. At the meetings with her, we could feel how much she loved us, like our mother."

Q: The Blessed Mother had some strong things to say about sin in your homeland. Has she mentioned the United States or anywhere else?

Responded the seer: "Saint Mary mentioned in her messages Slovakia, that Slovakia is awaiting a disaster, but if we pray it will move away. She did not mention any other countries, but she said that she came for everyone, not only Slovaks. She asked for many people to come to Zvir. The more people that would come and live by her message, the more happiness she would have."

What sins in Slovakia, I wondered, did Katka think most troubled the Virgin? Where did she think things were headed?

"It is hard to say what I think," replied the soft-spoken visionary. "According to what we see that is happening around us, it is not going in the right direction. But if we believe in the power of God and the courage of Mary, there is nothing to fear.

Chapter 16

SLOVAKIA BORDERED UKRAINE JUST BELOW POLAND, which meant it was prime territory for conflict.

And that one message, *"God's visit is already close:"* This also struck a chord because not far away, just west, in Slovenia, tucked between Croatia and the northwest of Italy, in the heart of Europe, had been another seer, since relocated to Australia, who'd used identical verbiage.

When Jesus said He will "visit," she told me, it meant with major events—and not necessarily pleasant ones.

These ostensible apparitions had begun after Easter in 1988, while the alleged seer was in mourning over a husband who'd been killed in a head-on collision.

It was April 4. Valentina Papagna had been in her forties when it happened. "I hardly slept at all because I was still very much grieving for my late husband but I was also praying," she said. "My son went to work, and I tried to do chores, but then I saw rain.

"So I went back to my bedroom and I opened my shades on the window and I sat on my bed and I said my morning prayers and then I said the Sorrowful Mysteries of the Holy Rosary. I should have said the 'Glorious' because Jesus had resurrected and it was Tuesday after Easter, but I find comfort in the sorrowful ones.

"I was looking through the window from my bed, sitting there watching the rain that was pouring, grey sky, very depressing. All of a sudden, I noticed it was quarter past eight and I thought to myself, what am I doing wasting time here? I should be up. I was supposed to meet a friend in Merrylands. She wanted me to meet her to do some shopping with her for her son, who was going to get married that week.

"The next minute, I put my legs down on the floor and as I was still sitting on the bed I heard this very, very strong sound of wind. It was really a harsh wind that was coming close to me. It was so loud I placed my hands over my ears. Yet when I looked towards the window, everything was standing still. No trees were moving. The wind was getting closer and closer and closer."

In a moment, the sound of that wind threw Valentina half off her bed sideways as air swirled furiously around her. Yet, she maintained tranquility. She told me it was like the roof— the ceiling—then opened in a corner of her bedroom and, astonished—moreso, in a state of shock—Valentina told me she had spotted a gold glow coming from afar as if from the stars—fast, "like lightning."

The next minute, claimed Valentina, the Blessed Mother was standing in the room, in a white dress with a blue mantle dressed as at Lourdes. "'Oh my God,'" I said, 'Blessed Mother'!"

That was a prelude. Next came visions of Christ. He was wearing a brilliant white tunic and over His tunic, "a very pale-cream vest, all the way to the ground."

"The Lord arrived right in front of me and said *'Can you tell me what country you come from?'*" claimed the alleged seer. "I said, 'But you already know.' He said *'Yes, Slovenia. I will visit your country very soon.'*

"I said, 'Lord, you will like my country. It is a very beautiful country!'

But there was that word "visit" again, which meant more than simply traveling to a place and the next week, recalled Valentina, there was "a tremendous storm" in Slovenia, "like a cyclone. The Lord told me the [extreme weather] is a punishment—not [a matter of] science, like they think."

"Tell people that many storms will happen all over the world such as you have never experienced," the Australian quoted Jesus as warning. As elsewhere, the climate was heating, swerving.

"My children, I am very sorry that you all had to go through a lot of suffering through this heat wave that came," He supposedly related, or words to that effect. *"My children, if you think that the heat wave was due to the scientific environment, then you are all very wrong. You can see that signs are given to you all over the world. The changes are coming everywhere."*

Referring to her new homeland, the Lord supposedly added, *"The city of Sydney is no exception. It is a very, very sinful city."*

Valentina told me that, in these supposed apparitions, Christ "took me into a supermarket and said, *'Take a close look, My child.'* Reality suddenly changed. Visions materialized before her eyes. "The next minute the store was completely empty—nothing on the shelves. He said, *'This is what will happen.'* Some parts [of the world looked] like desert, others flooded, a deluge; there was damage to crops. It's not just India or Africa but also America and Australia, where there will be shortages and famine. We have to go through this. He also told me America will be given a *'very hard test.'* It could be a comet, it could be anything. God spoke to me many times about America. The Lord told me, *'How can they do that* [referring to immoral marriages]?' He said He will 'visit' every nation until there is conversion."

The notion of "visiting" one nation after another was daunting and already unfolding: hurricanes in Florida, drought in the Southwest, floods in Bangladesh affecting millions. Ice shelves near the poles were in a state of collapse, permafrost was vanishing—destroying ancestral, centuries-old Eskimo ice cellars—and glaciers in Switzerland in retreat.

Of particular note had been the quake at Fukushima, which had triggered a major tsunami and destroyed a nuclear reactor, which unleashed radiation into the Pacific.

It all was beginning to fit the idea of seas and clouds "emerging from their limits."

Would Sister Lucia not have agreed, and was she aware of all the seers at places such as Akita, the messages of which paralleled her Enlightenment?

"Yes, I have heard speak of this," she said in 1993 of Akita (*"Fire will fall"*).

"We also have been with Vassula Ryden, and with Conchita of Garabandal," said a questioner, referring to a well-known Swiss mystic and the seer from Garabandal.

"Yes," said Sister Lucia.

"Do you have a message about apparitions to the world, about current apparitions?" she was asked (by a group led by Filipino Cardinal Ricardo Vidal).

"No, I am not authorized to send any official message to anyone," replied Lucia. "But I will tell you that we are in union of prayer, that may the Father, Son, and Holy Spirit bless you all. God has manifested Himself in miracles. He has spoken and speaks to His saints and we are so small that it is hard for us to comprehend. We must wait therefore, and hope, and see what God reveals to us before we make a pronouncement. The Virgin never spoke to me about other apparitions, but we know that God created other invisible beings, who are the angels. God could also perform other miracles. We are ignorant of these mysteries."

The guidance had been sought from Lucia in the midst of a veritable explosion in mystical claims; and guidance was desperately needed. Deception wore ingenious masks. Four years after the Enlightenment had been the apparitions in the Philippines at Lipa, during which a Carmelite named Teresita Castillo saw Mary as strange rose petals fell from the sky, with detailed religious images impressed on them. Soon others in that nation were also experiencing the petals, sometimes in a way that seemed suspect, other times in a fashion that was clearly paranormal. Was that preternaturality from the Good Source, or the legerdemain of a dark one? One noted that spiritual warfare had been attendant to the apparitions from the beginning, when three knocks, a hoarse voice, and a foul odor signaled an attack upon Teresita, along with sooty inhuman footprints. The demon was either behind the subsequent phenomena or trying to forestall or even prevent an appearance by the Virgin Mary, for on August 18, 1948, after several more attacks (including a bruising physical assault), the devil seemed to leave, his place taken by a beautiful woman who was dressed in white and emitted a lovely fragrance.

"Do not fear, my daughter," said the alleged apparition. *"He Who loves all things has sent me."*

I thought of Fátima and the time a crowd there too saw roses fall from the sky, but at Fátima they were ethereal roses that vanished before they touched the earth, while here they were tangible petals red, yellow, orange, anxiously gathered as keepsakes. A botanist found that some of the petals were of a kind only in Russia—linking this apparition, in a second way, to Fátima—and like Lucia, Teresita claimed to have been given Communion by an angel. Though she guarded "secrets" she too was allegedly given, Teresita said to a journalist forty years later, "I'll tell you this much: one [of the secrets] is for China, not Russia."

Teresita quoted Mary as directly saying, *"Pray, my child. The people do not heed my words. Tell my daughters that there will be persecutions, unrest, and bloodshed in your country. The enemy of the Church will try to destroy the faith which Jesus established and died for. The Church will suffer much. Pray for the conversion of sinners throughout the world. Pray for those who rejected me and those who do not believe and trust in me. Spread the meaning of the Rosary, because this will be the instrument for peace throughout the world. Tell the people that the Rosary must be said with devotion. Propagate the devotion to my Immaculate Heart. Do penance for priests and nuns. But be not afraid, for the love of my Son will soften the hardest of hearts and my motherly love will be their strength to crush the enemies of God. What I ask here is the same I asked at Fátima."*

Those three words, "be not afraid," would later become a key phrase in the pontificate of the Fátima Pope, John Paul II.

The warning about the Church came just as priestly abuse was first beginning to take root in seminaries—hidden but soon to reach a ghastly scale.

It came too as images of Mary seemed more and more to weep, including in Syracuse, New York, the year after the alleged apparitions.

This was very interesting, but the apparition was the focus of constant controversy, with various bishops rejecting it (though not the initial bishop, who was showered with petals upon arriving at the convent, intending to halt the phenomena), and in 2023, exorcists in the Philippines supported a priest who publicly criticized Lipa, warning that "demons can appear to be holy... mimicking anything they (believers) want."

This was a legitimate concern at many and perhaps even most apparitions, from the Philippines to Brazil to the U.S. I had seen my own cases of demonism. One seer's face transfigured into that of a witch during her ecstasy, and more recently, a priest spewing extravagant predictions at one point used the "f-word" from a pulpit (perhaps mistakenly; he mainly spoke French), while in Italy was a "stigmatic" with lettering on her arm that looked like an inexpensive tattoo (and who had an interesting personal history).

But who were we to judge? It had to be left to the Church, a quandary for sure because the Church was dominated by intellectual types whose "scientific" mindset all but precluded the supernatural (despite the fact that Christianity was founded on it).

Most problematic: a "stigmatic" in Brazil who later transitioned from male to female, and another in Italy whose "wounds" looked like crude skin graffiti (letters scrawled on her arms in blood with what charitably would be described as inartistic penmanship).

God, Jesus, and the Virgin Mary were more discrete and tasteful. Were they being aped—or mocked? That wasn't to say false seers couldn't be precognitive, that certain predictions didn't materialize. They weren't all "false" so much as mystics whose phenomena drew from the wrong well. One aforementioned "seer" had foreseen the eruption of covid in September of 2020 when she said, "Pray for China, because new diseases will come from there, all ready to infect the air by unknown bacteria."

That was a prophetic "hit," months before China revealed the outbreak. But a correct prediction said nothing about the force—dark or light—behind it. Had there not been Nostradamus, Cassandra, Edgar Cayce, Jeanne Dixon, and a slew of others, some of whose predictions came true but seemed occultic? Deep waters, these. Perhaps a mire. Certainly a jungle. Often, that hill or mountain to climb. No one wanted to dismiss a seer who might be the real thing, although controversy of some form surrounded nearly all of them. One, in Ireland, Christina Gallagher, I had known since 1992 and claimed the stern Voice of Jesus had said: *"Woe, woe, woe unto the one who blocked My words to the heart and soul of mankind who might have responded to Me."*

"Fire, pestilence, plague, famine, and the third world war will rage upon the earth until two-thirds of the world's population is wiped out. Those who will remain living will envy the dead. The man from the east will be evil, cruel, and show no mercy to the world's inhabitants. Oh, the foolishness of man, believing that when he has a vaccine, all will return to a normal behavior—as it was before. How foolish of such a 'man' who has failed to hear My call because if My words had been taken to heart, you would have the wisdom to understand how you have been deceived by those in union with antichrist. It will be the deception of the man-made powers to control and destroy you!"

Difficult indeed to discern. Some more recent views were strident. *"My Church is prepared for the entry of antichrist as there are those in union with antichrist active in My Church and there are those bringing about a one-world currency. As I have already told you, they will control your existence, dictating to you in the manner they desire and all that you own will no longer belong to you. As you, oh foolish people, behold all this unfolding before you, I want you to realize the many times I have echoed those words through My little one—but to no avail.*

"The stench of death will be everywhere because life will have neither meaning nor value for those of antichrist: you will be disposed of. I call upon mankind to pay attention and listen to what I say. Open The Book and read at chapter eight of the seventh seal of God..."

Now this also got back to the Third Secret and the later elucidation, for *Revelation* 8:3 explains that seal as involving an angel with the censer, filled with incense offered up *"with the prayers of all God's people,"* just as the Third Secret described the angel with the crystal aspersorium to convey the blood of martyrs and showed Mary empowered by prayers of the faithful—overcoming the fire of the angel's lit, wrathful spear; but then, as in Chapter Eight, depicting an angel hurling the censer to earth, *"and there came peals of thunder, rumblings, flashes of lightning and an earthquake,"* like what Lucia was told in 1944.

It seemed clear: both the Third Secret and its subsequent explanation were indicating arrival—seemingly imminent—of the Seventh Seal.

In several years would come The Event, and later what Medjugorje characterized as "chastisements."

We stood at the brink of the Seals, which would be followed by those seven Trumpets (8:6).

In Venezuela was one mystic who exuded convincing fruits. There was joy. There was warmth. There was healing. That again was Esperanza in Venezuela (the name meant "hope"), yet certain of her messages had to do with serious oncoming events, and she had correctly foreseen September 11—not only in a vision during the 1990s, before the *first* Trade Center attack, when she described explosions at two tall towers in New York, but then, in the winter, spring, and summer of 2001, when she repeatedly warned (including with a fax to our website three weeks before 9/11) that "enemies of the U.S." were "on its own soil" and preparing an assault.

September 11 then occurred—while Maria was visiting Manhattan.

(The mystic later had a driver take her to the Mother Cabrini Shrine and Saint Patrick's Cathedral, each of which she circled seven times praying for their protection. Had she "seen" them also as targets of Muslim wrath? And was an attack forestalled?)

Esperanza had once quoted Mary as saying (note use of the words "fire" and war"): *"Little children, today in these times, Jesus, wishes to renew consciences, for mankind is currently abusing the graces received and is moving toward perdition, and if there is no change and improvement in life, he will succumb under fire, war, and death. We want to stop what suffocates you, the evil of rebellion, and overcome the darkness of oppression by the enemy."*

Chapter 17

FASCINATING WAS ESPERANZA'S PREDICTION that the United States would suffer major earthquakes and that the "core of the earth," as she put it, "is not in balance"— which brought us roaring back again to the "axis" and Lucia's Enlightenment.

For if the core of the earth was unbalanced, there wasn't a seismologist on the planet who could tell what that would portend.

This was uncharted turf.

We couldn't even really say what the earth's core was.

It was hypothesized to be a molten center spanning two thousand miles in radius and rotating independently from the rest of the planet: a spin within a spin, leaving open unfathomable possibilities, among them (if it was out of balance) great surface turmoil.

It was 1,800 miles below our feet, the core, while the deepest hole ever drilled by men (in Siberia): a scant five. Scientists weren't certain what formed the deepest part. Was it really liquid? Might it not be solid? And who could know the effect of a fluctuation in its behavior—let alone a major shift? If the earth ever went off its axis, or if that degree of tilt ever changed significantly, it could alter nearly every aspect of our lives, starting—to bring us back to the LaSalette prophecy ("seasons will be altered") with the way the seasons work. If an axial tilt were to change enough to spin sideways on its axis, whole portions of the planet could be plunged into darkness or thrown into direct sunlight for months at a time. The continental U.S., in one scenario, would wind up with the same twenty-four hours of sunlight that certain places in the far north already receive eighty-two days a year. Some animals and plants would thrive for a little while, but crops planted in sun-drenched "temperate" climate zones would quickly vanish, and months of unending daylight would lead to severe sleep deprivation, anxiety, and other disorders.

Was this already being seen in places like Arizona and Texas, which recorded temperatures at a hundred or more degrees Fahrenheit for more than a month in 2023, or Maui, where fires created a miniature holocaust, killing hundreds, or Canada, which saw its Northwest Territories likewise surpass the 100-degree mark amid dangerously dry conditions, lightning storms, and new blazes that intensified the country's historically severe fire season—scorching twenty-three million acres (an area the size of Indiana)?

The more one realized the limits of knowledge, the more one chafed at its arrogance and its denial of God. *"My greatest nemesis is science, even more so than the media,"* said an anonymous locutionist in 1990, quoting the figure in a dream. *"The science that alters life, the science which creates a counterfeit heaven, the science that toils with the womb and genes, the science that has filled the air with the power of the enemy, the science which creates chemical witchcraft and fouls the earth, the science which seeks to create life but cannot in actuality even sustain it, the science which has denied God."*

"This will fall, and all of its creations with it."

The earth was not in balance, reflecting a state of spirit and mind.

While we often looked to crime and rates of abortion to gauge evil, seldom did we digest the totality of human offense when it came to the Lord. Merciful was He. Patient also.

Infinitely. And humble? One could but marvel at the Person Who created the universe or universes, our dimensions and countless others, whose vast star systems we could only pretend to comprehend, and yet maintained tolerance toward minuscule humans who denied Him.

Unfathomable mercy. The question was whether that tolerance could possibly last.

However tiny, all were important to Him. He wanted but love. *"The smallest of what lives is precious in My sight,"* was another message to the anonymous locutionist. On June 25, 2022, in her monthly message at Medjugorje, the Virgin had said, *"Dear children, I rejoice with you and thank you for every sacrifice and prayer, which you have offered for my intentions. Little children, do not forget that you are important in my plan of salvation of mankind. Return to God and prayer, that the Holy Spirit may work in you and through you. Little children, I am with you also in these days when Satan is fighting for war and hatred. Division is strong and evil is at work in man as never before."*

It stood out, those words towards the end. *Evil is at work in man as never before.* This was coming from a woman who was two thousand years old and now, near God, saw with the eyes of eternity. I had dinner with an excellent official exorcist at a major archdiocese who said that during a recent deliverance session, a demon speaking through the victim explained that the alleged hundred-year reign of Satan—again, prophesied by Pope Leo XIII in 1884—had actually begun in 1917. If the supernatural world adhered to human calendars, that would have brought it to an end in 2017. "At the 100th anniversary, he was bound in seventy-seven individuals and forced to undergo 111 hours of exorcism a week," the exorcist asserted. "He lost control of the other demons and what we see is chaos as groups of demons fight each other."

Chaos. There is that! Yet: is not Satan orchestrating that—

as master of confusion, the chaotic? I didn't pretend to know. I think of Medjugorje, which John Paul II called the fulfillment of Fatíma and where the Blessed Mother said (on September 25, 1991, at the beginning of the Croatian-Serbian war), *"Now as never before Satan wants to show the world his shameful face by which he wants to seduce as many people as possible onto the way of death and sin."*

She was saying that in the current era, darkness exceeded that of brutish man-apes, the cavemen, of Noachian times, of ferocious gladiators, of Pharaoh, of Caesar, of Attila, of Napoleon, of Mao, and again of the 1960s, when drugs, sex, rebellion, and music—often devilish, even mostly—were all spawned in a few short years.

She was confirming that the current level of evil in fact did exceed that of Stalin and Hitler—the Nazi holocaust, the horrifying Ukrainian famine: that it was worst than the world wars central to the first Fátima secrets, worse than even Hiroshima.

Evil is at work in man as never before.

What about the French Revolution and attacks on cathedrals and all Christendom?

Evil is at work in man as never before.

She was saying it surpassed the thunderous, murderous, blasphemous hordes of barbarians, the debaucheries of Nero, the bloodlust of Vlad (the Impaler). *Evil is at work in man as never before.* More than the brutal and lustful Romans of the first centuries A.D.; more than at Tenochtitlán, at Auschwitz: that none of these times was more or even as evil, when the entirety of modern apostasy was tallied.

Only Heaven could have that ledger. And with such a measure, how could major events not loom?

Would a merciful God allow it to continue?

Or was chastisement—purification—an aspect of mercy?

Might it be that Justice was not what came after Mercy but was spawned in and by it?

Many were those who scoffed at the notion of chastisement, and it was true, that it did no good to be overly negative. But Pollyanna also carried her risks.

Most negative was allowing immorality to continue its slow boil unwatched—for eventually those little rising plasma bubbles, left to their own course, were going to blow off the lid and knock down satellites. That actually happened in 2023, gases from an undiscovered undersea volcano disrupting telecommunications. An unnoticed dragon was slowly stirring from its slumber. Its fiery breath, those toxic gases, rose from the depths to claim their victims in our orbital arena. Coming was an event as cataclysmic as it was poetic, a reminder of the price of ignorance and the cost of immorality.

Thus, a message from nature itself, a warning loud and clear—avert the boil, tend to the pot, else we pay the price of neglect. For it was not just a volcano that erupted, it was our collective conscience that had been twisted, inverted, hot-started, pricked. An eruption sought to ask, "Have we tended to our own rising plasmas of immorality, or have we simply allowed them to simmer their way toward a boil?

True it was that looking darkly at everything could feed energy and make it darker. That had to be balanced with this: knowing we live forever. That was joy. There is eternity. Life was limitless. In her apparitions Mary appeared with a backdrop of flowers and meadows similar to the splendor, the ineffable beauty, too profound for utterance, too elusive for the chains of language, that was seen by folks in those near-death experiences. The colors alone were worth all earthly suffering, any trial. Awaiting the kind of heart were the peace and comfort of forever, the aromas unlike any on earth, and music like a thousand songs with exquisite strings and tinkling gold bells somehow orchestrated (and this was no fantasy) by angels.

There was that light, fantastic yet not blinding, the visual of God's Love.

Light emanated in purest form from all that resides in Heaven—even plants, grass, jewel-like edifices, and those who earned—who had loved their way to—an abode there.

Oh, cottages in most verdant of woods, mansions beaming rays of rainbow!

Light goes there from house to house, brighter, more resplendent, more multivariate with each loop; everything magnifying beauty.

"Suddenly, an enormous explosion erupted beneath me, an explosion of light rolling out to the farthest limits of my vision," said a woman named Kimberly Sharp, who had just such a vision. "It reached the ends of the universe, which I could see, and doubled back on itself in endless layers. I was watching eternity unfold. The Light was brighter than hundreds of suns, but it didn't hurt my eyes. I had never seen anything as luminous or as golden as this Light, and I immediately understood it was entirely composed of love, all directed at me."

"I wasn't sure when the light in the room began to change," said Dr. George Ritchie, a psychiatrist who experienced clinical death in youth at a military facility. "Suddenly I was aware that it was brighter, a lot brighter, than it had been.

"I stared in astonishment as the brightness increased, coming from nowhere, seeming to shine everywhere at once. All the light bulbs in the ward couldn't give off that much light. All the bulbs in the world couldn't! It was impossibly bright: it was like a million welders' lamps all blazing at once. I saw that it was not light but a Man who had entered the room, or rather, a Man made out of light, though this seemed no more possible to my mind than the incredible intensity of brightness that made up His form.

"The instant I perceived Him, a command formed itself in my mind. 'Stand up!' He said. The words came from inside me, yet they *had an au*thority my mere thoughts had never had. I got to my feet, and as I did came to the stupendous certainty: *'You are in the Presence of the Son of God.'*

"Again, the concept seemed to form itself inside me, but not as thought or speculation. It was a kind of knowing, immediate and complete."

"When I first saw Him, the light and the glory and the surging of power was so tremendous," added a woman named Margaret Tweddell. "It was like an avalanche of feeling over me. At the present time I just don't feel that I have found a way in which to describe what it was like—an indescribable contentment and uplifting, a tremendous ecstasy of feeling on all realms, being completely out of myself, an unusually vivid knowledge of the intense, sympathetic love around you—the warmth of it, the light of it—something that's not external but is part of you."

It usually starts as that small speck of light but grows—dramatically. Soon, it consumes all. There is no more tunnel. There are no more planets or stars. "It is like a sunrise on a mountain that is covered with snow, when the colors come down and reflect on you—a dazzling brilliance that would make you close your eyes and yet feel it in every pore of your body," said another. There is no earthly point of context in describing it. "It was so wonderful and beautiful and everything in my life was suddenly perfect: it was joy and bliss," said another, in wonderment even years later.

It was a light available to the extent that it could be manifest on earth when one prayed from the heart and asked Jesus to be right there beside and inside. Here and now. A personal Companion. He could go to the limits of a universe and be closer than your shadow. Render homilies that said that! Did a similar well-being come from the Rosary? Did it come during Mass? Potent prayers! Light streamed from the Eucharist, when we gazed on it with a soft yearning heart. It was a portal. It was a wellspring. Hardening of the arteries? Sometimes, the fruit of hard hearts. We worked too hard when we didn't work for God.

"His Light began to fill my mind, and my questions were answered even before I fully asked them," noted a woman from Seattle. "His Light was knowledge. It had power to fill me with all truth. As I gained confidence and let the light flow into me, my questions came faster than I thought possible, and they were just as quickly answered."

It is a Light that not only informs but shoos away demons like cockroaches in a dark kitchen when a bulb is clicked on.

"While I was enveloped by the Light, I knew the answers to the questions that had formulated in my mind," continued the previous testimony. "Secrets from the beginning of time to infinity were clear to me. Myriads of things were understandable. I understood, for example, that when I left earth I would leave with whatever spiritual growth I had attained there, and I would take that spiritual growth with me into this new world."

Said a woman from Alaska named Karen Thomas, during her brush with the hereafter (during spinal surgery), a spirit took her to the bank of a river—glistening, "living" water—where, on the side bank, she spotted deceased relatives who were watching and thrilled to see her: her father, who died when Karen was a child, a deceased brother, aunts and uncles, and four people she had never met but whom she knew were grandparents. They had passed before Karen was born. There was "a green lush gorgeous-looking area, grass, and bright flowers, all kinds of colors I had never seen before. It was mesmerizing. And I noticed this immense light I had come into was actually within every living thing I was looking at and emanating out."

God is Light and Light is Love and His Love and Light are more than all in the world multiplied by infinity.

One thought of this and how much time was wasted on politics, on Facebook, when Heaven beckoned, when there was Jesus to worship. Divided. Diverted. It was a classic stratagem of the enemy. Overwhelm with trivia. Divide and conquer. Block anything that brings light. Make humans waste precious moments that will never come again.

Every minute was of endless value and idle time was time for prayer. For life moved as a flash of neon. In our time, it had quickened.

In Heaven, everything would be now. There is no time.

"I wasn't blinded, but I was am*azed* that the luster and intensity continually increased," said a preacher named John Piper who was hit by a truck in 1989. "Strange as it seems, as brilliant as everything was, each time I stepped forward, the splendor increased. The farther I walked, the brighter the light. The light engulfed me, and I had the sense that I was being ushered into the Presence of God."

When we concentrate on the Light, we get Heaven.

"Seeing the light made me fearless," testified yet one more, a woman who had been in a state of depression. "In fact, I was filled with the most incredible peace I have ever known. The Person speaking to me knew what all my problems and fears were. All of my burdens slipped away. Suddenly the light went through me. It didn't reflect off of me or anything like that. It went straight through me. As it did, I was filled with unconditional love which was so complete and powerful that I would need to invent new words to describe it."

Wrote the great mystic St. Teresa of Avila, "It is not a radiance which dazzles, but a soft whiteness and an infused radiance which, without wearying the eyes, causes them the greatest delight, nor are they wearied by the brightness which they see in seeing this Divine beauty. So different from any earthly light is the brightness and light now revealed to the eyes that, by comparison with it, the brightness of our sun seems quite dim and we should never want to open our eyes again for the purpose of seeing it. It is as if we were to look at a very clear stream, in a bed of crystals, reflecting the sun's rays. It is a light which never gives place to night, and being always light, is disturbed by nothing."

That takes us back to Lucia, who described an angel who preceded the Blessed Mother as "transparent as crystal when light shines through it."

Chapter 18

THIS WAS HEAVEN'S ILLUMINATION. But in Light came truth, and the truth was not always what we wanted to hear. At the same time that a woman with a famous near-death experience described vistas she was favored to glimpse, she also was shown matters of a serious nature, and in our time, this woman told me, mankind was in a profound tussle with the enemy. Sin and its power had caused the world to jolt out of kilter, and the result was storms, fires, and quakes—quakes that, she quietly told me, will get much worse. Our inner imbalance was translating outwardly; more powerful than a cyclone.

"We live in troubling times," wrote this woman. "Time is speeding up. Like a magnetic force, this energy is beginning to pull and distort the earth's harmony, throwing natural forces off balance. If we do not return to the truths of God, seasons will continue to be altered, earthquakes will split the earth, and this will be a direct result of our collective disregard for universal laws. Our actions magnified by billions of souls will literally change our environment, first spiritually, then physically."

One had to be careful. He could deceive, could Satan, "even the elect" (*Matthew* 24:24). In this realm of afterlife sojourners was a woman from Sulphur, Louisiana, named Sondra Abrahams, whom I first met while doing a retreat for Archbishop Philip Hannan of New Orleans.

"I remember [Jesus] putting His arms around me," said Sondra, who clinically died during a hysterectomy from a reaction to medication in 1970. "The Lord wasn't a spirit; He was real. I was just my soul and it was dirty. I could feel His love—a consuming love. It was in every pore of my being. He told me that He was going to show me things. He turned and He moved His Hand. As He moved His Hand, I saw a review of my life from the time I was a tiny child up until age thirty. It was almost like a movie screen. I saw every time I did something good and I felt His love and joy. When I did something bad, I felt His hurt and the intense pain I caused Him. He showed me my whole life. But He never stopped loving me. His mercy is enormous. Explaining this is very hard. I came face to face with Jesus. He radiates love. He is more beautiful than any picture I have ever seen. I remember Him putting His arms around me. I could feel His love—a consuming love. Being a parent, I thought I knew love, but His love doesn't even compare. His love consumes you and you can feel it. It is the most beautiful, unusual sensation I've ever had."

"He [also] showed me Hell."

"It was horrible. It never ends. It is for all eternity. It is just horrible. I was so distraught about the souls going there. The souls looked like something in your worst dreams, almost monsters. They were cursing God, and never stopped. It was like a volcano: You can't imagine what these souls looked like.

"I cried out 'I will pray for them!' and Jesus shook His head. He showed me a horrible man who would curse God, mean, cruel, and prideful. To this day, I don't know who this man was. I have never forgotten this. And I knew right away that I didn't want to go to Hell. The suffering is so intense there. [This man] would slam doors in people's faces on purpose. He would see an animal and deliberately run over it on the street. The man's friends showed him that he needed to find God. And he said 'I don't need to find God. I am God.' He didn't recognize Jesus because of his pride.

"I saw my great uncle Creighton who died when I was four or five years old," Sondra also recounted. "He committed suicide by shooting himself. He was in the lowest level of purgatory. His soul recognized mine, and he asked me to pray for him. I heard his cry. He came another twenty years later after this experience to let me know he had been released."

"The Blessed Mother appeared with Saint Michael," Abrahams had continued. "She is gorgeous. When she speaks it's like little tiny bells chiming. It's so hard to explain. She told me that all the times I had prayed to her, she had heard every prayer. All prayers are heard. Saint Michael was something else. I remember thinking that I wanted to be on his side! I saw prayers of people carried back and forth to Heaven by the angels. The reason why we don't get what we pray for is that sometimes that 'something' may not be for the good of our souls."

In her prescience, Abrahams also saw a grave new sin and massive events, rising on the horizon. "[Jesus] showed me euthanasia and said many would die in hospitals and nursing homes," she recounted. "Then He showed me clear tanks with babies in them that all looked alike and they were attached to umbilical cords, but there were no wombs. Their eyes were blank. Jesus said *'Man will try to create life and they will destroy many. They cannot create life because only My Father can create and destroy life. Only He can put the soul into the body.'* I was shown that the soul enters the body at the time of conception and a guardian angel is assigned to that soul. A baby that has Down's Syndrome or another disability is not a mistake. They are here on a mission to show us compassion and love. Jesus said *'My father makes no mistakes. He knows every creation He has made.'*"

The babies in those tanks: in retrospect, it seemed like human cloning, which Sondra for years described as "duplication," for this was before the term "cloning" came into currency. In 2023 came photos in the news of egg-shaped plexiglass wombs in which would be fashioned genetically-altered, "designer" babies, or infants with three parents. Actual cloning hung over society like a sword of Damocles. And it hearkened to that anonymous "word" in 1990, which began: *"In four years there will arise a new evil the likes of which mankind has never before encountered. It will arrive almost imperceptibly, with few people noticing the depth of its evil, for it will appear to have beneficial and convenient aspects. It is an evil comparable to abortion—that is to say, that even if evils as great and widespread as abortion were to be eliminated, this is enough of an evil that it would present mankind with an enormous challenge. This evil is being allowed as a test because of the prayers inspired by Mary to put off chastisements. How mankind responds to this new evil will determine the extent, length, and severity of the first chastisements."*

Four years later was 1994, a landmark year, for great headway was made into the technology of cloning, and funding at a federal level was made available.

More astonishingly, in the early morning of September 11, 2001, the main headline in *The New York Times*, which arrived at newsstands hours before the Trade Center attacks, was, "Scientists Urge Bigger Supply Of Stem Cells; Report backs Cloning to Create New Lines."

The scientific community was demanding the creation, for purposes of harvesting their cells, of human embryos.

A similar story was the main headline in *USA Today*, just three miles from where a third plane struck the Pentagon.

Soon, researchers in South Korea announced that they had "cloned human embryos and extracted from them stem cells in a development that experts hope could spark a medical revolution," said a report. No one knew what was being done in secret in the larger moneyed nations.

But it was a harbinger, and I related it to a follow-up prophecy, in 2004, which warned that *"there is going to be a major disruption in a region of the world that will affect everyone.*

"The world is now seriously out of conformance with the Will of God and what He created and intended.

"There are those who would reconfigure the very creatures He has formed, and who meddle with the texture of life.

"For this reason, the Lord will allow a huge reorientation. If not for the action of Heaven, what God has created on earth will soon be damaged beyond recovery."

Continued the anonymous utterance, *"A very dramatic effect already is in progress as regards the support structures of what man calls nature. Such cannot be allowed to take the final realization of total realignment when it comes to the very way elements and life forces interact. The event to come will surprise everyone who has offered a prognostication, and will show even recalcitrant scientists, though not all, that there is a fundamental alarm in Heaven over their arrogant and wayward course. Nothing that is artificial in a way that disrupts what God intended will be allowed to stand.*

"Heed this too: the politics of denial will be struck as with a plague.

"The smallest of what lives is precious in My sight.

Days later—as a preview—was the Great Asian Tsunami.

Back in 1938, it had been the aurora. What would the next "huge light" be?

Abrahams, weeping, had said, "The one thing God told me was that when we tried to become God that He would come down on us. You noticed when all this cloning was announced, the weather got horrible everywhere? That's God saying He's still in control. The other thing I was shown was a war. And it won't be like any kind of war we've ever had before; it's going to be here on our land too. It won't just be a war of guns and planes but nuclear, and every little nation that has a nuclear weapon will get in on it. I've seen it. He showed it to me. Fires out of the sky, people burning, death everywhere. I can still even smell the smoke. I've never talked about it because I wanted to keep the focus on love. Peace can happen—it can happen—but we have to pray. If they do something crazy, China will join North Korea."

While South Korea was messing with clones, its enemy just north was readying nukes.

And the clones would appear how?

The "duplications," said Abrahams, "looked like babies, thousands of babies, in jars that were moving, like artificial wombs, and it was their *eyes*. It's always what I remember. The eyes were just dead. There was nothing there. And I kept hearing Jesus say, '*You see, man is going to try to become God,*' and over and over I heard that. I called it 'duplication' because they were all identical, they all looked alike. I didn't understand it until a few years ago, and then I realized it was cloning! That's what He was showing me."

"There were a lot of bombs and everything was turned upside-down and the whole world was a mess," said the Louisiana woman of her premonition. "There were lakes where there were not lakes, mountains were gone. There were little areas where people survived—remnants. Everything was turned around, like the earth was off balance."

This hewed close to Medjugorje, where a priest close to the seers had said those who survived the chastisements (would there be many? a few?) would be as peasants. Others too foresaw a more naturalist and simple way of existence. This once more called forth the anonymous divulgence which said, "*Your era is ending. Soon the world will not be the world you know. I am not speaking of a barren world, or one depopulated, but of the end of your technological era. Many inventions of mankind will be broken down and there will be more of a peasant attitude and way of life everywhere.*" It added, *"You think of the changes in very simple ways, without realizing the fundamental mistakes of mankind.*

"The very artifice of your societies is false and against the accordance of God's Will.

"This artifice shall not last.

"Your very conceptions of happiness and comforts are a great evil and falsity."

If the prospect of cloning—already underway in earnest with animals—was not enough, there was the truly macabre trend of euthanasia. Suicide, often cited, in near-death experiences, as a serious sin, one that brought dense afterlife darkness, was spreading to all corners.

Once a morbid quirk in Holland and Belgium, it had spread to Europe—even Portugal—and North America, particularly Canada, where one doctor who'd helped kill more than two hundred poor souls boasted of traveling to help a "patient" die despite a ruling that this person was neither sick nor mentally incompetent enough to reach such a decision. In visions, Abrahams had seen many elderly dying in hospitals.

In some cases, in real cases, in real-time, young people were opting for euthanasia as the remedy for depression (along with traditional means of suicide).

And some nations—so altruistic!—were euthanizing babies.

There was also the prospect of "baby farms": artificial uteruses that hearkened to future scenarios like that portrayed in *Brave New World*. Would we confront a time when man-made wombs, these sterile and mechanized cradles, usurped the majesty, the holy mystery, of natural gestation?

Lambs and mice (lambs!) already had been partly gestated in such contraptions.

And so there was the prospect of war, which I heard from many near-deathers, though one, Dr. Howard Storm, said he was told during his trip to the beyond that in the end, God wouldn't allow a nuclear war to destroy His Creation. During the tense 1980s, the Virgin reportedly assured seers at Medjugorje that a third world war, feared so greatly at that time, would not occur, a claim doubly fascinating because in her cloister (now Coimbra, Portugal, an hour north of Fátima), dear hidden Lucia would soon tell visiting prelates privileged enough to see her that, indeed, an "atomic war" nearly occurred in 1985 but had been prevented by prayer.

"The end of the world?" said Abrahams. "No. A punishment. There will be famine and extreme cold and we will not have medical supplies and we will have to go backwards. That's all there is to it. We've become so advanced with things like cloning and we think we're so smart. But [and this was said urgently] we have to go back to find God."

Chapter 19

GOD WAS FILLED WITH MERCY. He was also just. Justice *was* often God's mercy. "It is a justice that comes from love, from the depths of compassion and mercy that are the very heart of God, the Father who is moved when we are oppressed by evil and fall under the weight of sins and fragility," Pope Francis said in 2023.

"If people change their ways, Our Lord will still avail the world," was the way young Jacinta's had put it. *"Nosso Senhor ainda irá beneficiar o mundo.* But if they do not, the chastisement will come."

"If my people will not submit, I shall be forced to let fall the arm of my Son," Our Lady of LaSalette said. *"It is so strong, so heavy, that I can no longer withhold it."*

On her deathbed at Dona Estefania Hospital in Lisbon, Jacinta asked a nun named Mother Maria Godinho to "tell everybody that God grants us His graces through the Immaculate Heart of Mary, that they should ask her for them, that the Heart of Jesus wants the Immaculate Heart of Mary to be honored along with Him, that they should ask the Immaculate Heart of Mary for peace because God has placed it in her keeping."

Had there been events that already fulfilled this?

Jacinta spoke of "great world events that would take place around 1940," which turned out to be the year Brussels fell to Germany, there was a Nazi invasion of Iceland, Norway, and

Denmark, and the Battle of France began.

"Wars are nothing but punishments for the sins of the world," Jacinta had said.

In 1941 had come the ghastly Holocaust. "If men do not change their ways, Our Lady will send the world a punishment like of which has never been seen," she said.

"The sins that lead more souls to hell are the sins of the flesh," Jacinta added—a comment perhaps more relevant to our time than hers. "Fashions that will greatly offend Our Lord will appear," said the little prodigy. "People who serve God should not follow fashions. The Church has no fashions. Our Lord is always the same. The sins of the world are very great."

And the Church?

In vision Jacinta saw the Holy Father besieged by critics, holding his head in his hands, weeping, kneeling by a table. "Outside the house were many people, some of whom cast stones at him, others cursed him and said many ugly words. Poor Holy Father! We have to pray a lot for him."

"Pray much for priests! Pray much for religious!" Jacinta also urged. "Priests should only occupy themselves with the affairs of the Church. Priests should be pure, very pure. The disobedience of priests and religious to their superiors and to the Holy Father greatly offends Our Lord."

The first two secrets of Fátima had ended, as far as what was initially released, with the words, *"In Portugal, the dogma of the faith will always be preserved, etc. ..."* Those words were added by Lucia three years before receiving the Enlightenment, as she was pushing herself to recall everything and write it for the bishop.

For decades that verbiage—eleven words, so enigmatic—entranced Fátima watchers. What did they mean? Did they imply that Portugal would remain steadfast while the rest of the Church, or a great part of it, fell into apostasy? "In the translation, the original text has been respected, even as regards the imprecise punctuation, which nevertheless does not impede an understanding of what the visionary wished to say," was all the Vatican said.

So there was all that—foremost, the intimations of war, and a Church under attack, from inside and out.

The outward attack arrived viciously under Stalin. The Soviet tyrant slaughtered millions of Christians. Hitler wanted to create an occult version of the Vatican around a spooky SS castle. The "inside" one arguably took place, meanwhile, during the misuse of Vatican Two and the clerical sex scandals that ensnared at least 2,458 priests in the United States alone.

Clerics were openly defying bishops. By the 2020s, bishops openly defied the Vatican. This was foretold not only by mystics at spots such as Fátima and Akita (*"bishops against bishops"*), but by Emeritus Pope Benedict, who in 2015 sent a note to a friend saying, "We see how the power of the Antichrist is expanding, and we can only pray that the Lord will give us strong shepherds who will defend his church in this hour of need from the power of evil."

The evil was on all sides, cyclonic, the winds every which way. Good was called evil and evil good. Yet the devil was rarely mentioned in homilies.

How could one fight an inimical force without seeing where the enemy was?

And there was also, perhaps urgently, that other aspect of the Fátima Enlightenment to do with geophysics.

Again there were the near-death visionaries, including the famous one in Seattle who saw that city vanishing in a tectonic event, unnerving because it lies near to the boundary between the "North American" and "Juan de Fuca" tectonic plates, a 700-mile span known as the Cascadia Subduction Zone as it slashes from northern California to Canada, the Juan de Fuca trying to force its way under North America.

When the next massive earthquake hits, pointed out a newspaper, the northwest edge of the continent will drop by up to six feet and rebound thirty to a hundred feet to the west, "displacing a colossal quantity of seawater.

"One side will rush west, toward Japan. The other side will rush east, in a seven-hundred-mile liquid wall that will reach the Northwest coast, on average, fifteen minutes after the earthquake begins."

Added a magazine, the *New Yorker*: "In the Pacific Northwest, the area of impact will cover some hundred and forty thousand square miles, including Seattle, Tacoma, Portland, Eugene, Salem, Olympia, and some seven million people."

Added the magazine, "We now know that the odds of the big Cascadian earthquake happening in the next fifty years are roughly one in three. The odds of the very big one are roughly one in ten. Even those numbers do not fully reflect the danger—or, more to the point, how unprepared the Pacific Northwest is to face it. The truly worrisome figures in this story are these: Thirty years ago, no one knew that the Cascadian subduction zone had ever produced a major earthquake. Forty-five years ago, no one even knew it existed."

Chapter 20

BUT REALLY, WE KNEW PRECIOUS LITTLE. Where else might the hidden faults, too deep for discovery, spawn calamity?

Across America and around the world, major populations were in target zones.

If not quakes, it was hurricanes. What was Miami doing where it is? And New Orleans? Tokyo?

Storms. Tremors. No one could augur where or when the truly big ones would occur, just that they could and (without the Grace of God) would. When it came to natural events, the big stuff, we usually were surprised.

Were we now about to be shocked?

For guidance could we rely on mystics?

This was also problematic.

Many false ones had spread around the globe, and they spewed prophecy after dire prophecy.

Thus did Scripture say, "Beloved, do not believe every spirit, but test the spirits to see whether they are from God, because many false prophets have gone out into the world [*1 John* 4:1]."

But as it also says, "Test everything; retain what is good" [*1 Thessalonians* 5:21].

And testing was crucial, for many predictions were dramatic, apocalyptic, drastic, among the more gripping those of

James Wilburn Chauncey, a former military weather forecaster and cost engineer for NASA and the federal laboratories in Oak Ridge, Tennessee, who told me of a near-death experience as a child in 1946 when he was escorted first by angels and Jesus and then "radiant beings" in their late twenties.

"We went to the edge of paradise, like a cliff, and you could see the blue earth hanging there and when you wanted you could just zoom in on various places on earth," said Chauncey, whose "death" had been due to spinal meningitis. It was from this vantage point that he was shown not only what was currently transpiring, but what would occur in the world, and this entailed events that fit like confounding pieces of a jigsaw into the Fátima elucidation.

"Mountains had fallen; canyons disappeared; the courses of rivers were changed, and much land disappeared," he recollected. "Portions of Texas and Arizona were now lakes. What had been deserts of the west were now green and lush with trees and vegetation. Asia, Africa, Europe, and the world over became lush with vegetation, clear water, lakes, and rivers, and an abundance of fish, fowl, and the animals."

But getting there—cacophonous disturbances—was the trick, and many would not. This was implied in scenes he said flashed in front of him: pandemics, war, and volcanic eruptions as perturbations known to modern history rocked the planet, which he was shown would wobble before regaining equilibrium and ending up "totally straight" (which meant no more tilt on its "axis"). Along with the great new inland sea would be a gulf between California and the mainland, and loss of great chunks along the East Coast, especially Florida, to frothing, greedy torrents.

"I saw that we must not delay getting our lives in order," said another near-deather, Julia Rowe of California. "The time has come to... prepare for the days ahead. I was shown upcoming natural disasters on a scale unlike anything the

earth has ever experienced: earthquakes, hurricanes, torna-
dos, tsunamis, plagues, droughts, famines, pestilence, and all
manner of disease will be upon the earth in such a deep and
broadened scale that mankind cannot even imagine what
it will be like," she insisted, pointing to that set of tectonic
boundaries around the Pacific, the "Ring of Fire," which she
believed would generate a large seismic event like the first
"firecracker" in a series of catastrophes as the world beneath
our feet was "jostled," triggering many volcanoes and likewise fitting the idea of the earth's axis "unlatched."

This would be announced, she said cryptically, by an
event that occurs along the Wasatch Range at the edge of the
Rockies in Idaho and Utah.

Biological disaster was hardly out of the realm of possibility, though in the scenarios marshaled forth from future-gaz-
ers was every conceivable disaster, man-made or natural.
Food shortages. Exchanges between Libya and Israel. Iran.
Chauncey had "seen" people fleeing from the Vatican. Julie
Rowe saw the Vatican destroyed and a Pope killed. She also
saw an anti-christ arising as peacemaker in the Middle East.

In Utah, a woman named Sarah Menet predicted (in a
book, *There is No Death*) that there will be small "cities" of
refuge, where people will pray, share with each other, and
protect themselves from marauders who she warned will all
but take over the land. "There will be chaos in every part of
the world," she claims. "Many people ask me, 'Where will
it be safe?' but I also give them great hope. I saw pockets of
light on the earth. I know the power of God is greater than
any army of the earth."

Was this simply "tickling of the ears" (*2 Timothy* 4:3)?

In 2021, I was made aware of a young girl in Mexico who
was said to have visions that started in 2005 when she was
just three. "She dreams but also has apparitions in her own

room," Jaime Duarte, a prominent Mexican broadcaster, told me. "The Child Jesus played with her in her room. She has visions in a conscious state, and alone in front of Holy Sacrament, she sees the Virgin and dialogues with angels."

One night, according to Duarte, founder of *Cisne* Catholic Radio, the girl encountered Jesus Crucified and, trying to comfort Him, offered herself, in whatever way a youngster might, as a victim soul. As a result, she had developed red stigmatic marks.

At age nine, she'd informed her parents and a priest that world events were imminent, including a "warning" and "illumination" of conscience, the Mexican evangelist said.

"The warning is very close," he believed. "She says we have to prepare in four ways: 1) spiritual Rosary, prayer, not sinning, use of sacramentals, use medal of Saint Benedict, and also fasting 2) offering souls that are victims: sacrifices and pain 3) the Virgin asks that we are ready with food and clothing that would be necessary to survive some days during the warning and other things that will happen and 4) to meditate on a book written by Luisa Piccarreta on examination of conscience—to live the Divine Will of God." In the realm of prophetic utterance, an air of familiarity hung heavily, as if a ghostly chorus of countless soothsayers had already sung the same tune. Indeed, the echoes of parallel prophecies reverberated across the landscape of visionary accounts. One striking similarity bore a resemblance to the alleged foretellings that resonated through the enchanting hamlet of Garabandal. It was there, amidst the rustic charm of this Spanish village, that young souls were bestowed with extraordinary revelations—or so it was said—of an impending epoch, a time when the fabric of reality itself would unravel, unveiling a phenomenon of unprecedented proportions. These seemingly gifted youngsters were entrusted with a peculiar message, a revelation of a forthcoming event—a grand "illumination" that promised to cast a radiant light upon the souls of all humanity. In this Divine illumination, the witnesses would peer into the depths of their being, glimpsing their own essence as God Himself perceived it. The magnitude of such a notion, real or unreal, was simply awe-inspiring, for it held the promise of an unprecedented revelation, a collective revelation that would transcend the boundaries of ordinary perception. Moreover, Garabandal's enigmatic tale intertwined with the threads of the ethereal, for it harkened back to a distant day in the annals of recent history. In the final moments of the miraculous apparitions at Fátima in 1917, a moment of profound significance had transpired: Amidst the sacred grounds of Cova da Iria, the celestial manifestation of Our Lady revealed herself alongside the holy figures of Jesus and Joseph, showering their Divine benediction upon the throngs of fervent believers who had gathered there. And thus, it was at Garabandal that she chose to appear once again, assuming the ethereal visage of Our Lady of Mount Carmel. The resonance with the momentous climax of the Fátima apparitions was undeniable, a connection that heightened the mystique surrounding this grand tapestry. The intertwined narratives of these holy manifestations, bridging the gap between generations, whispered of a profound continuum that bound the celestial and earthly realms together in an enigmatic dance.

But was it true? Was this not the region of massive deceptive phenomena just three decades before, starting at a place called Ezkioga, where there likewise was talk of warnings, an "illumination," and great chastisements? The echoes of these prophecies, the overlapping motifs and sacred visions, painted a portrait of transcendence that if true and good parted the confines of time and space. A tapestry of Divine revelations unfolded before our eyes, intertwining the threads of history, faith, and the mystical yearnings of humanity. It was within this nexus of celestial whispers that the prophecies of Garabandal found their place in the eternal lore of Our Lady's apparitions, forever etched upon the collective consciousness of those who dared glimpse beyond the veil of the mundane.

As for the motif in which Mary allegedly showed herself, noted a priest named Father Alfred Combe: "Whenever Our Lady appears to her children on earth under a particular name, it is not without a purpose. At Lourdes in 1858, when a young Bernadette Soubirous asked the 'beautiful lady' who she was, the answer came: *'I am the Immaculate Conception.'* This was clearly a reaffirmation of the newly proclaimed dogma of the Immaculate Conception decreed by Pope Pius IX a few short years before, in 1854. When Our Lady came to Fátima in 1917 as 'The Lady of the Rosary,' it was to emphasize that most powerful prayer and urge us to use it in imploring God's mercy and gaining Our Lady's help and protection against the catastrophic events which were to come in the form of World War II and the global spread of atheistic Communism. Why then did the Blessed Virgin come to Garabandal as 'Our Lady of Mount Carmel'? What significance does this have for Christians today? If we go back to Lourdes we can begin to see a Divine theme being developed. The Blessed Virgin's last appearance at Lourdes was on July 16, 1858, feast of Our Lady of Mount Carmel. During the final apparition at Fátima, October 13, 1917, when the 'miracle of the sun' occurred, Our Lady first appeared as she had been appearing to the three shepherd children with her sorrowful heart exposed. And then she appeared as Our Lady of Mount Carmel with 'something hanging from her right hand.' We can safely assume that 'something' was the Scapular. Forty-four years later in the little mountain hamlet of San Sebastian de Garabandal in northern Spain, Our Lady appears with a large brown Scapular prominently draped over her right wrist."

In hot circulation was that prediction of a "warning," during which, said the Mexican girl (as relayed by Duarte), "We're going to see our sins, how God sees us. There will be an astronomical event. God wants that we should all ask God to forgive us. Everybody will see these extraordinary moments. It's going to be something really strong, very hard. That's why the Virgin asks us to prepare."

While the youngster said nothing about death during the warning, she related, according to Duarte, "some planet or something comes close to earth. It's not going to hit the earth. Some will fall on earth. Pieces will fall from it but won't harm us."

But fright? A hard moment? This traversed onto strange nervous turf, the notion of a "Planet X" or massive bolide menacing our solar system, at least the girth of Pluto, but of course in a belt of comets splaying itself millions of miles beyond what we normally envision as the solar system. During one experience, according to Duarte, the girl saw the moon, or some heavenly body, split in two, which the Mexican broadcaster took as a metaphor, like her augury of a "temple, half-destroyed," which he believed was the Church. "The Virgin said that after the warning, there will be the third world war," he said. "And there will be a new virus on earth. She doesn't know what virus it is. She made a drawing of it, which was shown to a doctor who said it resembled the smallpox virus. The girl also says she was told that in all the world is going to be a very powerful earthquake. There will be volcanic explosions and tsunamis. One volcano is a famous one in Mexico City and will have an eruption. She sees destruction and death in Mexico. The coasts are flooded. I don't know if these events will be before or after the warning. She sees or dreams of destruction caused by an earthquake. What's strange about this, on four occasions or so, hours after waking up or the next day, there always is an earthquake in some part of the world."

In one case, added Duarte, a nightmare the girl had of people with "dark skin and slanty eyes" amid death and destruction was followed by an eruption, a volcanic event, in Indonesia—no dream, this. An omen? Her parents believe it actually pertained to an event that remains in the future and involves a great coming quake preceded by "a six-hour warning."

Was this why there currently were so many hearing "hums," "rumbling," "booms": were these mere microcosms, a presage for what would later detonate into a louder cacophony—global echoes—occurring, without explanation, in a future not so far away?

Duarte wasn't sure if the girl had glimpsed as had so many others a tsunami or coastal floods for the U.S. "What she sees about the U.S.," he said laconically, "is world war."

I reflected back on Esperanza, who said it was "a crucial time, a decisive time for humanity," that a "hard moment" would come, a "good test," but a tough one, adding, "We cannot be concerned about money or houses or big cars. No. The moment is arriving when we must leave all those things. This moment is coming. Right now man is punishing himself through his egoism, through his lack of charity, through his lack of conscientiousness.

"There will be much upheaval. There will be some societal chaos. Our Lady is coming to lighten the chastisements. There will be problems and certain natural calamities. I see little quakes and certain others. A very difficult moment will arrive, but there will remain good because the Light and Grace of the Holy Spirit will always illumine those few who desire justice in the world—the truth and recognition of Jesus with His Love throughout all time."

Chapter 21

"LITTLE QUAKES."

Rumbles.

"Certain others."

And weather? The world in 2023 endured intense heat just about everywhere—in some cases, such as Arizona and Italy, life-threatening temperatures. Was this what a seer in Cuenca, Ecuador predicted would be "natural disasters created by man"?

Whatever the source—human or natural (that blazing sun, those solar storms)—it was unnerving to see some areas with temperatures that for weeks seemed like an oven set on "low warm." What would happen if electricity—and therefore air conditioning—went out during a heat spell of 120 degrees? Was it going to get even hotter?

As for war, the Enlightenment said just what Esperanza—who had not been privy to it—did. *"It is the purification of the world by sin as it plunges. Hatred and ambition cause the destructive war!'"*

And there was the anonymous locution, which in part said, *"Chastisements will differ according to regions, and like the great evil, will not always or usually be immediately noticeable for what they are. In [this] period also will be a warning that involves not fire from the sky but fear of fire from the sky, and strange loud rumblings."*

The notion was captivating: loud sounds from high above or deep under. One had to step back and form one's own inklings. Oh, the commotion! The undulating terrain! The agitation! A strange reverberation would occur, if there was truth to this, and a global quake? What would a tremor worldwide sound—and look—like?

Wide, roiled rivers, rollicking to a boil, a field of snap beans, disturbed, rolling like a blanket in a breeze. Rising, falling, billowing, rolling. Then, more distant rumblings and loud ones, far away and yet really just underneath. A blast from below, a temblor, a massive fissure. Ramparts slouching, tumbling into whitewater. The earth shaking fitfully; locally, regionally; with violence; water cascading into chasms—high cascades of water—as streams, creeks, and rivers flowed over hills. Towering water would seem to come from below as well as laterally—from the north; perhaps from the Great Lakes, if what occurred was in the Midwest (Lake Superior?), or a bay, a sea, if a coast was near the epicenter. Vapor and dust will swell and commingle, rise and plummet and elevate again, filling the atmosphere. Rumble after rumble, one deeper than the previous.

Or so one speculated.

Would America be singled out?

New York?

Wasn't New York involved in every new trend?

The "fear" (of fire)—if such prophecy spoke true—raised the possibility, too, of a large astronomic object approaching, coming into view, and splitting in half, causing great fright and perhaps global panic but not devastation. This would fit the bill as "not fire from the sky but fear of fire from the sky." It could also cause "skyquakes," "a strange loud rumbling," the threat of a massive celestial leviathan. An astral goliath in the far reaches of the great cosmos that dared to cross the boundaries of human complacency, jolting the world from the stupor of everyday existence. This celestial entity, born in the great factories of starlight, might split asunder upon arrival, bisected with the exactness of a divine mathematician. It would be a sight to behold, too majestic, too petrifying, its duality perhaps sparking a global tremor of the psyche, a terror not of destruction, but the mere specter of it. This seemed to align the cryptic prophecy—not a blight of combustion from the heavens, rather the very anticipation of such a cataclysm, a crippling dread of cosmic pyrotechnics that held the earth in its cold, paralyzing grip. A phenomenon that could be the source of tumultuous rumbles in the sky, the mysterious auditory stamp of the cosmic titan's descent. A strange, terrible resonance of Divine portent that carried with it the thunderous echoes of celestial disturbance.

Yet there was no devastation in its wake, only the potent cocktail of fear and awe stirred up in the hearts of the earthly observers. The true weight of the phenomenon lay not in the potential for destruction but in its capacity to rattle the collective psyche of a species, its audacity to shake humanity from the comfort of its celestial ignorance. A reminder of our infinitesimal stature in the vast, uncaring theater of the universe. At the Jet Propulsion Laboratory in Pasadena, an expert on comets told me the likeliest scenario when it comes to apocalypse was of an object wholly unanticipated suddenly appearing and hanging in the sky.

For long moments, mankind would hold its collective breath, waiting to see what course such an intruder from darkness unknown would take. As for the sounds: here again were forerunners in the skyquakes and rumbles from clustered Europe to remote forests of Canada, and across the United States. "After about a month of silence, Fort Wayne's mysterious 'boom' has returned," noted television station WANE-TV in 2017. "'You can't describe it,' said Helene Lilly, who heard it almost ten times. 'You think you're in a war.'"

In 2023, not far from New York, news outlets reported what one called "a loud, sustained rumbling" that "shook residents and buildings along the Jersey Shore, leading some to speculate on social media that an earthquake could be to blame." There was, however, this twist: The U.S. Geological Survey logged no sign of seismic activity in New Jersey, New York, or neighboring states as of 2:30 p.m. on January 13, 2023, about thirty minutes after the tremors rattled windows and houses.

"Residents from as far south as Cape May and up to Manahawkin along the coast and as far west as Glassboro in Gloucester County reported feeling the shaking on social media. The tremor lasted at least ten seconds."

Seismic? Cosmic? Perhaps the northern lights, strumming the atmosphere like a bass? Aliens?

Here we got into the bizarre, for such sounds often were included in reports—and they had become countless—of UFOs and strange "creatures." It was like portals to mystical dimensions—floodgates—were opening. In spot after spot, aerial lights and rumblings, along with legendary "cryptids," were reported near cemeteries, around places of *wicca*, at sites of ritual sacrifice, and especially, where there had been battles, massacres, or Indian activity, particularly burial mounds. Had such places been cursed, unlatching a vortex, or was it all raw demons, evil in masquerade, flaunting its capabilities of deception?

While the "mature" mind was wont to file it—skinwalkers, werewolves, bigfoot, lake leviathan, mothmen—as straight-up lunacy, there was Saint Columba to consider (he had once exorcised "Nessie," which later regrouped near the cottage owned by Crowley), as well, when it came to UFOs, as the fiery wheel of Ezekiel. Befuddling huge red-eyes hirsute man-apes were reported as unexplained lights—what the military was now calling UAPs (unexplained aerial phenomena)—

hovered overhead or zipped instantly to invisibility, often as if teleported or dematerializing, as did certain "yetis," and as did sinister, bulb-headed, gray-skinned "aliens," whose eyes (and here an exorcist might take note) were described as jet-black and almond-shaped: totally dark, no pupil, no soul, no iris, just coal. Hear this, from the Book of Wisdom: "In return for their senseless wicked thoughts, which misled them into worshipping dumb serpents... You sent upon them swarms of dumb creatures for vengeance... or new-created, wrathful, unknown beasts."

I noted that strange rumblings often occurred in relation to bizarre phenomena, whether abominable snowman, "UFOs," or old Indian haunts such as Moodus, Connecticut, where the Wangunk told colonists of sounds they took to be from angry "gods." Indeed, the town's name came from *"Machemoodus,"* or "place of bad noises." Reports of strange rumblings and lights in the sky dated back to early Spanish missionaries in the 1600s in Colorado, this the terrain of Utes, a tribe known for its legendary "medicine men" who supposedly could transform into wolfen creatures. Transylvania had nothing on Colorado! Had a veil there been breached, and were veils opening around the world?

In the Talala area ravaged by the 2004 tsunami, many who had taken to slumbering outdoors did so because they had felt tremors and heard "mysterious blasts" (according to the *Times of India*). Similar shocks had been reported from the Jamnagar district months before the Great Tsunami. The spiritual and geologic seemed intertwined.

Some geologists believed whole ancient continents had been "subducted" under the earth's current crust, and below even that were molten flows or great areas of metal that it was speculated slide like plastic.

No geophysicist knew how big an earthquake could get; no one knew what else might jolt deep below the surface. Could the earth, the entire planet, "shudder," to use Lucia's verb? What was the Enlightenment referring to? Regional shudder? Global? The question was magnitude. When I spoke to one of the world's leading authorities, Dr. Hiroo Kanamori, at the University of Tokyo, he told me it was impossible for scientists to speculate on the highest magnitude. "There is no real limit," he said. "Of course, if you break the earth in two parts, that probably would be the biggest one."

Quakes could come in swarms. They did in ancient Asia, the Middle East, and Mesopotamia: one could set off another. There were a shocking number of hidden faults beneath Los Angeles; a visible one shot up a hilly street to Columbia Records at the famous Walk of Fame in Hollywood.

Similar breaches could be below any state and any city, including America's largest.

Could there be a global storm of them?

In ancient Turkey ("Anatolia") tremors one after another wiped out early settlements, and the same may have occurred during the Bronze Age in Egypt and Israel.

Indeed, some scientists believed quakes may have set off the brimstone at Sodom.

Chapter 22

THE FIRE WAS, AND WOULD BE, AS SCRIPTURE SAID: from the celestial vault, heaven, as seemed to occur in Central Wisconsin in 1871 when the "mother" of all wildfires, a truly historic one, rendered that million acres ash, twelve short years after a warning (of chastisement) from the Blessed Mother (near Green Bay). Of monumental curiosity, and yet as ignored by historians, it had been the same day, the very same, as the greatest urban blaze in history roared two hundred separate miles south, in Chicago, engulfing 17,000 structures; and also, back to forests, in Western Michigan (near Port Huron), which caused speculation that a comet's blazing prolongation had touched—torched—several Midwest spots, falling from above the tree lines, from the celestial canopy.

No cow kicking a lantern, this.

It was impossible not to see this as a microcosmic harbinger, a cousin, of the Third Secret's angel with a spear aflame.

Would it repeat?

"Fire will fall."

On a grander scale?

The more salient questions: "where," "how," and urgently, "when."

One day, would searing heat descend upon the earth, this time across a vastly greater expanse? Would it be from the rise in global temperature—igniting desiccant brush—or reflecting on the Enlightenment, and geophysics, would the earth "bob" off center and trigger volcanoes?

There were those rumbles of it: sounds in New Jersey (the Pine Barrens) like giant tuba; low, rattling rumblings in Louisiana; a hum in England; a metallic echo in Moscow; many reports evoking the uncanny soundtracks of *Close Encounters* and *Star Wars*.

In Czechoslovakia, a deep vibration.

"Hell's bells," a witness elsewhere said.

Or was it the lion's roar (*1 Peter* 5:8)?

But mainly it was a throbbing bass, and intriguing was that certain global echoes resembled the "shofar," an ancient horn that summoned warning, and repentance, from the thick boiling clouds on Sinai (*Exodus* 19:16). Now, a dirge, a haunting echo, was heard without sure explanation in the modern world: In most cases officials ruled out sonic booms, distant traffic, the grinding noise of factories, quakes, heavy equipment, sewer belches. Some of it perhaps—only perhaps—was by way of an aurora borealis and its electromagnetism, which can strum the earth's upper reaches, as energy streams from a flare—the eruption of tornadic magnetism—on the sun.

"In our opinion, the source of such powerful and immense manifestation of acoustic-gravity waves must be very large-scale energy processes," a scientist named Elchin Khalilov had ventured, explaining the sounds. "These processes include powerful solar flares and huge energy flows generated by them, rushing towards earth's surface and destabilizing the magnetosphere, ionosphere, and upper atmosphere. Thus, the effects of powerful solar flares: the impact of shock waves in the solar wind, streams of corpuscles and bursts of electromagnetic radiation are the main causes of generation of acoustic-gravitation waves following increased solar activity."

Here too one could extrapolate the metaphor of a "flaming spear," and in fact, one recent flare resembled the profile, no pareidolia here, of an angel ready with trumpet.

And mystically, there were all the "miracles of the sun" at sites of apparition, the plunging, colored solar orb at Medjugorje, at Betania, or Kibeho, and Fátima. Yes, the sun or another astronomical force could be the jolt, could unlatch the axis, as could the hot blade of a comet.

But unless the world's end, it was not a bolide, for one large enough to unlock the hatch would jettison torrents of debris to the point of shutting off the lights and killing photosynthesis, plunging earth into an endless winter night. Though other mystics saw an event that would cause three days of utter darkness, Lucia had not, nor, it seemed, had Medjugorje: at a conference on September 9, 2001, in Sacramento, a seer from there ribbed me for proclaiming during my talk that fire was about to fall on America, afraid, she joked, that the next thing I would declare would be those "three days darkness."

When, less than two days later, fire did fall, it was on Manhattan.

Oh New York, with Babylon towers, with bronze bull! Had it learned no lesson, even when trounced by a virus? Had it seen no irony, this paragon of mammon, in the name "World Trade Center"? Did it not see aluminum cladding collapse into heaps of tortured metal.

And the devil? Demonic visages raged from the smoke that Tuesday, angry devils, exacting their measure, several beyond pareidolia (the imagining of an image). It wasn't the mind-playing tricks! God had allowed hell to deliver ashes to the front door of the new Nineveh and without warning (except in prophetic circles, where there had felled towers in paintings and dreams), fire had fallen, as if from Heaven, but really from the force of hell.

God had allowed it—spears had touched it—because it was the ultimate of what Jesus preached against: materialism. Did we think God was joking when He warned of it? Glitz. Wealth. Celebrity.

Noah.

And so it was that in the vaporous days after 9/11, a man never identified somehow slipped beyond the barricades of the NYPD and in haunting fashion played a trumpet on a street devoid of cars, of pedestrians, of clattering deliveries. Who was this mysterious stranger, this soloist, sounding an actual horn in the cement canyons, mournfully? When a photographer tried to take pictures, reported a radio station, his camera—and this was a professional—inexplicably jammed. It was the singular figure of an unidentified man who managed to slip through the cobwebbed cracks of the NYPD's rigorous barricade. He, alone, on a street scrubbed clean of the ceaseless bustle, an urban orchestra silenced; the tempo of automobile tires on asphalt, the staccato footfall of pedestrians, the grinding bray of delivery trucks—all had hushed in respect of this unanticipated requiem.

Perhaps his name was Gavreel, a mystery name for Gabriel, or Raguel, angel of justice. It was a unique exercise, imagining an angel with prophecy walking the streets of the world's nerve center. If he did, perhaps he would leave a rarefied old Bible, the Latin Vulgate, by John E. Potter and Company, for someone to thumb through and notice parchment that was torn or missing, pages that held clues to the future.

When I lived in New York I ran into several mysterious strangers and I imagined if I ran into another, on the streets of Midtown, or Lower Manhattan, he might appear at first glance like a homeless soul or simply a clever clean-cut pan-handler and leave, in his wake, that Bible with hints of the future—absent passages that lent clues to the future. Once I actually had encountered a mysterious elderly woman who simply and suddenly was there in front of me on Third Avenue, unfazed by the pedestrian crush, looking right at me while making the Sign of the Cross, and then vanishing into the crowd.

I imagined one missing page to be 585, *Isaiah* 45:2 (XLV), which among other things says: *"I will go before thee, and will humble the great ones of the earth: I will break in pieces the gates of brass, and will burst the bars of iron."*

The New American and King James versions say "bronze" instead of "brass," but either way, there were plenty of those closely-related metals in Manhattan and there was the bronze bull—emblem of unfettered capitalism, of Wall Street—and there was the brass of posh apartments in Midtown, not to mention the omnipresent bronze at Rockefeller Center.

There were bars of iron—grates—over the windows of old brokerage houses and bank vaults made of iron. Skyscrapers, subways, and bridges were fashioned or their cement reinforced with "bars of iron."

In some translations of Scripture to do with bronze was the word "sunder," which meant to cleave, rend, to divide, and sounded wroth. There were 140 search results for the word "bronze" in the Bible and eight for "sunder."

A different version said, *"I will go before you and level the mountains; bronze doors I will shatter and iron bars I will snap."*

"I will go before you and make the crooked places straight," the King James had it. *"I will break in pieces the gates of bronze And cut the bars of iron."*

More to the point was how instead of *"make crooked places straight,"* it said *"level the mountains."*

Chapter 23

THAT CAUSED ONE TO REFLECT ON THE WORDS OF THAT SEER in Africa who relating her vision had said, "I saw mountains crashing into each other. Stones coming out of the earth, nearly as if they were angry. I saw storms crashing against each other and fire coming from them. I don't know what this means. I was told that people are causing this and that it is coming..."

Since she and fellow seers had foreseen the historic genocide in the 1990s (incredibly, even warning the nation's president before it occurred, and also listeners who heard radio streams from the apparition site), I paid close heed to her utterance. *"Crashing storms"; "fire coming from them."*

As in *Isaiah* 9:10, "bricks" had "fallen," but the response to it, to 9/11, and then to the coronavirus, was pride and defiance, the vow to build even better, taller buildings in New York.

A Bible search for "tower" turned up case after case in the Old Testament whereby God's judgment was witnessed in the destruction precisely of towers.

Yet New York—the world—would have none of it. There were 340,000 millionaires and 107 billionaires, the richest man there, Jeff Bezos, at one point making four to nine million dollars an hour, or $6,541,666,666 a month (while minimum hourly wage for Amazon workers was fifteen dollars).

At the low end of his range, the Amazon guru made $66,666 a minute, more than the average American worker made in a year, while the founder of Microsoft was "worth" more than the annual gross national product of Puerto Rico— and neither of these two was as rich as Elon Musk.

Oh, those sixes! The tale was told in neon. A block or two from the bronze of Rockefeller Center stood a building where William Friedkin had edited *The Exorcist*, and at the summit had been a restaurant called "Top of the Sixes," complete with rooftop sign playing on the tower's address (666 Fifth Avenue).

Such was the world: two thousand richest controlled more wealth than five billion lesser souls.

The only surprise about the bronze and brass in New York was that it wasn't solid palladium instead, or at least gold.

It was also a surprise that there had not been riots, though civil unrest, from each end of the political spectrum, and points between, seemed in the prophetic mix—all but inevitable—and would come quicker if there were natural disasters.

Perhaps, if there was a prophetic Manhattan angel, offering riddles, another page (in that old Vulgate of mine) would be 592: "But the wicked are like the raging sea, which cannot rest, and the waves thereof cast up dirt and mire" *Isaiah* (Chapter 57).

More than missing pages, there would be visions—cast onto the mind's eye from a cosmic projector: Hordes of rioters, first in one city, then another, perhaps starting in New York, as they did after the slaying of George Floyd, moving next to the plazas and cul-de-sacs of suburbia; then exurbs; then farmland. This is what would occur in quick succession if a major disaster or series of them broke down our fragile, susceptible infrastructure.

They'd be best described as marauders: moving house to house, modern barbarians, like vandals of ancient Rome, for history must replay itself, when sin—gluttony, wanton sex, abuse of Creation—do likewise; in the plunder, residents who stocked food: now robbed of it. Especially sought: sugar, liquor, pasta, canned food, and rice, if food ran out; McDonald's could get no supplies, nor Costco, nor Walmart. Those stores will be emptied. The angel would show me this: gunshot from parts in curtains on suburban drives, as ruffians materialized first on one street, then on tree-lined others, accepting miniatures of liquor from those who had them to barter, raiding pantries and attics and the garage. Nothing frozen to rob, no, but freeze-dried food would be sought and gardens raided of what was to be had. Who to call? Where to seek help, if phones, radios, and laptops had been rendered useless; oddly—in the "vision"—a klatch of miscreants, sifting through coins, plucking out nickels (for their true silver: the only coin worth its weight), unless there was gold.

In the backdrop: buckled streets, punctured roofs. Chasms. Receding floodwater.

In the Bible, bronze was used for shackles after a city was plundered and that, among other places, was on a missing page (641) from *Jeremiah* 15.

This was not just the dark bidding of dystopia. If not in detail, often there was the truth of essence—a *feeling* and sense—in prophecy. Despise it not (*1 Thessalonians* 5: 20)! If it seemed strange, so was much of the Old Testament. Goliath, a bronze helmet, bronze armor, bronze javelin (*1 Samuel* 17). A huge man —a giant—slain.

"Giants" once had roamed earth—and there were those who claimed, perhaps wildly, they were being fashioned again.

Towering hybrids. Part human, part alien (fallen angels). Nephilim. Mysterious remains had been found in parts of the U.S. during the early 1900s, with countless articles in *The New*

York Times hinting, with other news outlets, that the origin of humans (or at least some) was more complex than scientists knew.

Also, more bizarre.

Only God knew. Only His angels.

Ohio, Illinois, West Virginia, Minnesota, California, Missouri, Texas, New York, Pennsylvania, Florida, Mexico, South America, spots in Eurasia: these are where odd huge skeletons had been unearthed, and quickly hauled away by the Smithsonian.

The Times on February 11, 1920: "GIANT SKELETONS FOUND; Archaeologists to Send Expedition to Explore Graveyards in New Mexico Where Bodies Were Unearthed."

Were these just mistakes, cases whereby scattered bones had been measured as much larger than they really were, or hoax? Had scavenging animals stretched skeletal remains? Would scientists have been so gullible a hundred years ago?

That could be argued. Or did one have to spend more time meditating on the era of Noah (*Genesis* 6:4), or some other page that might be missing? *2 Samuel* 21:20: "There was war at Gath again, where there was a man of *great* stature who had six fingers on each hand and six toes on each foot, twenty-four in number; and he also had been born to the giant."

The world was a mysterious place. Upon death, there would be much to learn! There'd be surprise after surprise. We had no idea about very much. If there'd been gargantuan humans, where were their bones? One researcher had amassed more than a thousand accounts of outsized skeletons unearthed in the U.S., and at least five hundred elsewhere, and it turned out that many early explorers such as Ferdinand Magellan and Sir Francis Drake had said they witnessed giants in the New World. When Lucas Vazquez de

Ayllón ended a voyage near the Santee River in South Carolina, he wrote that "the natives are white men. Their hair is brown and hangs to their heels. They are governed by a king of gigantic size, called Datha, whose wife is as large as himself." The first Spanish explorer up the Mississippi described entire villages inhabited by them, and when Buffalo Bill Cody ventured into Wyoming, he said the Pawnees brought him a human thigh bone three times normal size. "These giants denied the existence of a Great Spirit, and when they heard the thunder and saw the lightning they laughed at it and said that they were greater than either," Cody wrote in his autobiography. "This so displeased the Great Spirit that he caused a great rainstorm to come" until, according to Indian mythology, "it drowned even giants who had fled to the mountains." Noah. Ventured Dr. Dennis G. Lindsay, a researcher, "The giants mentioned in the Scripture may have been a remnant of a once expansive, human giant race, beginning before the great Flood of Noah's day, but also reappearing after the Flood. Moses, who wrote the Book of Genesis some 850 years after the Flood, reveals these giants had been around for a long time," and added that: "the Bible gives warning that giants will appear at the end of the age."

Were these then keys to the past—and the future? Said the prophet Enoch, "And it came to pass when the children of men had multiplied that in those days were born unto them beautiful and comely daughters. And the angels, the children of Heaven, saw and lusted after them, and said to one another: 'Come, let us choose us wives from among the children of men and beget us children.' And all the others together with them took unto themselves wives, and each chose for himself one, and they began to go in unto them and to defile themselves with them, and they taught them charms and enchantments, and the cutting of roots, and made them acquainted with plants. And they became pregnant, and they bare great giants, whose height was three thousand ells: Who consumed all the acquisitions of men. And when men could no longer sustain them, the giants turned against them and devoured mankind."

Really, no one knew if *Enoch* was valid.

If it was, the giants, it seemed, were poised for re-entry.

And in it, an angel of prophecy?

Gavreel, once in Judea, now on the pavement of New York?

That was one thing: giants, extraterrestrials, orbs.

The other was their origin.

Is it another planet, a different dimension; did sin open portals to this? And the occult, as in the beguiling records of Enoch: was this—rituals—why New Age meccas and coven seclusions and Indians grounds were "haunted"?

Or was it simply a manifestation of hell?

In *Close Encounters*, the base had been in Devil's Tower.

The fallen angels as in *Genesis*, materializing again?

According to a book of messages, Marija Pavlović-Lunetti of Medjugorje recalled how she and fellow seers, asking Mary, in the early days, a flurry of questions, had queried: "Is there life on the planets?" Our Lady's response: *"That is not for you to know now."*

Oh, strangeness! Missionaries claimed a demonic creature haunted the swamp near Lake Vufao in Peru, while in the U.S., rock stars insisted that they had encountered flying saucers (when they weren't on hallucinogens).

In both cases the smell of sulfur.

Chapter 24

IT WAS AS IF—WITH HORROR MOVIES, drugs, music, sex, contraception, rebellion, feminism, sodomy, transvestites, and of course the occult—a *kraken* had been unleashed.

"You see," Gavreel would say, walking the street, "there have been five major periods in this era, which soon will end. These are the ferocious epochs of temporal rule, brought about by the desires of the flesh from which the taint of sin is never absent. One was a dog, fiery, but not burning; another a yellow lion; another like a pale horse; a fourth like a black pig—your current period—and the last resembling a grey wolf."

Brushing by pedestrians, the mysterious stranger would explain how the first period involved attacks on the Church, whether Masonic or by some other name, as the "synagogue of Satan" formed, with great upsets in Europe, leading into World War One.

This was fourteen years after "The Beast" Crowley had gallingly pronounced an end to the Age of Jesus and replacement with the pagan deity "Horus." Seven years later, Hitler was meeting with the occult Templars, reading the dark works of Theosophy (in part inspired by Crowley), and offering his soul to a spirit he "felt" at a museum exhibiting the spear of Longinus (a centurion who, legend has it, pierced the side of Christ). "The air became stifling so that I could barely breathe," Hitler would later recount. "The noisy scene of the Treasure House seemed to melt away before my eyes. I stood alone trembling before the hovering form of the Superman—a spirit sublime and fearful, a countenance intrepid and cruel. In holy awe, I offered my soul as a vessel of his will."

In that mix had been Fátima.

It was the beginning of great electrical achievements, mass production, and the contrivances—not all good—of chemistry.

Edison was fond of spiritualism, and Tesla was born at the very stroke of midnight, during a fierce lightning storm in Croatia.

Who needed the Holy Spirit when now one only required the flick of a switch for illumination? And wasn't the telephone bringing to mankind virtually supernatural communication?

Who wanted to live without it?

"You think of the changes in very simple ways, without realizing the fundamental mistakes of mankind," Gavreel would say, repeating the 1990 prophecy, waving around at the buildings, at flashing neon, perhaps up at the old sign on a skyscraper that said "666." "The very artifice of your societies is false and against the accordance of God's Will. This artifice shall not last. Your very conceptions of happiness and comforts are a great evil and falsity. They will not stand."

"Look at your laboratories," the angel would explain—(*did* explain, in that anonymous locution): "The greatest nemesis of God is now science more so than your vessels of communication, more than media, the science that alters life, the science that creates a counterfeit heaven, which toils with the womb and genes, the science that has filled the air with the power of the enemy, the science which creates chemical witchcraft and fouls the earth; the science which seeks to create life but cannot in actuality even sustain it, the science which has denied God.

"This will fall," said Gavreel, in this iteration, "and all of its creations with it."

Oh that period of the sixes, of the Sixties. At its very onset had come approval in the United States of the Pill—capitalized, like Catholics used upper case for Eucharist—followed a decade hence by abortion.

"Yet evils arise equal to that," said Gavreel. "Men will kill and yet aspire to be Creator. When your laboratories now move to creation of living things, Heaven cannot tolerate this. It is the high sin of Lucifer."

Was the "pale horse" the pallid complexion of AIDS? And had not that pandemic also been brushed over, as simple happenstance, as now with corona?

Defiance. Rebellion. One cooked the other. Lust.

"Note how it began in those parts of Africa where the prostitutes plied their trade along the highway," an angel pounding the pavement of Fifth Avenue would say. "And that brings you to the 'black pig.' Of that a saint of yours, Hildegard, had prophesied, 'This epoch will have leaders who blacken themselves in misery and wallow in the mud of impurity. They will infringe on the Divine law by fornication and like evils, and will plot to diverge from the holiness of God's commands.'"

Chapter 25

IF DEMONS SEEMED LIKE THEY WERE UNDER EVERY ROCK, it was because often they were.

Did Jesus go anywhere without confronting them? Was it not this—exorcism—a key part of His mission, often *the* key part? Did not early French missionaries warn that forests in Upstate New York (see Auriesville) were filled with them? There Saint Isaac Jogues, a French missionary, in 1643 wrote: "How often on the stately trees of the forests did I carve the most sacred name of Jesus, so that, seeing it, the demons might fly, who tremble when they hear it! How often, too, did I strip off the bark to form the most Holy Cross of the Lord, so that the foe might fly before it; and that by it, Thou, O Lord, my King, 'might reign in the midst of thy enemies' (Ps 109:2), the enemies of thy Cross (Phil 3:18), the misbeliever and the pagan who dwell in that land, and the demons who rule so fearfully there!"

Jesus said He would know believers by their casting out of demons (*Mark* 16:17)!

Earth was not a playground; it was a *battleground*. Had it gotten to the point where modern society as spawned by the Sixties, refined in the Seventies, and marketed during the Eighties onward had become the equal of Sodom, as bad as the times of Nineveh? That seemed very possible, even likely. *"Division is strong and evil is at work in man as never before,"* the Virgin said on June 25, 2022, at Medjugorje.

"As never before" included the time of the Ark as well as Gomorrah.

Oh, that pale horse, wild, unbridled.

No wonder in 1953 in Ukraine at a hill called Seredne Mary said, *"My daughter, my daughter, my daughter, you see what a fullness of grace I possess. But I have no one to give my graces to, for there are so many daughters and sons who have turned away from me. I wanted to obtain a great forgiveness for poor sinners, for disaster is upon us as in the times of Noah. Not by flood but by fire shall the destruction come. An immense flood of fire shall destroy nations for sinning before God. This is the kingdom of Satan. Rome is in danger of being destroyed, the Pope of being killed."*

Despite that, the Virgin came with peace and joy. She knew we were on a tough battlefield, a place of testing, but that goodness and brilliance awaited us in the eternal, if we battled successfully, if we avoided or erased the taint and tinges of a passing world.

Nothing was as powerful as the Name of Jesus. No evil could win against it.

But *try?*

Evil if nothing was tenacious, persistent, unrelenting, until its defeat. It was up to us to carry forth to that end. With Jesus, the road was straight. We simply had to exercise faith, and persevere. The Lord wasn't out to scare. And while some found the prospect of future events espoused in His Name frightening, far more alarming was what happened to sinners after life on this planet was over.

Heaven came through love, and no love was remotely as pure as that of Jesus. What it took for Heaven was kindness, charity, patience, forgiveness, truth, humility, courtesy (*1 Corinthians* 13:4-8). That was love and with love, all fear was cast out (*1 John* 4:18). When one feared, especially death, one had to ask if it was because the subconscious wasn't ready for the afterlife and knew it. Here the closeness of Christ was urgent. For no prophecy is truer than this: all of us will die. Life on earth is less than a blink. This "passing world" (*1 John* 2:7) is better described as fleeting. But then comes existence forever. Through prayer, one conquered all; one reached the right destination. This was God's lesson. He wasn't trying to scare. He wasn't trying to coerce, and neither were authentic prophets. To prophesy was to proclaim the truth, and the Truth always involved the Name Jesus.

But here was our query: Due to all the contamination and the potential for losing so many souls, was God about to cleanse humanity, His Creation; the face of His earth?

Reputed seers were everywhere, especially Brazil, where one named Pedro Regis on May 22, 2021, related a message he claimed was from Mary that said: *"My Jesus awaits you with open arms. Courage. When everything seems lost, great joy will arise for you. Remain by my side and I will take you on a safe path.*

"You are living in a time worse than the time of the Flood. Men have defied the Creator and are walking like the blind leading the blind. Do not allow the flame of faith to be extinguished within you. A great darkness is approaching and many of the consecrated will fall. I suffer because of what comes to you.

"Be attentive. This is the message that I give you today in the Name of the Most Holy Trinity. Thank you for having allowed me to gather you here once again. I bless you in the name of the Father, the Son, and the Holy Spirit. Amen. Be at peace."

The following month the Queen of Peace (as he called her) presumably added, with some reiteration: *"Dear chil-*

dren, you are the Lord's possession, and you must follow and serve Him alone. Turn away from worldly things, and turn toward paradise, for which you were created. My Jesus loves you and expects much from you. You are living in a time worse than the time of the Flood, and my poor children are heading for the abyss of self-destruction that men have prepared by their own hands. Pray much. Seek strength in the Gospel and Eucharist. The days will come when many will repent, but it will be late. Do not forget: it is in this life, and not in another, that you must testify for Jesus. I suffer because of what is coming for you. Turn back quickly! Do not put off what you have to do. This is the message that I give you in the Name of the Most Holy Trinity."

Was it legitimate? Were the words extramundane? One took from voluminous locutions—and Pedro's were certainly frequent—what seemed good, what was edifying, and rang authentic, and left the rest (*1 Thessalonians* 5:21). *"Dear children, I am your Mother and I love you. I ask you to seek to imitate my Son Jesus in everything. He is the fount of every blessing and your true liberation and salvation is in Him alone. I am the Mother of Grace and Mercy. Open your hearts and accept the Lord's Will for your lives. You know full well how much a mother loves her children. Be obedient to my call. Difficult times will come for the righteous, but the Lord will be with His own. Do not retreat! The Lord has called you and expects much from you. You will be persecuted and rejected for loving and defending the truth, but do not be discouraged. Heaven is watching over you. At this moment, as the Mother of Grace, I shower you with Heaven's blessings. Onward without fear! This is the message that I give you today in the Name of the Most Holy Trinity. Thank you for having allowed me to gather you here once more. I bless you in the Name of the Father, the Son and the Holy Spirit. Amen. Be at peace."*

Yet another message that same month: *"You are heading for a future of great spiritual darkness. The smoke of the devil will cause spiritual blindness in the House of God, and many dogmas will be denied.*

"I suffer because of what is coming for you. Bend your knees in prayer. Trust in Jesus and you will be victorious. Onward in defense of the truth!"

Long before, another reputed mystic named Marie-Julie Jahenny had claimed she'd received a message, in this case from Joseph, saying even more pointedly, *"My children, plagues of all sorts are reserved for the earth. Plagues and calamities will come with this time. To indicate mortality, in some places, they will place the pall on the Church! It will be that corruption and lawlessness will issue from these plagues. I warn [about them], since my Son orders it."*

One thing for sure was that while the Spanish flu was more severe, Covid-19 still had not fully run its course (there were the long-term effects yet to be reckoned, along with possible vaccine casualties), and whatever the case, the world truly had come face to face with a disaster of epic stature. If nothing else—if the body count didn't come close to the pandemic of 1918-1920, not to mention the medieval Black Death (which killed at least one in four in Europe, perhaps one in three)—there was the enormous psychological mayhem. The populace, unaccustomed to hard times, was first shell-shocked, then made angry, then indifferent, lethargic, a feeling of helplessness with division and hostility that spread dark tincture across the land. Bitter debate over everything seeped into the soil of society, painting a nightmarish canvas of cabalism with its brooding palette. There was refusal to accept it as a warning, admonishment, and turning point at which a long period of Mercy transitioned into Justice—a time in which "forerunners" and "pre-warnings" entered a larger venue.

And here one came to an African preacher by the name of Emmanuel Makandiwa, founder of a large Pentecostal mega-church called United Family International Church in Zimbabwe. According to biographies, "Prophet Makandiwa," who was born on Christmas Day, in 1977, was sleeping under a sun-shade at his parents' farm as a boy when the canopy caught fire. It turned out the slumbering young man was caught up in a "vision," and when onlookers rushed to douse the blaze, they were amazed to see the wood planks still intact and Emmanuel peacefully somnolent, without a scratch or burn.

Whatever the final verdict (and certainly he had missed the mark with some prognostications), Makandiwa had made an extraordinarily accurate prediction of the coronavirus on November 20, 2016, when he told tens of thousands at the City Sports Centre in Harare that in a vision he had seen "diseases that are coming, many diseases—know that we are praying about it—and another disease more deadly, and I saw it coming from the sea. If they investigate, they will find that it comes from the ocean, more deadly than HIV and cancer.

"Very fast, very aggressive," he said. "How does it come from the sea? Is it a creature in the ocean, I don't know. Is it from food from the sea? It will originate from under the waters, from the ocean. And thousands and millions, perhaps billions, will die. This is something we can pray against, because it isn't good news," he told the rapt crowd.

"Imagine sitting and watching TV and seeing millions and millions die — thousands in one city in one day. It's a plague. It's serious. It's something that you will see like it flies in the air. We need people to pray, because we can prevent it, we can slow it down. But we can't cure it."

Two months (and eighteen days) later, Makandiwa returned to his warning.

The virus he was speaking about, he now said, was "coming closer and closer, a disease from the sea that will kill more people than any disease we have fought before—very fast. I saw people falling like leaves and dying. They will do everything to investigate where's it coming from, and they will not find out, but eventually they will confirm what I'm telling you. Something will bring that disease from the ocean to the land of the living.

"It's a plague that only God can stop.

"They will do everything, but God will give power to His people in the midst of global upheaval."

Most astonishingly, Makandiwa, "We need to pray. China. China. China."

That was on January 11, 2015.

Six years later to the month, on January 9, 2021, the World Health Organization announced a mysterious pneumonia had taken hold in the Chinese city of Wuhan, with speculation that it had spread from the local seafood market, where everything from fish and crabs to dogs and hedgehogs was sold.

It was a wide array (by one count, a total of thirty-eight species), and while bats, which is where the virus actually is birthed, were not sold, there was a facility very near, the Wuhan Institute of Virology, that handled just such animals, from which it was extracting the exact virus—SARS-CoV-2—behind the fast-moving and soon global pandemic.

Had someone from the lab been infected and then spread it at the wet market, which was in walking distance? Had a bat escaped? And most urgently: had it been extracted from bats and then genetically enhanced, either to test vaccines (in the event of a corona outbreak) or for bio-warfare purposes?

We knew only that Chinese officials—frantic and knowing more about it than the rest of the world—immediately instituted draconian quarantines, detained talkative scientists, burned the corpses of victims (sometimes, it was claimed, before the person quite died), and nailed the apartment doors closed. If technicians there had amplified the transmissibility and lethality of the virus—which almost certainly they had—this explained its bizarre effects, and left mankind guessing as to final outcome.

On television was footage of Chinese paramedics in space suits transporting coughing gasping victims in plastic isolation chambers to destinations unknown.

Makandiwa was right: millions were to die, by the end of the first year three, and at last count seven. *"Imagine sitting and watching TV and seeing millions and millions die—thousands in one city in one day,"* the prophet had said—years before the outbreak.

And where did the funds to engineer the coronavirus come from? A company in Manhattan.

In New York, of course, as harbinger, hospitals were overwhelmed, as were morticians, the dead stacked in refrigerated trucks as mass graves were excavated.

"It's a plague," the prophet had said. "It's serious. It's something that you will see like it flies in the air. It's a plague that only God can stop. My question is, who is safe now?" he said to his followers before the contagion. "It is going to continue happening, over and over and over again. And it will not be the last of its kind.

"Whatever you see happening far away is not going to end

there," Makandiwa said ominously. "It is really catastrophe, it is chaotic. It is a demonic spirit that is going on a rampage."

A demonic spirit: During the Middle Ages, bizarre phenomena including lights in the sky accompanied waves of Black Death.

And unpredictable? Strange?

The SARS-CoV-2 virus, which was also accompanied by outbreaks of the paranormal, and caused everything from a cold to organ collapse, seemed to linger for months after symptoms dissipated, and even those who had no overt illness felt strange. Loss of smell. Hearing defects. Brain fog. In some cases, with the severely afflicted, blackened skin. Everyone knew someone who had succumbed to it, especially elderly: When it manifested as pneumonia, it was tantamount to drowning.

A rampage indeed. The world gasped collectively. Satan (prince of the power of the air) loved the respiratory tract. No one had been prepared psychologically. It could ruin the kidneys, sear the liver. All of a sudden, everyone had myocarditis or atrial fibrillation. And if not from the virus, from vaccines.

Yet most often it was no more than a sniffle, a raw throat. No one could prove when it actually began.

Oh, yes: we yearned for normalcy. It was not to be rendered. A spirit of division that had been incubating for years broke into the wider domain, slash and burn, detonating even health policy. Makandiwa said there would be "chaos" and in fact institutions buckled, stock markets swerved, unemployment surpassed those of the Great Depression. Added Makandiwa cryptically, "We need to pray because this time there is a place somewhere where these guys are working on the nuclear."

Chapter 26

AT THE CORNER OF SULLIVAN AND BLEECKER, Gavreel would have stepped into view in front of the sidewalk flowers at a deli and pointed to the young pedestrians, many wearing masks, though not for a virus. "Now it is smoke," he might say. "Residents of this island are being told to stay inside for the third time. This is, shall we say, an 'indicator,' and though it will be only fleeting, remember these words: When you see the great smoke rise, Satan will have touched the earth. His manifestation will be near. He will seek to destroy what Christ has built, as Jesus came to destroy the work of the devil. In the end, the Cross will predominate, but not before the end of an era that has strayed."

There might be another page missing from the wood-covered old tome. And it might be 65, torn, one would learn later, at *Exodus 19:18*. ("And all Mount Sinai was on smoke: because the Lord was come down upon it in fire, and the smoke arose from it as out of a furnace: and all the mount was terrible." The more modern translation said, "the whole mountain quaked violently.")

While this was fictive, perhaps it was also something else: true. Not imagined was the strange way that smoke from wildfires in Quebec five hundred miles distant had descended in 2023 on New York and then elsewhere, at the same time volcanoes began to fume at Kilauea in Hawaii and south of

Mexico City in the highlands near an old and exquisitely holy shrine dedicated to the Archangel Michael.

If the devil came around—oleaginous of complexion, major grease—there was always Michael, mystery name Sabbathiel, to drive him off.

Smoke.

In Ukraine, water.

A dam collapsed. It was an apocalyptic nation.

The mystic Josyp Terelya had told me that.

But for now, there was a tendency to focus on New York because no one thought it could suffer more than it had on September 11 and now, before all eyes, with the coronavirus, it had. The city had been a "ground zero" again. This was not a good omen. Everyone recalled the torrents of smoke from its tallest towers on September 11 and I also remembered crossing the Whitestone Bridge on the way to deliver the eulogy for a close friend who perished in the South Tower and looking to the skyline and how, though it had been weeks since the attack, a strange fog shrouded the island, unlike any I had seen flying dozens of times from LaGuardia, JFK, and Newark or witnessed through the bay windows from which I peered every day when I'd lived in Manhattan.

It was a "cloud," and the prophecy had been just under a dozen years before.

Was New York the portent? Was its suffering from coronavirus, not a second harbinger?

Was it perhaps telling us with symbols in microcosm about the future of the world or at least America?

The evening of 9/11, cable news was rife with New Yorkers lamenting destruction of what one after another called the city's "pride" (*"Do not go there. The pride there will be broken."*)

Now that symbol was gone, as broken as anything could be broken with one exception: a nuclear detonation.

Were all the events a precursor for what larger events would look like? For years after 9/11, Manhattanites had softened. They were more polite. They were accommodating. You could approach a cop for directions now.

But was the big-city hubris and coldness returning, and not just in New York but the entire country, which had become the "Manhattan" of the world?

Swift. Big. Fast. First. And flush with cash.

That was the creed of New York and America.

Had humbleness reigned and had honest work returned? Or was there just more paper, more mammon?

The fear was that the latter was true and while it'd been hard to imagine anything the equal of 9/11 that would come as a chastening for materialism, with the virus one witnessed something beyond the "smoke" of 2001 and likewise—now invisible—a nefarious scent through the air. No sackcloth here! No ashes (*Jonah* 3:5-6)! Instead, the United States—and really the entire globe—was tempting fate again.

On September 11 the article on cloning in *The New York Times* had said, "A panel of scientific experts has concluded that new colonies, or lines, of human embryonic stem cells will be necessary if science is to advance," adding a few paragraphs later, "The report by the National Academy of Sciences, perhaps the nation's most eminent organization of scientists, is scheduled to be made public on Tuesday [September 11, 2001]" at a news conference in Washington.

That never came to be.

Did anyone notice?

"In four years there will arise a new evil the likes of which mankind has never before encountered," said the anonymous

prophecy eleven years before 9/11.

Four years later had come federal funding and technology paving the way for embryonic cloning, and so yes, a new and great evil had arrived, one that was "comparable" to abortion (a comparison made even by a secular academic) and touted for its "beneficial" applications. Some said it was even the distraction of embryonic stem cells that allowed terrorists to mount their attack unnoticed by the White House.

Science, in its arrogance, tossed the roulette of unmitigated peril. This arrogance—a hubris imbued with an unnerving degree of myopia—was too blind, too swollen with self-importance, to perceive its own ignorance.

The simple fact was that it had veered off like a rogue wave. It had sailed, not towards the sunset of calculated destination, but off towards the midnight of the enigmatic and unpredictable. It had, in essence, become a vessel adrift on the waters of caprice, an unwitting captive of the mercurial tides of chance.

And New York was where so much of its seed money was harvested. The skyline of Manhattan was a monument to Man. And in its pace, in the quick-rhythm of its steps, was "innovation," always explained as "beneficial." It was now dispensing birth-control pills for free. How soon would pills for euthanasia be distributed with equal magnanimity?

New York—a city with so much excellence, just soaring potential—played with fire, and in its deeds were clues for the future. It wasn't just abortion and materialism, though these ranked high. It wasn't blue-blooded insolence. It wasn't just that New York—oh, great City that it once was, and could still be!—was the center of new-world-order diplomacy (the United Nations), spiritless media, entertainment (beyond television, print media, and Broadway, it financed much in Hollywood and Silicon Valley); it wasn't just fashion (which, as Jacinta said, sent many to hell). No: it was also the role New York played in promoting the occult on the one hand and secular humanism on the other, covering all dark bases. There was a group in town that once had called itself Lucifer Publishing and a cathedral in Manhattan's upper western reach that in audacity had displayed a naked crucified female Jesus ("Christa"). No wonder—and this was an actual finding—the city, the cement, the steel, the bronze, the asphalt, was sinking under its own weight. It had gotten more cordial of late; there were good aspects; and certainly, good people; sharp, diligent; hardworking. But a refined edge was the sharpest and skyscrapers were its temples, the higher the better, all but defying Heaven. Once I had seen an advertisement in the *Village Voice* for human skulls, and each year was the Halloween parade in Greenwich Village with men dressed in drag or as prophylactics or as priests, as nuns, and smirking behind demonic masks.

Chapter 27

BUT WERE THERE NOT ALSO ANGELS, mysterious strangers, roaming mean streets?

Near Washington Square Park was there also not Saint Anthony of Padua Church?

Was not God there to assist?

"This will fall, and all of its creations with it."

That's what the anonymous prophecy had concluded in its complaint against science—after its warning about New York.

With the pandemic, the city again had been at an epicenter and so one wondered whether the disaster in Gotham, folks collapsing on subways, gasping for breath in hospital hallways, with the city out of rooms: was this a follow-through, an augmentation; the next act in a tragedy? Had the Lord allowed a "demon" to "rampage" because, instead of conversion, instead of humility, Manhattan and the United States had resumed old ways after September 11, its steel and glass scraping the heavens with renewed audacity, this time with more mammon and a taller Trade Center, consuming the steroids of ego?

One could speculate. This much was sure: New York wasn't alone in transgression, just the most innovative, the most blatant, and as for science, since 1990 it *had* become a greater antagonist than media: A Pew Survey showed scientists half as likely to believe in God as the general public, and if they did, just thirty-three percent bought the notion of a personal deity. They had tooled together that new religion of Scientism, nudging God from His Throne (or trying to), with the public slowly but surely and sheepishly following. By 2022, belief in Him, always well over ninety percent, had dipped to eighty-one, and religious affiliation was in dwindling supply (replaced by yoga, *wicca,* and "none"). Was it a coincidence that God's Creation—nature—was degraded by these same forces of "progress" and in apocalyptic fashion?

Plastics, pesticides, "chemical witchcraft": the contrivances of science.

A synonym for contrivance was "artifice," ironic because, to reiterate, that anonymous message (if one believed it) had said, *"You think of the changes in very simple ways, without realizing the fundamental mistakes of mankind. The very artifice of your societies is false and against the accordance of God's Will. This artifice shall not last."*

Another way of saying this was done so by the Virgin, who at Medjugorje, again in earlier days (October 1981), had said, *"The West has made civilization progress, but without God, as if they were their own creators."*

What else would science concoct that was "beneficial"? Hybrid creatures? Humanzees? Cyborg humans?

Coincidental it was that whether in Tibet, in the rarefied air of the Himalayas, or in an adobe, at an arid reservation in Arizona, mystics of all faiths were clanging the same alarm. Some elders—Hopi, Navaho—flatly saw events as the signal that the end of times was at hand. In December 1990, the same month as the anonymous prophecy, a dreamwalker reported "purple flowers and a pear-tree blooming in the winter," an omen, he felt, that the "final war fought with the gourd of ashes (H-bomb) had begun."

In 2023 came the report of seismic readings—undulations, waves—that showed earth's inner core had stopped spinning and might now be reversing rotation, although scientists were quick to reassure that this probably happened every six or seven decades and should affect very little on the surface.

Yet, it brought out the irony of a ceremony those same elders had held "to stop the earth from turning over."

Added to all this—also across cultures—were those "cryptid" reports: strange creatures that thousands of witnesses, many reliable, insisted upon. Most prevalent was "bigfoot": Though touted as a missing link, bridging humans to apes, in many cases the legendary hairy creatures were linked to lights in the sky—"UFOs"—and paranormal phenomena. The "creature" itself was most often gritty and robust but in telling accounts seemed simply to vaporize, in a few cases before the tormented eyes of hunters and others who described the fear it engendered and, like "aliens" (and demons), left as calling card a faint hint of sulfur in the nostrils, the scent of the devil's perfume, a terror seizing witnesses unlike that evoked by a simple bear. Bigfoot was one of many "monsters" in our time, so many it was beyond summary, a variety that spoke of games played by mischievous, devious entities. This question emerged from the shadows: are we the artists, the beholders, painting these chimerical beasts with the colors of our subconscious dread, emanating from the darkest depths of our own pit, or merely spectators of ultramundane reality, the intersection of otherworldly dimensions? While states such as Colorado, Oregon, and Pennsylvania had their versions of the yeti, Tibetans fretted over mythic water serpents and energy forms called "nagas" that in Native American lore caused earthquakes and other upheaval. Tempting it all was to dismiss, and perhaps warranting just that, but the idea of an aquatic leviathan brought to mind not only the Bible (where "leviathan" is used six times, most notably in *Isaiah*; a sea monster), but also popular mythology of again Loch Ness and other spectral specimens insisted upon by hunters, campers, cops, homeowners, from all corners. Throw into this poltergeists. Whether the "Flatwoods Monsters" in West Virginia or werewolves in Kentucky, or "Champy" on Lake Champlain, the question was whether folks were seeing something actual, a merging of dimensions, or envisaging in their minds what was rising from spiritual domains. No one could dispute that the endless extent of space allowed for the possibility of bizarre life forms elsewhere, and civilizations that tuned into our dimension via machines appearing to us as flying ones or perhaps indeed mastering fantastic interstellar physical travel were possibilities, but a bigfoot commandeering a flying saucer? Didn't this seem a mockery? Or truly, as the veil thinned, were spirits of all ilk climbing out of portals? Whether the History or Travel channels or YouTube, crypto-animals seemed everywhere, a special nuisance atop mountains, near graveyards (especially Indian burial mounds), and in woods.

There was a story in every county (if not more than one).

The occult was coming out of the woodwork. Light was fighting dark. Monsters at the same time that there were sun miracles.

In the West, witchcraft was growing in bounds and leaps as the young exited organized faith, kids who had grown up on vampires, New Ageism, and Harry Potter.

But it was more: it was a general spiritual tsunami. The evil one was exercising greatly enhanced power just as forewarned at Medjugorje (*"the hour of the power of darkness"*) and by Sister Lucia (that *"decisive battle"*), and as had been prophesied by Leo XIII. How else could the world be so confused, exemplified now by those who believed humans were not born with a real gender?

A few short decades before, such a notion would have consigned a person to a psychiatrist's couch (or that of an exorcist).

How possibly could there be greater confusion? But also, how could "Christians" hate? How could poisoning drinking supplies be a corporate right? How could it be right to carry assault rifles? How could letting a baby die on a cold sterile stainless-steel tray (after a failed late abortion) be tolerated by anyone who was humane, or a youngster to starve to death across Central Africa, in a world of nearly three thousand billionaires?

Christ *wept* for many reasons, in addition to abortion. Oh, but a spectacle it was. Paganism, that primal, earthy vein of belief we thought was buried in the crucible of time, had awakened from its slumber with a roar that pierced the veil of our understanding. The eddies of myth and legend spun about, obscuring rationality with veils of mystery and unfathomable knowledge, giving a life of its own to the strange dance that unfolded before our eyes. It was as though the annals of time had been unceremoniously ripped apart, each page flapping in the gales of history, spilling forth the relics of the old gods. The whispered tales that once swirled around campfires were back, flourishing in the limelight, creeping into the cracks of our civilized facade. We bore witness to occult mythology, rituals, and beliefs yanked out of the shadows of the forgotten ages, a dance between the ancient and the modern, the material and the ethereal, the transient and the eternal. The raw power of forgotten deities was resurrecting before our incredulous gaze, the forgotten runes, the clandestine rites, and the cosmic connections long dismissed as the misdirected understanding of the early men: They were now brazenly splayed in the open, as if flaunting their survival against our amnesia. It was as if the past had splintered from the hardened crust of history, fractured and fragmented, only to be forged anew in the present. Paganism, like a phoenix, was stirring amidst the smoldering embers of antiquity, ready to soar once again into the liminal spaces of our consciousness. And it all progressed, steadily and in great earnest, undeterred by the horrified or curious gazes of modernity.

These were not just echoes of the past, faded whispers of bygone eras, but a vibrant and terrifying and real resurrection. The earnest procession of this was overwhelming, intoxicating even. The paradox was stark: old gods in the age of silicon. But yet, it advanced, the monolith of forgotten ages, and catacombs, dragging itself into the murky light of the present, stirring the air with its primal energy—and real spirits. A grand tapestry of the arcane and ancient bloomed with renewed vibrancy, the past reviving within the throbbing heart of the present.

And so Indians saw signs. Were they superstitions, or did they meld with the observations of Eskimos who during the "Polar Night" season, traveling by sled in pursuit of seals, now found that instead of the standard one, they had *two* sunlit hours a day unlike their ancestors and even their own grandfathers. Superstition? These were people who grew up observing the pattern of snow and stars and sun as a matter of livelihood. What they were seeing was bothering them: While the sun still rose where it always had, now it was setting in a different spot: not behind the highest peak nearby, they said, as it had all their lives, but to the side of that peak. Perhaps the earth had "tilted on its axis," said an Eskimo who was interviewed by a reporter. He used those words. For some reason, the sun was striking and heating differently. And there was no longer a north or south wind; it was the east wind that now claimed dominance. There were huge banks of snow called "tongue drifts." These were used as travel markers shaped by the north wind, and these had changed. Said another Eskimo in a YouTube clip: "Today stars also look different. At night, returning from a hunt using the stars, it's noticeable; they are no longer in their proper positions. Our earth has changed, land, sky, and environment. Tongue drifts now point in a different direction. The shifting wind has caused this. When moving east, we crossed them sideways. Today, heading east, we go *with* the drifts. "

It seemed there was no longer a north or south wind; it was the east wind that now predominated—hardly a factor at all in past decades and known to bring bad weather. Now an ill wind was blowing. Ancestral ice cellars were melting. Roadways, street signs, and telephone poles were collapsing as permafrost turned to mud. Asphalt sank, buckled. Polar bears roamed new territories. If one ran into Gavreel might the Bible he left in an igloo, in an ice shelter, be missing page 561, *"And they shall make a noise against them that day, like the roaring of the sea: we shall look towards the land, and behold, darkness of tribulation, and the light is darkened with the mist thereof"* (*Isaiah* 5:29-30)?

That same time-worn biblical page, yellowed at the furls, held between those wood covers, would say in the preceding verse, *"Their roaring like that of a lion; they shall roar like young lions: yea, they shall roar, and take hold of the prey; and they shall keep fast hold of it; and there shall be none to deliver it."*

Curious it was, how the name "Osama" meant "roaring lion."

That was on the etymology websites, and that was another omen New York—9/11—had for us.

"I will bring up many nations against you," said *Ezekiel*. "They will destroy the walls of Tyre and break down her towers."

"How have you perished, city most prized!" (*Ezekiel* 26).

Again page 585: "I will go before thee, and humble the great ones of the earth: I will break in pieces the gates of brass, and will burst the bars of iron (*Isaiah* 45:2).

The day of wrath was a day of "clouds and darkness, a day of trumpeter and battle cry against the fortified cities and the high corner towers," warned another missing page.

"I have cut off nations," said *Zephaniah* 3. "Their corner towers are in ruins."

And besides "towers," besides the name Osama, these signs also: when the Trade Center collapsed, it sent seismic pulses that widened cracks in the masonry of Federal Hall on Wall Street, where George Washington had been inaugurated, where the Bill of Rights had been signed, and where the first Congress convened. When an earthquake hit Richmond, Virginia in 2011—one further noted—it shook Washington D.C. to the point of causing a serious fissure in the Washington Monument.

The monument—such a national icon—had to be closed for more than a year, and the same happened to Liberty Island in New York, which had to be shuttered the following year due to damage from the hurling, vengeful surge, the spectral hand of nature, called Hurricane Sandy.

And still fate was being tempted—in fact, more than ever. On the island of Manhattan, former woodland, former Indian territory, once farms, stood now 309 towers over forty stories, and seven thousand standing higher than a hundred feet, a density of nearly seventy thousand penned souls per square mile. They lived on an island that now boasted a new naked gold statue of a woman with tentacle arms and hair coiffed into horns as she emerges from a lotus on top of a city courthouse next to Confucius and Moses and symbolizing the fight for abortion. It made sense in a city responsible for ten percent of national pregnancy terminations.

New York Babylon. Los Angeles Babylon. Washington Babylon.

As America babbled on.

Satan was always among idols. "I know thy works, and where thou dwellest, even where Satan's seat is: and thou holdest fast my name, and hast not denied my faith, even in those days wherein Antipas was my faithful martyr, who was slain among you, where Satan dwelleth," says the Book of Revelation.

Wall Street Babylon. Hollywood Babylon. Las Vegas Babylon.

When events came in response, they were ignored or brushed off. New York had absorbed 9/11 as tragic, epic, but in the thrum, the whoosh—once the smoke cleared—devoid of deeper meaning. Manhattan was too cool for omens. I pondered how on Wall Street—defiant, brazen, brass-knuckled Wall Street, even during the pandemic—there had been the denial of signs. The fortress stone bank edifices, with iron grates, seemed unshakable, impenetrable, looking every bit as immovable as the most unyielding mountains, as intractable as the deepest-rooted oak. Bravado was in the very calcium, the bone, of The City. Yet during plague, the financial sector proved naught but fluff stuff: in the scheme of things, hollow, minuscule. For if real calamity like many in earth's past were to climb from the crypt of prehistory—"planet-changers," as would happen if there was all-out nuclear or: the interior of earth shifted—the fantastic soaring constructs of Man would be deleted with a clack from the cosmic keyboard.

The "Brazen Charging Bull" was not a mere totem. In ancient Greece it had been a device of torture, the condemned locked inside, a chamber fashioned to look bovine and a fire was set under, heating the bronze until the condemned, shouting, shrieking, was broiled. In Pompeii had been at what archaeologists called the House of the Bronze Bull, so named after a small statuette that stood at a fountain and was associated with Dionysus, the Olympian god of pleasure, festivity, frenzy, which brought to mind New Year's at Times Square.

As for Pompeii: it had been another mother "spiritual" center of the Roman Empire, and the calamity that struck there around 79 A.D.—Vesuvius—involved the kind of fire and tremor one fretted as our own destiny, if mystics such as Padre Pio were correct. (When asked about the future, he once said, "Can't you see the world is catching on fire?").

Chapter 28

POMPEII. SODOM. ANCIENT ROME. FIRE. But a quandary remained: how did the axis of the earth and warfare—fire—go together, for while flames could come from a geologic eruption, the Fátima Enlightenment mentioned "war." Certainly then, warfare was in the mix, and it was likelier by the year. Even if hostilities in Ukraine didn't metastasize, the spirit of division was manifest in all corners, and Medjugorje, which John Paul II called the "fulfillment of Fátima," had dialed into the idea of great military conflict when on January 25, 2023 in her monthly message Our Lady said, *"Dear children! Pray with me for peace, because Satan wants war and hatred in hearts and peoples. Therefore, pray and sacrifice your days by fasting and penance, that God may give you peace. The future is at a crossroads, because modern man does not want God. That is why mankind is heading to perdition. You, little children, are my hope. Pray with me, that what I began in Fátima and here may be realized. Be prayer and witness peace in your surroundings, and be people of peace. Thank you for having responded to my call."*

It was extremely similar to what she'd said in 2022 on the day Pope Francis consecrated Russia, the idea of Satan, war, a "crossroads." And it meshed with the Third Secret and its fiery sword.

In the imagination—from that Bible with missing or torn pages, left as clues—here perhaps it would be page 213 in the New Testament, which brings us to *Revelation* (8:5): "Then the angel took the censer and filled it with the fire of the altar, and threw it to the earth; and there followed peals of thunder and sounds and flashes of lightning and an earthquake," which sounded like *"the tip of the spear as a flame."*

Geology and meteorology, yes, but also: a nuclear event in New York?

It wasn't just Manhattan. Symbolically, Manhattan was the *world*. So yes, New York was high in risking its future.

But so did other places, especially in Asia, particularly mega-cities in Asia which were not as altruistic as New York and where atheism had such a stronghold as to evoke or resurrect their history of fantastic ancient catastrophe.

From the dark dense past would not only come those idols, that Mongol brutishness, but also quakes powerful enough to cleave earth into lakes or detonate volcanoes that could be heard at a distance—this had happened at Krakatoa in Indonesia—of two thousand miles.

If Gavreel were to show this, it would be chasms spewing tornadic geysers of grit and mud and massive sinkholes growing yet larger—gargantuan—a group of peasants in China near Guangzhou or in India or on the veldt of Africa, a look of deep fright carved into their faces, squinting down as farmers half a world away, in Peru, or a windswept bog in Ireland, gape and gasped with equal scare as hollows the size of Hells Canyon opened on yawing terrain. Creeks and trees swallowed. Rivers emerging from their limits. Dams instantly toppled. Therefore floods.

Surely, if this was in our destiny, Gavreel would show the hologram of a volcanic blast with heat-driven winds suctioning trees, the blast tunneling twenty-five miles up while it yanked out roots far below and everything in between.

Was this one of the "whirlwinds" Sister Lucia recorded? What if volcanoes popped in thunderous unison, dozens of places, a deafening orchestration of pumice clogging harbors hopelessly, floating even on roiled tides of the ocean?

War, geophysical events, and something—seen or unseen—from the cosmos?

Might unknown pulls of gravity tug at the uprights of earth?

That would mean that deep below, somewhere in the cement footing of earth, in the support beams of continents—of oceans, above molten rock—gales of great sinew would blow, first in a keen, whistling at distances that were uncanny, quickly offering up a roar that alternated booms and echoes in poise for the final act of tectonic wrath. Times deep ago were recorded in sounds deep below. The only position was in prayer on the knees. And the only ones who knew were the unlearned mystics who relied not on what overloaded the studied academic cerebral circuits of our "geniuses," but on what was whispered to simple intuition, in locution, or in the throes of disparate dreams. Write them down before they vaporized into the ether: What was echoing below was in the very anterooms of the human spirit.

On the same "missing" page: "The third angel sounded, and a great star fell from heaven, burning like a torch, and it fell on a third of the rivers and on the springs of waters" (*Revelation* 8:10).

Already we see in the news forewarnings of geology. "A Russian TV crew flying over the Siberian tundra this winter spotted a massive crater thirty meters (100 feet) deep and twenty meters wide—striking in its size, symmetry, and the explosive force of nature that it must have taken to have created it," reported articles in September 2020. "Scientists are not sure exactly how the huge hole, which is at least the ninth spotted in the region since 2019, formed. Initial theories floated when the first crater was discovered near an oil and gas field in the Yamal Peninsula in northwest Siberia included a meteorite impact, a UFO landing, and the collapse of a secret underground military storage facility. While scientists now believe the giant hole is linked to an explosive build-up of methane gas—which could be an unsettling result of warming temperatures in the region—there is still a lot the researchers don't know, and the other holes have gone unexplained."

There had been a flurry of small earthquakes in Iceland—thousands. Unusual. Europe had felt temblors. Turkey. In Iceland were at least a hundred and thirty volcanoes, many capable of turning that frost into the gruel of a seething caldron.

And if an angel were around, perhaps as the Tiber threatened Rome, he would lament that the Church no longer could guide with power because it no longer believed in the mystical dimension, it no longer subscribed to prophecy. It is why so many left: no longer did they feel the Holy Spirit, only the cold calculus of theology. Only if it returns to its supernatural heritage—the mystical body, its true roots—will it recover from what it has been through since the Enlightenment. That is an ironic name for it," an angel might muse. "The secular 'Enlightenment' was one of the darkest periods in modern history. It was when mankind put on blinders. It is when unenlightenment—Descartes, Voltaire, Bacon, setting the stage for Nietzsche, Darwin, scientism, Marx—cast its spell upon mankind."

The real Enlightenment had come to Sister Lucia though a minuscule fraction—an infinitesimal few, even of Catholics, even of devout ones—had heard of it.

It wasn't just a shortcoming, a minor point: the tedium of sermons. No: along with homosexual scandals, it had played a huge role in decimating attendance, causing a vast swath of the flock, especially the young, to lose closeness with Jesus. That distance opened both the laity and Church to demonic onslaughts, one after another. The general societal trend of irreligion, plus religious feminization and clerical aloofness—including portraits of Jesus that made Him look almost genderless (far softer than what one saw with the Shroud or in the words He spoke)—served to further estrange males. When it came to the real Lord, powerful was the description of George G. Ritchie, a Virginia psychiatrist who as an army recruit in his youth had a "near-death" experience during which he claimed to have encountered the Lord. "This was not the Jesus of my Sunday school books," he recounted. "That Jesus was gentle, kind, understanding—and probably a little bit of a weakling. *This* Person was power itself, older than time and yet more modern than anyone I had ever met. Above all, I knew that this Man loved me. Far more even than power, what emanated from this Presence was unconditional love. A love beyond my wildest imagining. This love knew every unlovable thing about me—the quarrels with my stepmother, my explosive temper, the sex thoughts I could never control, every mean, selfish thought and action since the day I was born—and accepted and loved me just the same."

A sterile, academic Church, often at odds with itself, had left the flock with a distorted image of the real Jesus.

Oh, there were good priests. Many. There were great priests. Many also. And the younger, the more devout. There was plenty of room for hope.

But for the moment there was sterility, made worse by division: Satan was doing his inventive best to turn both liberals and conservatives against Rome (as well as each other), and disheartening was how Christian commentators felt free to treat the Supreme Pontiff like any political target. (This was especially true in Catholic bloggery, which too often was toxic).

It was true that Pope Francis was different, from a continent that never before had generated a Pontiff, a region that spoke differently with greater (and sometimes chaotic) candor. Also, Francis was a Jesuit. The surprise was not that he had liberal tendencies (along with some decidedly conservative ones); the surprise was that a Jesuit had been chosen in the first place.

Controversy had taken place almost before the last wisps of muted gray from the Sistine chimney.

Adding to the angst: in 1965, Garabandal seer Conchita Gonzalez had said a "great miracle" (similar to what was later indicated at Medjugorje) would coincide with "a singular event in the Church that happens very rarely, and has never happened in my lifetime."

"It is not new or stupendous," she added, "only rare, like a definition of a dogma—something like that in that it will affect the entire Church."

Interesting it was that Garabandal occurred from 1961 to 1965, paralleling Vatican Two.

An angel like Gavreel would bring visions not only of what was to come, but of the past. I saw flashbacks of the Middle Ages. I saw the dark corridors, the haunting specter, of the Great Bubonic Plague. I saw villages where no one survived and there was no one, local or visiting, to inter the dead, bodies stacked like firewood. I saw corpses so repulsive that wolves wouldn't scavenge them. And the Church? Monasteries emptied. So did dicasteries. Priests, bishops, seminarians were counted among the dead. Once vibrant sanctuaries of faith now stood hollow and void, their holy occupants succumbing to the relentless grasp of mortality. I saw that physical infections have spiritual precursors. There were sex scandals before the Plague hit. Indulgences were sold, as was the right of clergy to marry. Cash was piled high at the papal palace, which had moved to France. There was narcissism. There were stage dramas instead of liturgies. It was the era they invented the vanity mirror. The parapets of palaces were bronze. Some were gilded. Peasants owned embroidered shoes. Starkly apparent it was that the physical afflictions besieging humanity in those dire times sprout from spiritual rootstock. The shadows of moral transgressions cast themselves before the arrival of the Plague. "Like your own time," said Gavreel, "everyone felt rich. There had been warnings. They had been given signs. The Plague was preceded by storms, rumblings, phenomena. Tremors rang the bells of churches in Italy. Lightning struck steeples, which were made of bronze. If you look into it, you'll find the origin of *bacilli* in cemeteries near Lake Issyk-Kul in Kyrgyzstan, an area known both for ancient tremors and whispered tales of enigmatic UFO sightings, which likewise taunted Europe, where strange balls of light were recounted and where there were meteorites and weather had turned erratic, as in your time, as in this time when again everyone is rich."

Meteors?

I learned that a train of small asteroids is thought to have hit the eastern Atlantic in this general era, causing tidal waves, especially in Portugal.

I was stuck on meteors, seeking to map myriad threads of this tapestry spun by Gavreel.

Gavreel's celestial voice would resonate, imparting the wisdom of far-bygone days. "In that era," he might speak, "warnings were heralded. Signs were bestowed upon mortals, a prelude to the impending catastrophe. Plague arrived on the heels of tempests, thunderous rumblings, and anomalies that teased also the European populace. Strange orbs of luminescence danced across the night sky, and the day too—in at least one instance, exorcised urgently by a bishop, manifestations married to nature's gasps, as the very fabric of weather turned capricious.

"Such parallels echo your present time, where opulence reigns supreme and embroidered shoes have transformed into luxurious pickups and SUVs. Once again, prosperity surrounds all, but its evanescence remains an ever-looming specter. In your occult—in your psychics, in your astrology, in your tarot, in your trance mediums, in your crystals, in your Santeria, in your mantras, in your witchcraft you ladle the cauldron of ancients, your revive darkest gremlims, whose device it is to orchestrate calamity."

After a pause, he would continue: "Epidemics can follow great disruptions, or shout their arrival," Gavreel might explain. "In your epoch, they precede what is to come, as does the strife of your disobedience, of rebellion, which is as witchcraft, as disrespect shown authorities, including the Pontiff, who kneels in supplication as stones are thrown at his house, as Jacinta saw in a vision."

The Angel of New York might then show a swirl of black smoke, one that circulated the earth. Around and around. A coiling snake. Another clear spot would open, then close; close then open. A region in this world would learn devastation—a region relied upon for resources. When Lot looked toward Sodom, said *Genesis*, he saw it go up "like the smoke of a furnace" (1-28).

Were there not mysterious strangers at Sodom?

Did they not come to warn, guide, and protect? Was one of them Gabriel?

Within the realm of this earthly plane, a particular region would bear the weight of unfathomable devastation—a region hitherto regarded as a bastion of sustenance, a provider for the many. This land would become a crucible of destruction, its very foundations shattered and its lifeblood tainted.

Would angels show herds of animals stampeding on the veldt of Africa, amidst a constant earthen regurgitation of noise, soon a roar? Might the stars seem somewhat askew as the planet turned channels? Cosmic order, once unwavering in its harmony, would undergo subtle yet perceptible shifts. Like a grand celestial puzzle, the arrangement of stars would hint at an enigmatic rearrangement, a choreography in sync with the metamorphosis unfolding below. About the end of time, Saint Vincent Ferrer prophesied (in the year 1401), "You will see a *sign* and you will not know it, but note that at that time women will dress like men and will behave according to their tastes and licentiously and men will dress vilely like women." In Grottaferrata, Italy, in a monastic settlement, an Orthodox saint named Nilus (1005) was said to have prophesied that toward the end of the next millennium (the 1990s), "the people of that time will become unrecognizable. When the time for the Advent of the Antichrist approaches, minds will grow cloudy from carnal passions, and dishonor and lawlessness will grow stronger. Then the world will become unrecognizable."

Likewise was a prophecy—variously attributed to Saint Brigid, Saint Columbus, and even Saint Francis of Assisi!— that said, "The sign of these events will be: when the priests will have left the holy habit and will dress as common people, women as men and men as women."

This was difficult turf. The internet was good at fabrication.

But the drumbeat of apocalyptic predictions meant something, and when it came to cataclysms, one scanned upward, at the great unknowns of this cosmos and perhaps universes beyond it.

Here, forces were in motion that could have untold effects on the galaxy, in stellar infrastructure, not to mention our minuscule planet. At Garabandal seer Conchita claimed the "warning" would be a cosmic event, "like two stars... that crash and make a lot of noise, and a lot of light... but they don't fall. It's not going to hurt us but we're going to see it and, in that moment, we're going to see our consciences." (Many years ago, I had called Conchita but she steadfastly declined to say a word about the secrets.)

And elsewhere?

In Pasadena I was told at NASA that the likeliest "doomsday" scare would be a large comet materializing from around the blind side of the sun, entirely unanticipated. Gavreel would stare down at the sidewalk as he intoned in a low solemn cadence, "If man goes to the extreme, so will nature, and one day a comet will hang in the noonday sky, before your television cameras."

And so the doomsday prophecies spun. Would such events even occur? Or would humans snap back into a morality that'd prevent disasters, beseeching a God Who kept all in order, Who fine-tuned gravity?

But for God's Grace—and that was available in abundance—anything could happen.

How many knew that a decadent spit of land off the Rockaways called Hog Island (and patronized by gamblers, corrupt Tammany Hall politicos, and those seeking the services of prostitutes in the Rockaways) disappeared (in waves of thirty feet) in a hurricane in 1893?

Boiling, churning gas and ash.

Seismic events. Astronomical ones.

"They do not know the punishment that is coming their way," said a reputed seer named Amparo Cuevas in Mexico, quoting Jesus on February 11, 1988. "The punishment is near, it will consist, my daughter, of the stars that will collide with the earth, they are about to destroy the majority of humanity. The star Eros will illuminate all humanity, it will be horrible, my daughter, it will seem that the world is on fire, it will only be a few seconds, many of the humans will want to be dead at that moment. Even the just will see it, but it will not affect them at all. Many humans will also die from that great impression; it will be like a rain of fire, the whole earth will tremble, my daughter, it will be horrible."

Few were the prophets who *weren't* doomsayers.

Before her death in 1961, a beatified Italian sister, Mother Elena Aiello, quoted the Lord as lamenting that *"in the dark they continue to live in their sins and move further away from God; but the punishment of fire approaches to purify the earth from the iniquities of the wicked. A firestorm will fall on the earth. This terrible punishment that has never been seen in the history of mankind will last for seventy hours."*

"The bad example of parents trains the family in scandal and infidelity, instead of virtue and prayer, which is almost dead on the lips of many," she had said. *"Stained and withered is the fountain of faith and sanctity of the home."*

New York, yes. But also Los Angeles: Oh, Gavreel would have much to project in visions here. He would have much to show in every city. He would have much to say to celebrities who mocked the Church, naked, with black candles. He would speak to those who hoarded money while Africans starved. He would address televised spectacles, the award shows flaunting their decadence for all to witness—the singers gyrating in garish attire of blood-red leather, dancers weaving through themselves in circles that called to mind the unhinged revels of Saturnalia—or worse, the clandestine congregation of a satanist's ritual. Conclusively he would see through the cheap veil of entertainment for the worrisome idolatry, the alchemy, it was. It was all coming out into the open. Satan was showing what the Virgin of Medjugorje had called *"his shameful face."*

Little wonder, then, that all the crazy beasts were reported, the skinwalkers and chupacabras and bigfoot and mothmen and aliens and giants and dwarves and ghosts and fairies and mapinguari and living dinosaurs, so very often in conjunction with the equally ephemeral sightings of UFOs. Here too was often an occult underpinning. Why would a man-ape leave behind—as was also true here—that sulfur smell or something comparably repugnant? How could so many be spotted—again like "UFOs"—without leaving final physical evidence (or at least, none that we yet knew)? In the case of mothman, who was first spotted in West Virginia, in 1966, the description was of a winged, red-eyed "man" who appeared just before a massive bridge collapse in Point Pleasant (which killed forty-six). Why would UFOs be spotted where bigfoot was— if both were not part of the same scheme (at least in many cases)? How brilliant it seemed, the part of the 2010 message that urged "the uncovering of those spirits which now install themselves as guardians for those who have invited into their hearts falsity" and said that "only those in union with God will be able to see in the darkness which so many expected and that already is upon the earth" while adding that "the dark spirits are now allowed to materialize in full due to the pretense and aspirations of man." The world was not only stranger than we imagined but stranger than we could imagine, stranger than science. And deceptive.

It was the "final battle" Lucia had warned about.

It was not difficult to imagine "extraterrestrials" arriving as saviors—and as original Creator.

Anti-christ.

"Oh! how sad is My Heart to see that men do not convert (or respond) to so many calls of love and grief, manifested by My Beloved Mother to errant men," Mother Aiello had quoted Jesus as saying. *"Roaming in darkness, they continue to live in sin, and further away from God! But the scourge of fire is near, to purify the earth of the iniquities of the wicked. The justice of God requires reparation for the many offenses and misdeeds*

that cover the earth, and which can no longer be compromised. Men are obstinate in their guilt and do not return to God. The Church is opposed, and the priests are despised because of the bad ones who give scandal."

She allegedly saw the Madonna dressed in black with the seven swords piercing her chest, saying, *"My Heart is sad for so many sufferings in an impending world in ruin. The justice of Our Father is most offended. Men live in their obstinacy of sin. The wrath of God is near. Soon the world will be afflicted with great calamities, bloody revolutions, frightful hurricanes, and the overflowing of streams and the seas.*

"Cry out until the priests of God lend their ears to my voice, to advise men that the time is near at hand, and if men do not return to God with prayers and penances, the world will be overturned in a new and more terrible war. Arms most deadly will destroy peoples and nations! The dictators of the earth, specimens infernal, will demolish the churches and desecrate the Holy Eucharist, and will destroy things most dear. In this impious war, much will be destroyed of that which has been built by the hands of man."

"The overflowing of streams and the seas" returned us, posthaste, to the Enlightenment of Fátima, where simplicity had so roundly trumped sophistication.

"Clouds with lightning flashes of fire in the sky and a tempest of fire shall fall upon the world. This terrible scourge, never before seen in the history of humanity, will last seventy hours. Godless persons will be crushed and wiped out. Many will be lost because they remain in their obstinacy of sin. Then shall be seen the power of light over the power of darkness. The rulers of nations make so much ado and speak of peace," Mary said. *"Tremendous will be the upheaval of the whole world, because men—as at the time of the Deluge—have lost God's way, and are ruled by the spirit of Satan. Defiled in the mire, mankind soon will be washed in its own blood, by disease; by famine;*

by earthquakes; by cloudbursts, tornadoes, floods, and terrible storms; and by war. But men ignore these warnings and are unwilling to be convinced that my tears are plain signs to serve notice that tragic events are hanging over the world and that the hours of great trials are at hand."

Chapter 29

MANY PREDICTIONS SEEMED PREMATURE. Aiello had recorded her messages in 1950, saying the scourge was "near" and that blood soon would be on the "streets of the world."

That had not come to pass—not in the way it was portrayed. But this was a common puzzle when it came to a prophetic pulse: How much was simply in error, or simply the seer's presumption, and how much was "premature" due to the timelessness of the spiritual realm?

One thing for certain: if Mother Aiello was transmitting actual missives from On High—a reckoning—it had not yet materialized. Or did it simply loom?

"See how Russia will burn!" the Madonna supposedly told Mother Aiello on Good Friday. And before the nun's eyes, "there extended an immense field covered with flames and smoke, in which souls were submerged as if in a sea of fire."

"And all this fire is not that which will fall from the hands of men, but will be hurled directly from the Angels," narrated the Madonna.

As in the Middle Ages, prophets had risen on all sides, including psychic ones. During the summer of 2008, a soothsaying medium published a book that said, "In around 2020, a severe pneumonia-like illness will spread throughout the globe, attacking the lungs and the bronchial tubes and resisting all known treatments. Almost more baffling than the illness itself will be the fact that it will suddenly vanish as quickly as it arrived, attack again ten years later, and then disappear completely."

Were we in for another contagion?

Such folks spoke frequently of "earth changes," including the most famous of them, Edgar Cayce, who "channeled" visions of the future in a hypnotic clairvoyant state and pronounced cataclysmic events that, occult or not, brought to mind the Fátima Enlightenment. "He claimed the polar axis would shift and that many areas that are now land would again become ocean floor, and that Atlantis would rise from the sea," noted Wikipedia. "The belief that the California coast would slip into the sea—a common feature of Earth Changes predictions—originated with Cayce's alleged prophecies. Belief in earth changes is also found among Native Americans, some of whom refer to the concept as 'the Great Purification.' These beliefs have occasionally been associated with Christian millennialism and beliefs about UFOs. Some New Age adherents believe that earth changes will preface a 'Golden Age' of spirituality and world peace."

Said the director of Cayce's own institute—further calling to mind Lucia's verbiage—"We like to think of our planet as a stable home, but, in fact, its crust is always moving, it wobbles on its axis, and it is flying around in a space containing other objects, two of which [asteroids] passed so close in 2010 that they were inside the orbit of the moon."

On May 28, 1926, Cayce made a link between temperature changes in deep ocean currents and weather changes on the surface. "As the heat or cold in the various parts of the earth is radiated off, and correlated with reflection in the earth's atmosphere, this in its action changes the currents or streams in the ocean," said the "sleeping prophet."

Did the connection to psychics negate similar Christian ones, tying them into New Age) and raising question of *their* source, or—in a left-handed way—confirm them?

It was tricky territory. The devil certainly had glimpses of the future. And certainly, something was afoot. Average temperature in the United States was 54.62 degrees Fahrenheit in 1998, which placed it in a virtual tie with 1934 as the warmest year in records dating to 1895. It only got warmer in subsequent years. Climate swerves were always a sign, and despite all the politics, when I spoke to the director of the National Climate Data Center, this man who had served under both Republicans and Democrats and had access to the world's greatest store of readings told me point blank that temperatures were arcing higher than they had not in centuries but in thousands of years.

In 2023 oceanographers were stunned by spikes in Atlantic heat, warning rightly or wrongly of unknown consequences as temperatures neared what they feared to be a historic and unpredictable "tipping point."

"Prophets" were less reserved. *That day will be most fearful in the world!* Mother Aiello, now beatified, had relayed. *The earth will tremble, all humanity will be shaken! The wicked and the obstinate will perish in the tremendous severity of the justice of the Lord. The world will be once more afflicted with great calamity; with bloody revolutions; with great earthquakes; with famines; with epidemics; with fearful hurricanes; and with floods from rivers and seas. But if men do not return to God, purifying fire will fall from the Heavens, like snowstorms, on all peoples, and a great part of humanity will be destroyed!*

"Russia will march upon all the nations of Europe, particularly Italy, and will raise her flag over the dome of St. Peter's. Italy will be severely tried by a great revolution, and Rome will be purified in blood for its many sins, especially those of impurity! The flock is about to be dispersed and the Pope must suffer greatly.

"But soon terrifying manifestations will be seen, which will make even the most obdurate sinners tremble!

"If the people do not recognize in these scourges the warnings of Divine Mercy, and do not return to God with truly Christian living, another terrible war will come from the East to the West. Russia with her secret armies will battle America; will overrun Europe.

"The river Rhine will be overflowing with corpses and blood."

The most potent in modern times had been a magnitude-9.5 in Chile, which in 1960 generated a tsunami and killed thousands, felt as far as Japan.

That had been followed by a magnitude-9.2 on Good Friday in 1964, in Alaska, a jolt lasting for four and a half excruciating and roaring minutes.

The most forceful recorded quakes went back only to the 1930s; we knew only that in ancient times, civilizations had mysteriously and completely vanished in places like coastal South America, Egypt, and Turkey.

Might there occur a magnitude-10—more than five times stronger than Chile? And really, was there a final limit (short of the earth splitting in twain) when it came to magnitude?

It forced one to contemplate the raw, chaotic power of the very ground beneath our feet, a seemingly stable foundation that, in truth, belies a boiling cauldron of roiling energies waiting to be released. We already knew that Manhattan was sinking under the weight of all that steel and cement, and that extraction of groundwater around the earth was causing it to wobble slightly. Are we then, mere dust motes in the face of such monumental fury, impotent to do anything but speculate on the unthinkable, tremble at the unfathomable?

But for God: yes.

There were those who fretted that "tectonic blocking"

pausing great quakes was ongoing but soon would end.

Might a quake be felt by everyone in the world at the same time?

Was this one of the things that could occur if the angel Lucia saw unlatched the axis?

Or if Gavreel did?

One could also visualize the angel of New York waving a hand to materialize the holograph of a sinkhole beginning a rapid, voracious expansion, sending startled onlookers—residents nearby—to flight and swallowing an entire countryside. The desert shaking. Cascading into it. Like rapids into a vortex. One day, might we read of sinkholes in places such as Siberia or Louisiana or upper Canada or New Jersey along with the desert locales where such chasms would plunge a thousand feet deep?

How about more if something in the vasty depths, in earth's unknown cellar, were to implode?

In New York, we can envisage the pedestrians, those undulating waves of bobbing heads, first quizzical, then apprehensive, if suddenly the ground beneath them were to telegraph deep rumbles. On Fifth Avenue, many would flee to Saint Pat's, staring with anxious, yearning looks at the stone vaulting along with the exquisite woodwork behind the high altar under the bronze baldachino—peering up as if watching for anything falling. From a pew one would hear shuffling feet, the distant ding of an inopportune text, the whispers from a group that looked like tourists from the Midwest. No more clacking of cameras. The missing page from the Bible here, 219, New Testament, a chapter called "The Fall of Babylon: Kings and Merchants Lament Over Her," which when found would read, "And kings of the earth, who committed fornication, and lived in delicacies with her, shall weep, and mourn over her, when they see the smoke of her burning.

Standing afar off for fear of her torments, saying, 'Woe, woe that great city Babylon, that mighty city: for in one hour is thy judgment come" (*Revelation* 18:9-10).

When one considered, in that same chapter of the Apocalypse (17:1), a "great harlot, who sitteth upon many waters," one thought of the Hudson, the East River, the Harlem, the Bay of New York, and the Atlantic beyond. When one saw a "kingdom which hath dominion over the kings of the earth" (17:2), one saw the United Nations on one of the waters. When one saw "all manner of precious stone" (18:11), one looked to West 47th Street and the diamond district. When one saw "fornication" or "sodomy," one saw this (18:1-3) in callgirls, streetwalkers, hookups, porn productions, gay bars all over town. When one saw a "great city, which was clothed in fine linen," one saw storefronts on Madison, or 57th Street, or the models. When one saw "merchants made rich," this *was* Manhattan. And when it came to the Tower of Babel (*Genesis* 11:1): this was seen in towers, in high rises, in hospitals, at universities, in the hood, in corporate headquarters, in corner stores and delis, in train stations and airports, for every language in every dialect was spoken here.

"Woe, woe, that great city, wherein all were made rich, who had ships at sea, by reason of her prices." Again, check.

In one hour (*Revelation* 18:19), "desolate."

New York, and what is symbolized, was going to fall.

There might not be anyone else in the pew, wood vibrating, a steady quiver, then a wobble and undulation that suddenly but inauspiciously halts.

Tremors would begin anew, this time with greater intensity, the flames of candles strobing, as if to indicate in one direction after another, as if fanned and then deprived of oxygen. A prance of erratic shadows. One would look toward the narthex and see befuddled tourists consulting other befuddled tourists and natives no longer cocksure, their confidence gnawed by the unknown. Was it noise from beneath, a subway explosion, or *Isaiah* 24:12-13: "Desolation is left in the city; and calamity shall oppress the gates. For it will be thus in the midst of the earth, in the midst of the people."

Chapter 30

FAR OFF, IN THE CONGO, Our Lady had been appearing since May 3, 1988, in Church-approved apparitions under the title, "Mary, Mother of Disarmament," and brought no cause to dismiss apocalypse, in New York or wherever.

The seer: Raphael Minga Kwete of Kinshasa. The opening message: At this time in history, Raphael says he was told, the devil wanted to start a nuclear war.

And so once more visions of fire danced a cerebral ballet, for the moment supplanting tectonic thunder.

This was allegedly in a nation consecrated to Satan in 1975 and now a boil of sorcery, drug use, violence, and lust, along with warlike preferences.

The story was as straightforward as it was dramatic: As a child, Raphael had been blinded (by disease or injury it was not said), and it was then that Jesus appeared to him for the first time—restoring his sight *a la* Saint Paul. During that vision or apparition, the Lord had asked Raphael to read chapter twelve of *Ezekiel*, which began on page 659 with, "And the word of the Lord came to me, saying: Son of man, thou dwelleth in the midst of a provoking house; who have eyes to see, and see not; and ears to hear, and hear not: for they are a provoking house."

Pestilence and famine were mentioned. So was "Babylon."

The Lord was followed during a third apparition by His Blessed Mother, who, testified Raphael, "showed me some kind of sign that read: *'Holy Virgin Mary, Mother of Disarmament,'* and said, *'The days of great tribulations are near. You will notify the authorities when I give you permission.'*" She also gave Raphael a biblical passage, *Corinthians* 6:3-11.

That was page 143 New Testament, and started with, "Know you not that we shall judge angels? How much more things of this world." After a warning about the selfishness, lawsuits, defrauding, and contentions of this world, advising longsuffering, it said, "Know you not that the unjust shall not possess the kingdom of God? Be not deceived: Neither fornicators, nor idolaters, nor adulterers, nor the effeminate, nor sodomites, nor thieves, nor the covetous, nor drunkards, nor railers, nor extortioners, shall possess the kingdom of God."

Not just adulterers but fornicators. Sex outside of marriage. Idolaters: worshippers of money, celebrity, homes, cars, entertainments. (Worship of the sun without recognizing the Son behind it.) Effeminates: trans. Sodomites: partaking of unnatural intercourse, which also applied to heterosexuals (even married ones). Railers: the rancorous commentators, harsh judges. Extortionists: those who gouged, coerced, and threatened, defrauded, who held a person—or society—hostage for wealth.

How many were the detractors! How many fornicators!

"I came to disarm Satan and his henchmen because they are preparing a real catastrophe and worldwide apostasy," Our Lady said. *"Let the Church's leaders meditate on what I have just told you."*

This was addressed to a hierarchy that had not heard of these apparitions and by all odds never would, immersed, as was their wont, in a worldly version of Christianity.

It was she, said Mary, who had inspired John Paul II to consecrate that year of 1988 to her *"so that I might make this revelation to you, for I know what will happen throughout the whole world."*

Yet from the Catholic hierarchy, from bishops, from the Vatican: *silenzio.*

Clerics met for conferences in what looked like stockholder events, the hallowed resonance, the sanctified aura, the transcendent ambience all but extinct.

On April 14, 1989, in Kinshasa, five rainbows appeared in connection with the apparitions—symbolizing just what, no one could be sure—and three days later, a luxuriant tropical tree lost its leaves and dried out despite abundant rain. Our Lady explained that the tree symbolized the crisis in Christianity and the uselessness of men who had no faith.

Above all, however (she always imbued hope), it was a sign of Mary's presence.

Oh, yes: God could speak in rainbows. For Noah, it was after the Flood. It was as the world lay in ruins. It meant purging. It reminded us of His covenant. The Lord would refurbish His Creation. He was recounting *Genesis* 9. Raphael was given a prayer: *"Lord Jesus Christ, King of Peace, now that we venerate publicly Your Blessed Mother and ours, Immaculate Virgin, as Mother of Disarmament, send upon us a shower of peace, justice, grace, love, hope, faith, perseverance, fidelity, unity, and mercy. May the exploitation of man by man be annihilated and erased worldwide. Amen."*

Greed—materialism—was a root of God's displeasure. Extortion.

On March 30, 1996, the Virgin announced that a sign would occur in Nzete Ekauka and indeed, on the appointed day of April 17, a crowd estimated at 35,000 gawked and cheered and prayed on knees as the sun danced and turned on itself, a sign that repeated itself for months after: A fiery chariot of the sky, so profound, so miraculous, that the very concept of reality seemed to shatter. It pirouetted in the mid-day sky, spinning like a celestial top, bending the laws of nature to its radiant will. This was not just an event; it was an orchestration of cosmic proportion, a Divine interaction that like Fátima suspended the notions of our reality. It was the sun moving from its post in the sky, its performance more entrancing than the most profound symphony. The profound wonder of Nzete Ekauka transcended its earthly confines, proving that the miraculous could, and indeed does, intersect with the everyday.

It was a nation, the Congo, torn constantly by civil strife. Millions of kids neared starvation. There were thieves. There were extortionists. Approximately four hundred thousand women were raped here every year. Disease and famine were endemic. Tribal conflicts were reminiscent of neighboring Rwanda, where Mary had appeared in 1981, warning, in the gentle way only she could, of a horrid coming genocide, which killed more than 800,000; and where, after one apparition, half of the sky had suddenly and inexplicably and totally darkened.

So dark thousands had trouble finding their way home.

In the Congo—the mysterious, voodoo-drenched jungle—were tales of a crypto-beast called *mokèlé mbèmbé* (the "animal that stops rivers"). A Loch Ness neck. A massive frilled tail.

It was first mentioned in the West by a French missionary priest named Liévin-Bonaventure Proyard.

Many were the reports of strange creatures—none leaving bone or skull, none a definitive hair, nor hide—around the globe. This too was a sign of the times, what seemed like a precipitation of evil into physical form. In recent decades, sightings had intensified. It was a symptom of the age, it seemed, a coagulation of malevolence given crude and troubling flesh.

The smoke—sulfur, the devil's perfume—was now curling from the pit and taking physicality. Nature was confused. In the Alps, in Antarctica, near the poles, glaciers were melting. A walrus was spotted off Cornwall in the United Kingdom, two thousand miles from the Arctic Circle and disoriented.

It was as if the world was running a fever, her cool compresses failing. And what was the cause? It seemed the world was, at last, bringing forth into substance that which it had been nurturing in its soul. And if this was the case, then we must all prepare for a time of reckoning.

Had magnetism changed? Or ocean currents? Might the blanket of warming air cause the Gulf Stream to lose momentum, inhibiting downward flow of cool water and with this lost dynamic, causing the massive upper oceanic current that transfers warmth to collapse—bringing sudden cold to North America? The scenario was harrowing—a seismic shift in the aquatic order, the collapse of the grand conveyor, a plunge into frigid despair. And if such an event came to pass, North America, our expansive homeland, might find itself locked in an icy embrace, a sudden and cruel winter.

And quakes: they seemed to align with cosmic radiation—from the sun and elsewhere.

Much was shifting, altering, gyrating. One flare, a "piece" of the sun, broke off in 2023, creating a massive polar vortex, stunning astronomers; years before, another flare, blasting from the solar surface, from the furnace, took a form that looked much to those who saw signs like a blazing orange seraph holding trumpet at ready, a beacon of cosmic radiation. The universe was speaking. The question remained whether we had the courage to listen.

Once more were those words from LaSalette: *"The sea-*

sons will be altered, the earth will produce nothing but bad fruit, the stars will lose their regular motion, and the moon will only reflect a faint reddish glow.

"Water and fire will give the earth's globe convulsions and terrible earthquakes which will swallow up mountains, cities, etcetera."

Meanwhile, the more recent "prophecies" kept on keeping on, like the scroll of chyrons in Times Square.

"God the Father will send two terrible punishments," said a hotly controversial seer at Escorial in Spain. "One of them is revolution, drought, famine, and disease. God will allow Satan to sow discord between rulers, in society, and in the family. Another punishment will come from the sky, a devastating earthquake in various countries, and the onset of absolute darkness for three days."

We stood, a speck on the galactic tapestry. We awaited, with bated breath, the universe's cryptic reply. Were eddying currents in the liquid core, in the dynamo of the earth, creating instability? Were there cosmic forces entirely unknown to our detection devices?

Whatever the legitimacy of such locutions, the currency of a global quake grew in light of Lucia's message. And in light of the earth's deep past, during which there had been quakes rocking and swaying, cracking and raising, huge swaths of the Near and Middle East. In one fifty-year period, from 1225 B.C. to 1175 B.C., at least forty-seven cities around the Mediterranean had fallen to seismicity, with massive destruction across Turkey and Greece; while in Israel—where Solomon had bowed before profane gods and children sacrificed to a god called Molech—huge marble pillars had been knocked on their sides, men buried beneath. Some believed there may even have been a quake, a shimmy, a rattle of global proportion. Something similar also had happened around 2300 B.C. in Syria, Egypt, Iraq, Turkey, Palestine, and Crete, structures built in honor of demon-gods imploding, crumbling, as if under the sandal of a giant crushing god, into belches of grit. In Mesopotamia—in the land of Baal and Ra and Isis—an excruciating drought followed, cropland vanquished, rivers in retreat. No ordinary desiccation, this. The drought lasted for three hundred years, interrupted briefly by erratic, torrential rainfall, the torrents of flood. Sodom and Gomorrah—thought to have happened around this period—may not, after all, have been isolated events.

Were those quakes felt globally? Would future ones be?

"The demons of the air together with the Antichrist will perform great wonders on earth and in the atmosphere," Melanie Calvat of LaSalette quoted Mary as warning (causing one again to ponder all the strange lights, the orbs, the UFOs, in addition to bizarre creatures). *"Woe to the inhabitants of the earth! There will be bloody wars and famines, plagues and infectious diseases. It will rain with a fearful hail of animals. There will be thunderstorms which will shake cities, earthquakes which will swallow up countries."*

"Dear children," said that man of many messages, Pedro Regis, of Brazil. "You live in a time of great spiritual confusion. I am your Sorrowful Mother and I want to tell you that God is in a hurry. Bend your knees in prayer. You will still see horrors on earth. Do not live far from the path of conversion. Dense darkness covers all the earth. Seek the Light of the Lord. Be enlightened by the Holy Spirit and you will be victorious. In these difficult times, be attentive: The devil will act against men and women of faith. They walk into a future of great confusion, and so many will lose faith. Courage. Do not feel you are alone. My Son Jesus is with you."

Yet, lonely it could seem. And was Satan not laughing? Did he not bear the countenance of hearty mirth as he relished the agony of human disorientation? Was that not the toothiest of smirks on his drawn gray elongated red black face, observing those who chose to reverse the gender God gave them, defying nature with assignments such as "bisexual" or "non-binary" or "genderless" or "mermaid"?

And children: they were allowed now to reconfigure gender?

Sodom had never seen this, nor Nineveh, nor Babylon! Not in Gomorrah were there glass enclosures for the purpose of euthanasia. Doctors now prescribed death!

The Lord would judge. We all had cleansing to do. And yes: anyone who hated or hurt a homosexual or "trans" or abortionist, a euthanasia nurse, a street thug, was not in the Christian walk. No. Not fully. Difficult it was to avert the eyes or turn a cheek.

But the sin: that could be judged. *"The world is without faith and light because it no longer does the Lord's will; has abandoned Him; and insults him every day with terrible sins,"* was a message from another Brazilian, the late Edson Glauber of Itaparinga. *"My children, there are terrible sins upon terrible sins. The Divine Chalice has long been overflowing upon the world, and now the Angels of Heaven, by Divine order, are prepared for the greater punishments through which humanity will have to pass very soon."*

"Very soon Italy and the United States will be punished in a way never seen [before]," Glauber had gone on, in later, unsanctioned missives (his initial ones were approved). *"A great light, like fire, will be visible in the sky of Italy. Pain and sorrow will be great, and when this happens only the Rosary and my maternal heart will provide hope, refuge, and protection for many. Italy will be shaken because men did not respect what is owed to God, did not honor His Holy Name, did not obey His Holy Laws. Enormous pain will also come quickly in the United*

States, causing a particular region to be practically destroyed."

A "great light" put one in mind of Cora Evans, a California mystic up for beatification who once said "the greatest apparition of all" would occur with a magnitude and beauty that will be "beyond human understanding and wisdom. The whole world seemed to be swallowed in the light of a golden vapor, which in no way bore any resemblance to the glow of the earthly sun. It resembled in its mystery of light a huge monstrance tipped over the earth to such a degree that the Host could be seen by everyone in the world," she wrote, after a supposed vision of it.

Meanwhile, in Minnesota, a priest, Father Joel Cycenas, at St. Joseph's in Taylor's Falls, informed me of an anonymous locutionist, mother of four children, who—encouraged to spread her messages by Monsignor Pawel Ptasznik, head of the Polish Section in Vatican's Secretariat of State—said, *"The days are growing shorter and great light shall soon fall upon mankind. Nations will rise and crumble and you will see a great collapse in your financial institutions. My Church will be cleansed of its filth when I weed out those who are not My true chosen sons. Those who have failed [due to] selfish desire will see each and every soul they have neglected. Go forth and cleanse your soul, for the hour is drawing closer before the awakening of mankind. My people, take heed of the signs, take heed of the times in which you live. Mountaintops will awaken and the rock of the earth will split. My people, the mountains that have been sleeping will soon be awakened and this will ripple all across this world. Nations will soon rise up against one another, and this country that I have blessed with many fruits will be awakened by great fire, and ash will cover the valleys and the seas will no longer be calm."*

Even mountains deep in the sea, she was told, will be roused from their slumber.

"I come to warn you that vessels that have been sleeping will soon awaken, sending great fire and ash.

"My Creation is no longer My Creation in the eyes of man, for it is man who believes he is dictator of his own destination. It is because of the blood of the innocent that you will be plagued with great trials and suffering.

"The forces of evil will rise from the ports of the sea and will present the mark of the beast.

"My words of warning have come to the time of expiration. Streams of light will soon pour forth from Heaven and shine into the souls of mankind. My people, those of you who stand for man engaging with man and woman with woman are a witness to evil. Those of you who choose to take away life at any stage are a witness to evil. Those of you who commit adultery and choose to destroy a marriage that is united in Me will see your hour of judgment.

"Those of you who choose to idolize money and power will come to see that your ways are not My ways and your ways will become simplified.

"My words are soon to expire, for the wall that holds back the seas will soon come down. You will be covered in ash and darkness," the messages repeated. *"My people, this world will no longer be as you have come to know it. All must prepare for the time is drawing near."*

Structures, said Jennifer, quoting the Lord, would *"come tumbling as the roar of the lion intensifies."*

"My people," this woman identified only as "Jennifer" quoted the Lord as warning, *"so many have begun to keep a watchful eye to the sight of many earthquakes, yet you do not realize that the great shifting of the earth will come from a place that has been sleeping.*

"This earthquake will cause much chaos and destruction and it will come and catch so many off guard, for that is why I have told you to take heed of the signs.

"Your winter will rise with great force and for some it will present times of hardship.

"When you see the sign of light come from the east, know that the Son of Man is about to come and awaken your soul," it repeated again. *"It is in the calmness that mankind will be caught off guard."*

Right now, she seemed to be relating, the Lord was working gradually. There was a deliberate, gathering force. In time it would not be so piecemeal. *"One by one, I will send forth signs that man will not be able to justify,"* Jennifer quoted Christ as telling her. *"The bells of My Church will be silenced"* (an ironic remark in light of a story of a church in Scandinavia that, around that time, was ordered by a court to halt the ringing of its bells).

"Behold these times which you have been given, for your time of warning is near."

"I could see millions of people from nations from all the lands," said Jennifer at three p.m. on Christmas Day in 2004—the day of the Asian Tsunami in Sumatra, Indonesia. *"Many seemed confused as they were looking up toward the sky."*

Chapter 31

IT ALSO BROUGHT TO MIND THAT ANONYMOUS LOCUTION, an addendum of which, days before, on December 22, 2004, had said, *"There is going to be a major disruption in a region of the world that will affect everyone,"* adding, to repeat: *"When the huge light is seen, I will act in a way I have not acted before."*

This was the same series of locutions that had intoned: *"When you see the great smoke rise, Satan will have touched the earth. His manifestation will be near. He will seek to destroy what Christ has built, as Jesus came to destroy the work of the devil. In the end, the Cross will predominate, but not before the end of an era that has strayed."*

A huge light and smoke could result, one imagined, from the strike of a comet or the distant eruption, perhaps in Sumatra, of a massive volcano under the sea.

There was the notion in various locutions of a great "unraveling," a revelation to souls and lifting of blinders, a "great separation" (the wheat from the chaff) and his was clearly around us.

"My child, the world has entered into a time of transition," said Jennifer. *"The day, the hour of Revelation is upon mankind when the scales of deception will be removed, and My people will see all that they have been blinded by."*

Towards the end of 2021, she added, *"This world is greatly divided. There are those who trust out of fear and there are those who fear to trust. You are to love the Lord your God with all of your heart, mind, and soul, your whole being without reservation. When a soul lacks any of these things, it cannot truly trust. In order to trust, you must surrender everything. The days of great mourning are coming. Many will not be able to seek My Mercy because they do not truly know it. Mothers will yearn for their children, and fathers will weep because they will see how they have blindly trusted the author of deception. This world is in great need of My Visitation."*

There was that word "visit" again.

In February of 2022: *"My child, there are great signs from Heaven that come with the changing winds. I tell My children that the enemy no longer hides but seeks to show his power by taking custody of your soul. It is time to awaken because the hour of greater unraveling is here. If the world does not awaken to My Mercy, it will only arise to My Justice. Great change is coming, for the world can no longer sustain itself in the lies of the enemy. When the earth was created, I ordained day from night, light from darkness. I ordained male and female for there is no in-between. Those who seek to ordain anything that is outside of that are not of Me. My Child, governments will crumble and when you see France, Israel, Italy, and many others fall, know that the time of My Visitation is near."*

The last message from her: *"Now go forth, for I Am Jesus and be at peace, for My mercy and justice will prevail."*

In South America—where one did not expect it—Glauber had claimed that Our Lady "told me that if the Brazilian people do not listen to Her messages and do not live her appeals, a great earthquake will happen in Brazil that will shake the whole country a lot. This earthquake will kill many people who will not be prepared. The earthquake will hit a lot Rio de Janeiro, São Paulo, as well as other states. As a result of this earthquake, there will also be a great tsunami, which will head to Rio de Janeiro.

"When Our Lady showed me this, there were many people running, fleeing desperately, because they were not prepared. Referring to the Amazon, Our Lady said that as a result of all this, a great flood will come, leaving many homeless. After this flood there will be many plagues. It will be like plague that spreads more and more. These plagues will come one after another, one as a consequence of the other."

Could one quake not set off another?

When I interviewed Dr. Lucy Jones, chief of the United States Geological Survey office in Los Angeles, she speculated that "frontal faulting" at the base of mountains northeast of that mega-city could cause a magnitude-7.5, even an eight or higher, if it ruptured from San Bernardino to Santa Barbara.

Faults could set each other off, Dr. Lucy emphasized, and if several faults ruptured at the same time—major fissures—there would be a cataclysm. A magnitude-six that set off a seven that set off another seven or vice versa, or higher—something unexpected, a *storm*, perhaps including the San Andreas—was the seismologist's singular nightmare. If the whole San Andreas fault went and there was a triggering of faults closer to or *under* Los Angeles, we were talking uncharted turf, we were talking a magnitude-8.5.

Such a scenario was considered unlikely, by some implausible. But was it? Was anything? Another official cited earthquakes in places such as Chile that were followed or preceded by distant ones in regions like Alaska.

There were all kinds of faults, many as yet undiscovered, that, as in Manhattan, ran directly under downtown.

This wasn't the vaunted San Andreas. That was miles east. This was right there under asphalt, beneath Tinseltown, under Beverly Hills. And it was incredible: Just as voodoo and the petrochemical industry had planted themselves in the crosshairs of hurricanes in New Orleans and Houston, and as hyper-consumerism-materialism-sensuality had planted itself in harm's way at Palm Beach and Key Biscayne and Miami (*hurucan*, Mayan for "evil spirit of the air"), so had California's film stronghold found itself perched atop the single most dangerous known urban fault, which rose like a hillock behind Capital Records at Hollywood and Vine and below coursed along the Walk of Fame not far from Paramount.

Studios. Tattoo parlors. Grauman's Chinese.

All were subject to the seismic leviathan, which snaked under Sunset, edged alongside a house that had belonged to Ozzie and Harriet, and meandered on to Beverly Hills, forming a scarp at the entrance to a huge Mormon Temple. It could set off a host of neighboring faults, including one smack under Dodger Stadium, a peril to most if not all of what in brighter times had been known as the "Our Lady of the City of Angels" (before Junipero Serra and other brave missionaries were "canceled").

Yet when it came to scenarios for an apocalyptic seismic blast, San Francisco Bay was at least L.A.'s equal, riddled as it was with "strike-slip" and "blind-thrust" faults that with the strength of Apollo heaved one chunk over another or raced past each other, obscured in the mountains.

While the San Andreas was a major threat here too, there again was a flock of smaller faults that had potential to exceed the famous quake of 1906, when the city's promise was canceled and crumpled and set ablaze by the yawning dragon maw of the earth.

Of greatest concern was one called the Hayward, which cleaved rock at the southern end of the bay up through Oakland and out to San Pablo Bay before turning into a devious fissure beneath Berkeley towards Santa Rosa up where they held the secret dark effigy-burning owl-speaking cabalistic annual confab of international movers-and-shakers, key powerbrokers—Bilderberg types—at Bohemian Grove.

This curiously placed fault was described by a spokesman for the United States Geological Survey as "the most dangerous fault in the United States."

And it had a thirty percent chance of erupting in the next decade or two.

"These big earthquakes are close," another expert at the agency told me. "They're going to happen, and they're going to be catastrophic."

To mind came part of the anonymous locution from more than three decades ago which arcanely but boldly confided that *"the seat of Satan in America is north of San Francisco."*

And New York?

It took little research to learn that a very major geophysical event could indeed afflict the city, and not just in the way of a tsunami. No: buildings could actually topple—find themselves horizontal—from a shaking underneath Manhattan itself or due to riven areas to the immediate north and west.

While one rarely thought of the "Big Apple" as prone to seismicity, faults ran not only alongside the city (for example, at the New Jersey Palisades along the Hudson, so visible from the George Washington Bridge), but also directly under Manhattan.

Sodom. Babylon. Throw in Pergamon.

New York was an amalgam.

Miles below the surface, one fracture ran from the Rockaways to Manhattan, splitting north and south around Murray Hill or a bit north.

The latter would place it on the East Side precisely in midtown not far from St. Patrick's and perhaps a bit southwest to Tribeca.

The financial district?

Slashing diagonally, faults ran from the Brooklyn Bridge to Hell's Kitchen and from the Brooklyn Navy Yard to the southwestern corner of Central Park: under the feet of millions. If those were ever triggered, the destruction would be as obvious as it was unspeakable.

Another fault was thought to be near Forty-Ninth Street where the bronze statue of Atlas stood as if defying the spires of the cathedral and as if it—Apollo, not God—held up the cosmos.

A single small fault could topple towers and collapse water mains, sewage, power lines, tunnels, subways: forty billion in damages, at minimum. Power lines, the pulsing neural network of civilization, falling prey to this apocalyptic malady. The once vibrant hum of electricity snuffed out, replaced by a chilling silence that roars louder than any explosion. Darkness, an unwelcome guest, creeping in, a blanket of oblivion smothering the city's pulse. It would be a testament to our hubris, a stark reminder of the delicate threads upon which our towers are built and upon which they perilously stand.

Would the Lincoln Tunnel survive? The Holland?

Counting subways, there were two thousand tunnels and bridges in the City. One could but gasp at the crumpled steel, the contorted girders, the waterways clogged with what once seemed imperishable. If they collapsed, millions would find Manhattan a stone-cold debris-piled prison yard, silent but for pleas. The toll from covid had been chalked at 45,000— more than thirty-eight times New York loss on September 11—and if the curve continued the same ascent, if 45,000 were multiplied by another thirty-eight, it would be—God forbid—1.7 million.

Chapter 32

IN THE SILENCE, A VOICE. Is it the Lord—as the anonymous locutionist believes? *"I will come in the simplicity of ruins, when no light shines but mine. In the outer reaches of the world will be seen the power of goodness itself, which illuminates according to the good within. Those of darkness will find the pain of truth, for in them will the Light cast but shadows. In this truth will be the destructions of men and Man, in the throes of destruction and persecution, which will lead the righteous to promised lands. Go where the heart finds not riches but the sustenance of God, Who watches all things and will control the smallest eventualities. The rumbling of the time will reflect movement in the foundations of the earth, which will rock with woe. Go where the heart hears goodness and the spirit connects to what is eternal power."*

The harbingers—often the case—were there. When Hurricane Sandy hit New York, walkers-by recorded uncanny sounds as air whistled and groaned and roared through the beams of iron of the Freedom Tower, which was under erection. The wind, an omnipresent phantom, sang in an eerie chorus that filled the corridors of Lower Manhattan with disconcerting song as it poured through the nascent skeleton of the edifice: keening whispers, mournful groans, and commanding roars from the iron girders that stood in its path. And so, the Freedom Tower reverberated with spectral song that would forever echo in the hearts of those who bore witness to it. Yet, as anyone with the measuring stick of history knew, this was nothing next to what could descend.

Might hints of what "next could descend" be found half a mile from One World Trade Center at a strange windowless datacenter rising 550 feet at 33 Thomas Street, built in 1974 and long rumored to have secret hallways originally constructed without glass to withstand proximity from a nearby nuclear blast? Is that why it's devoid of windows?

In the intricate folds of time is no coincidence. There is cosmic embroidery, a design we can't fathom through worldly blinders, here in the "earth zone," like looking at the bottom of needlepoint and seeing only knots: It only makes sense, forms beauty, when viewed—as will be the case when we die—from above.

Dated July 23, 2023, at 5:41 a.m., the latest addendum to the anonymous prophecy now added: *"A crisis will come that will test the consciences of all. This is the enlightenment of the soul, its illumination in the stress of threat, in an era that will see too manifestations in splendor of the Lord."*

There is going to be an event that grabs the attention of the world. It will be an event bigger than Fukushima or the Great Asian Tsunami—although it may not affect as wide an area. More than anything, it will draw attention because it is unusual. It is not something we have seen happen, not in our lifetimes, and perhaps not in our books of history, geography, or astronomy. It will be an incident scientists did not anticipate. It will be startling, yet will pass without global destruction. It will reboot human orientation. For those it does not, the times to follow will be that much more difficult. The initial event will cause light in the soul more than in the stars, than in the sun, the sky. It will seem out of nowhere yet we will discover its origin. Someday, it will be understood. Like all of Creation, it is natural and supernatural. It will alarm many, awaken others, cause some destruction, inspire untold numbers. Faith is the insulation against fear. With it, wonder replaces woe.

So this will be.

Were the sounds from the Freedom Tower, which rose so defiantly (just as like the cedars in *Isaiah*, page 563, Old Testament), in any way related to the even eerier ones, the hums, the buzzing, the booms or rumbling, reported around the world?

Much was echoing around us.

And bronze?

Across from St. Patrick's at "626-636 FIFTH AVENUE," which was the entrance to Rockefeller Center, were bronze and brass in profusion, with words, on the façade, that quoted *Isaiah*, reminding us of that other "missing" page and its quote. (*"I will go before thee, and will humble the great ones of the earth: I will break in pieces the gates of brass, and will burst the bars of iron."*)

Might not a mysterious stranger, the angel of Manhattan, Gavreel, show up here? Might he be there to duel with the huge bronze statue of that titan god holding up the heavens in front of the building?

It was one thing that Rockefeller Center was a hub for mammon and media—home to RCA, which gave birth to NBC, movie studios, radio, records—and another fold of synchronicity that the statue there, of pagan god Atlas, had given title to the famous libertarian-uber-materialist novel, *Atlas Shrugged*, by atheist Ayn Rand.

Arms raised, the statue even could be taken as mimicking the Crucifixion.

Waiting for the next appearance of Gavreel, one would leaf through the antique Bible and searching up another missing page (559), find *Isaiah*, first chapter, saying, *"Your country is desolate, your cities are burned with fire; strangers devour your land in your presence; and it is desolate, as over-thrown by strangers. Unless the Lord of hosts had left to us a very small remnant, we would have become like Sodom, we would have been made like Gomorrah"* (1:7-9).

When the angel waved his hand next, it would be to present a holograph of dirt, sand, and rocks erupting from a breach in a desert, a sand geyser, towering, faraway yet frightening, a ghastly depiction of earth's raw determination. It would be something—on the Mojave, or perhaps the Sahara—modern geologists had not logged before: a gusher of hot debris tumbling with yowl a mile above the dunes, a whirling dervish fashioning a massive cloud with the smell of sulfur.

In 2022 an eighty-two-foot-wide hole mysteriously appeared at Tierra Amarilla in the Atacama near an excavation (perhaps ending its mystery), but it was jolting. As a story put it, "The terrifying phenomenon took place close to the Alcaparrosa mine and is thought to be more than 650 feet deep. Officials from Chile's national geology agency have been dispatched to investigate the unsettling spectacle."

If there were a profound shift inside our planet, such holes would grow and unsettle all the more, plunging much deeper, collapsing areas much wider—perhaps under a major megalopolis. Already a sinkhole had burst in front of the ancient Pantheon and its pagan deities, revealing paving stones from a thousand or two years ago—in a growing number of such collapses in Rome.

Among the gods in the Pantheon was Apollo.

Gods. Goddesses. The delta variant. Did we not notice the root cause of distress, and that money, clothes, and cars, food, celebrities, were idolized?

How many cities—Manila, Tokyo, Beijing, Cairo, Amsterdam, Mexico City—stood on nature's sharp edge? *"Now Nineveh was an enormously large city; it took three days to go through it. Jonah began his journey through the city, and had gone but a single day's walk announcing, 'Forty days more and Nineveh shall be destroyed,'"* was page 725.

One could cite dozens of relevant passages. A Bible missing the pages would be a greatly thinned one. Wildfire lapped right up to the sign that said "HOLLYWOOD," below which was a convent—on the precipice now of shuttering—where nuns long spent days praying for the carpet of murky glitter below, the endangered urban spectacle that seemed without horizon.

To the north was Napa Valley, where tremors occurred with disarming regularity, and Silicon Valley, tech capital of the world, and yet farther north, past emerald bigfoot mountains, into Oregon, then Seattle, yet more wunderkinds of electrical alchemy were planted on turf seismologists believed might be at greatest risk of anywhere in North America.

That was due to a gigantic fault offshore at the Juan de Fuca tectonic plate boundary, where one massive oceanic plate was grinding beneath (subducting) the North American one, upon which sat the entire continent.

Throughout its past, shifts in the earth had raised and dropped this part of the Northwest like a plank and Indians handed down legends of great tsunamis that had washed over the peninsula.

Here it might reach higher, perhaps magnitude-nine.

This, the Cascadian subduction zone, was "storing strain energy to be released in future great earthquakes," wrote two government scientists, Thomas H. Heaton and Stephen H. Hatzell, who fretted candidly about "a sequence of several great earthquakes of magnitude-8" that could rumble and roar on for years—what another geologist, George Carver of California State University, called a "decade of terror."

Perhaps it would be Seattle. Maybe Vancouver. Possibly Alaska. One might see in vision dogs, goats, and chickens, migrating fowl—an ominous premonition nestled in the secret language of the beasts, with frenzy before the shaking began—and a great upheaval of the earth. A plank beneath the ocean dropping like the back ramp of a truck.

Elsewhere, from horizon to horizon, what I can only describe as a veil of red dust. This is not an end but an upheaval, the great convulsion of the world, birthing not new life but a new world order of chaos and despair, for those lacking faith.

Endless miles of woods flattened as if by percussion, trees snapped in the same direction. Pedestrians in some major city, perhaps Tokyo, falling to the ground as all was shaking and heaving, intent on unprecedented destruction.

"Remember that pride follows pride, and pride deceives itself," an angel might inform the listener. "When the Lord looks at the heart, He searches for pride and love. He wants to find love only. Lack of love is the root of all evil. It leads to pride and it is pride that brings a nation's fall. Earth spirits will be vanquished. Indian grounds of ritual will be no more, nor circles of *wicca*. Nor the Masonic cornerstones—at the U.S. Capitol, at the foundations of Wall Street." Anything occult, he would confirm, "is part of Mystery Babylon," adding, "Those who stray follow themselves. Hatred has the energy of enticement, in the name of good. True goodness follows the way of Jesus and puts no stock in the fantasies of men."

The Juan de Fuca and San Andreas were part of the great "Ring of Fire" from New Zealand up through Indonesia and the Philippines to Japan before arching up to Alaska and down mightily through western Canada, the United States, Mexico, and Chile. It was the result of nearly unimaginably huge slabs of deep earthen crust jiggered together, a gigantic puzzle that fell into place grudgingly. About ninety percent of earthquakes occurred along the 25,000-mile ring, which also hosted a molten string of four hundred and fifty-two volcanoes—at minimum.

In that fiery geology was Mount Rainier, where a pilot named Kenneth Arnold in 1947 spotted boomerang-shaped aerial objects prancing and flitting at fantastic speeds, each moving in formation like "a saucer if you skip it across the water," said Arnold (thus the moniker "flying saucer"). That was just before Roswell. Mount St. Helens was in the ring, known like Rainier for "bigfoot," which edged back into the twilight, particularly a place called Spirit Lake.

Was this where The Event or events, the big seismic stuff, would burst forth from disgruntled movements of the axis? Was there a reason volcanoes and highlands were mystical places of power, venerated by natives? Did dimensions part there, as at Sinai and Tabor and Fiji, or occultwise, Shasta and Kilauea? What was it, what dynamic, what energy, that tied spiritual spots with geological or meteorological ones? Was the seismic juggernaut really poised to detonate from the restless pivoting of our world's very axis? What mysterious calculus offered such locales as theatres of destiny, the apertures of fate itself? Did the reason lie beneath the skin of our understanding, encoded in the millennia-old reverence paid by our forebears to the solemn volcanoes and imperious highlands? These were the oft-esteemed abodes of gods and spirits, held in hushed reverence by the native peoples—was their veneration, then, rooted in ancient wisdom or primitive superstition?

Was it merely a metaphorical weave spun by poets and seers or did it cloak a truth, a dynamic, an energy, buried within the layered realities of the universe? Were they cosmic crevices tearing apart the fabric of the known, a parting of the veil, summoning forth entities, powers, or energies unseen

and unfathomed? Were they heralding the dawn of a new epoch or the twilight of the old?

And if there was any reality to all this:

Were portals indeed opening?

A seer named Lorena claimed a prophecy from Gabriel
that said: "There will be major battles over the opening of 'stargates' throughout the earth. Such stargates connect the earth
to outer reaches of the universe and other dark dimensions—
all of them closed at the time of the Flood of Noah. However,
throughout the centuries, a few of these stargates have been
opened due to occult means. This agenda of hell will then ac-
celerate under the reign of the antichrist, as he will attempt
to open all the stargates on the earth. The antichrist will attempt to achieve this by amassing demonic power through
the black mass, which will be accepted and celebrated. Then,
finally, the opening of many stargates on earth will culminate
in the great Battle of Armageddon, taking place on the plains
of Israel between all the forces of good and evil."

In the hidden corridors of reality, in the creases of time
and space, was there more than Einstein or any vaunted
physicist imagined?

One imagines Gavreel might add, "The phantoms of your
time seek disorientation to divert mankind onto errant paths.
These entities operate at both spiritual and physical levels.
They come from sources of evil that seek to send religion to
the dustbin of history, with strange creatures bearing no affinity for humans, or God. In this way will they seek to discard
the works of Jesus."

He might say further: "From a hidden level, they will
cause a disorientation similar to the consternation of homosexuality, but now also in the realm of science and spirituality—connecting them with a bond of falsity."

One only had to watch television, where there were accounts of phantom wolven dog packs and tall furry man-ape monstrosities, eyes hot-red or phosphorescent green, gawping into windows on second floors no actual biological creature could reach: Such yeti-like proto-humans, which could appear and disappear at whim, were documented in nineteen or more Pennsylvanian counties in 1973 and 1974 by police and researchers, the cryptids spotted time and again with UFOs, luminous spheres, saucers, or "cigars" that swept across the starlit canvas of sky or hovered with blue, yellow, green, red, or white lights, in rare cases on the ground, issuing—also tellingly—a hum or rumble or *boom*, the rotted fetor again of sulfur and evading all laws of aerodynamics. "Flew" did they hundreds—thousands—of times faster than an F-16, or more impressively, simply vanished, leaving behind—this a farm in Fayette County, where both bigfoot and flying saucers were together, the silhouette of a dark-cloaked figure toting a sickle.

Did anyone really believe the grim reaper was an extraterrestrial pilot?

Yet there it was, a figure draped in mystery and fear, ready to reap what humanity had sown in fields of confusion, offering only the chilling whispers of visitation.

In certain cases, large unexplainable footprints were left to haunt and taunt (not usually cloven—often three-toed—though there were cases of cloven prints in England), markings that like "UFOs" started out of nowhere and ended abruptly nowhere; materialized and dematerialized; teleported. Or there were extraordinary circular swirls in wheatfields or meadows ("crop circles") and gruesomely mutilated animals, blood, eyelids, genitals surgically excised, as if ET was conducting a biological experiment or intervention (nephilim?).

Tellingly, a preference they showed, these phantoms, these malefactors—whether bigfoot, mothman, vampires, Nessie, or ufonauts—for cemeteries or places where accidents or horrific crimes had occurred.

Morbid fantasy, or did it speak again to *Wisdom* 11 ("new-created, wrathful, unknown beasts")?

There were cases where witnesses found themselves with "psychic" abilities afterward, were missing time (as if taken somewhere), and now had presages of the future.

The latter of course had to be taken with salt—visions that the world would end—for neither Jesus nor Mary had spoken with such finality in sundry major apparitions and Satan owned a quick hand in the prophetic, did he, confusing and diluting, discrediting the real stuff, or simply ladling deep psychological eddies of fear.

Was it then true inspiration, demonic interference, the subconscious? That was the time-honored question.

Most "prophets" were a mix.

Wild stuff.

Wanted: discernment experts.

Daunting was the glimpse of the future claimed by a West Virginia woman named Sharon Milliman who was struck by lightning in 2005. Escorted by Jesus to heavenly locales, she asserted that there had been a city of light, indescribably extraordinary colors so often mentioned by these type folks, and beautiful "vibrational sounds" out of everything, from below, sideways, above, keeping with thousands who bore similar testimony to the pervasive aroma of roses and lilies, the crystal-clear pools that healed, the pure-alabaster sin-cleansed robes, the sentient plants, grass waving in unison, the transparent gold roads, gargantuan structures, the splendid angels, and the beloved joyous deceased loved ones, smiling; the breathing of "water" and drinking of air and tasting of music—which is as if from the most exquisite strings of a Stradivarius, yet as penetrating and loud as a trumpet: these were things witnessed with remarkable consistency, choirs singing a thousand melodies at once, weaving in and out, the utter sense—overwhelming—of well-being: this and more were regularly reported, including by doctors who, during heart attacks, stroke, or accident, had the experience for themselves. Could anything on earth frighten when this was our true home? "The trees had a sound, the rocks had sound, the water had a sound, the grass had a song," confided Sharon. "When you take all those sounds and put them together, you have the most magnificent choir and orchestra that you've ever heard in your life and everything is singing praises to God.

"After I heard the music, I could see what I called the Glorious City, and it was off into the distance. There was a bright wall of gold that goes around the city. In the middle of the city is a round building. There are lots of buildings, but there was a big round building in the center and it had a golden dome on it. All these buildings are made of like alabaster, marble, and just beautiful. And the architecture is just like these columns and archways and intricate detail carved into the marble. And I saw what I call the 'hall of knowledge.' It was like a library and it had a bazillion books, from top to bottom, from ceiling to floor. And they were about every topic that you could possibly want to know about and you could get this knowledge. And I saw these beautiful healing pools like swimming pools out in the back behind it, and oh my gosh, it was just absolutely beautiful and it was like living water, it was absolutely alive and it was a spiritual hospital for people who have died from a traumatic death or suicide, and there's mentors and teachers and angels and people who are there to help these people come to an awareness of what happened to them. They're loved into wholeness, loved into understanding what happened.

"Jesus walks out of this grove of trees and He comes up to me and what He said to me was, *'I love you, I'm with you, and don't be afraid.'* He was solid. It wasn't just an image. He had this long, dark-colored hair and dark olive complexion and kind of looked glowing. He had beautiful brown eyes and I mean He was just breathtaking. He leads me over to this wooded glen and there was light coming through the branches. There was a log lying there and a stream. I sat down on the log, Jesus walked away, and there was a man sitting on the other end of the log. I knew that man was God. So that huge loving formless Presence that God was at the beginning of my experience had now taken on a form. And I knew that form was the Face He chose for me to see. He was beautiful too and was like an older version of Jesus. He was totally different.

Added the West Virginia woman, in a book called *A Song In the Wind*, "Then these two angels came and they took me to this lake and it was so beautiful. It was like looking into glass, but it was so calm. And so I leaned over and I looked into the water and I could see the earth below. And I could see all these things happening.

Recall that this was back in 2005. But she was seeing things happening "right now."

"I saw future events, the collapse of money, and terrorist stuff, and I saw just lots of things. I didn't know what to do, when I saw that, but the angels were saying these things don't have to happen, it's up to you all. The collective human selfishness is really what's causing all these bad things to occur, and you can change this so these bad things don't have to happen.

"To my surprise, they began showing moving pictures of future events on earth. I still felt wrapped within God's loving embrace so I was able to endure these revelations with a certain amount of non-attachment. Perhaps my detachment stemmed from underlying shock, horror, and disbelief of what I was watching. It all seemed surreal. What was shown to me were horrific events that stemmed from or were a result of the 911 attacks that have led to other terrorist attacks against our country and throughout the world. Specifically, they showed me people being killed by bombings and shootings. I witnessed our financial institutions crumbling. In the end, our money was not worth the paper it was written on. In money's place, I was shown silver and gold coins being used to make purchases. They also said that in time we would return to the barter system, as we had done long ago. They also showed me many natural disasters, such as earthquakes, volcanoes, tornadoes, and storms. Then I saw six huge waves of water covering the land. I witnessed a woman and a little boy in a car being swept off the road because of flood waters. As her car was being immersed, I saw that God had sent angels in the form of people to pull the woman and child out of the water. Next, they revealed how corrupt governments will become and their central role in destroying peace in our world. They were so poisoned that I saw dark clouds surrounding their capitols. In response to the corruption, I witnessed coups and rioting. I witnessed governments in different countries being overthrown and huge riots taking place in the streets. They showed me one particular riot where a man threw something through a storefront window while a nearby building burned. I also heard the sound of gunshots and saw a man lying dead in the street. They revealed small pockets of light where loving people huddled in places called 'safe havens.' These safe havens are mostly in mountainous regions.

"The very last thing they showed me was a 'silver ribbon' splitting the United States apart. I was told that this 'ribbon' was a river. With increased flooding in the Midwest, I wonder if we are now seeing seeds of events to come. I felt that it was the Mississippi River, but they gave no explanation as to the meaning of this 'ribbon' other than that the ribbon becomes larger over time."

What Milliman "saw" aligned with others who'd had near-death visions, particularly James Chauncey, who had seen the great quakes that would create a massive lake in the Midwest; disappearance of much of the East Coast (especially Florida); and that gulf between the mainland and California, along with volcanic eruptions and epidemics as unprecedented perturbations afflicted the earth, which he was shown would—and here was that word again—*wobble* before regaining equilibrium and ending up "totally straight" (instead of its current tilt). Like Milliman, Chauncey believed a purification or reshaping of earth would transpire, but probably not until after his own death (which occurred in Georgia in 2013). The chastisements would be followed, he said, by a renewal as survivors instituted society afresh and simpler, and after years of desiccation, normal rainfall would finally resume.

Into the cacophony of various forms of demise, before, during, or after natural events, was the niggling notion, the logical concern, of not just foreign intervention, but hot civil strife. Were some of the dramatic visions of geologic upheaval—especially the idea of the earth splitting—metaphors for an approaching civil war?

That was precisely what was "seen" during a near-death that involved Kenneth Leth, a bearded grandfatherly type who had his experience as a boy of eight and had seen the earth rock and crack and wars and more to the point, in the U.S., people marching in the streets in the midst of mayhem. Would disasters lead to societal upheaval, or was such discord now inevitable, part of the prophetic matrix, a scenario that would play itself out with or without cataclysmic damage? Leth had seen an image of what he later recognized as the Supreme Court Building, where he said he was shown "it would all start," which he later took to mean the 2015 ruling that legalized gay marriage and led to a climate in which Christians averse to such things were forced to cater gay marriages and take wedding photos. It would be resentment to such things, he believed he had seen—six decades before—that would create a chasm in society as gaping as any along the Mississippi, any involving quakes and the Great Lakes, but in a twist of fate—or a metaphor contrived by Heaven—would involve America's main river as a dividing line between two armies, one rising far to the west—he believed in California—and the other in the heartland or South.

"I saw all of this eruption coming out of evangelical churches, and politicians raising a big [protest]," said Leth. "There was that county clerk who was going to get thrown in jail [for not issuing gay marriage licenses], and they were protesting and they were really offended by the whole thing. I saw that as the beginning of the turmoil."

When he'd seen the army growing in the West, he didn't know who they were. "I wasn't told," said Leth. "But I saw them fighting and pushing from the west toward the east... and it looked like the Mississippi River was important, a dividing line. I saw fighting go totally out of control, fighting everywhere. I just couldn't stand to watch it. It was severe enough that I turned away. Things just got crazy. I saw people being pulled out of their homes in the middle of the night, like in raids, and arrested. I saw myself in a basement of sorts and there were other people with me and we were looking outside, like 'Things are really terrible outside.' It was almost like the beginning of a civil war. They marched across the United States, but they organized about where I'm living like through Nebraska, because we're just west of the Mississippi here. Eventually the army from the west will win and the fighting eventually will end. I saw somewhere in the

Deep South and like another government building because it was fortified. And I saw people fighting and demonstrating around that and eventually the building is overcome.

"But what's uncovered in that building is tremendously evil. When it was blown up, it looked like a ghost of some kind rising up from that building because finally it was destroyed. It didn't really have a human form, although it had a face. It was big, like a balloon. The best word that I can come up with is a demon, an agent of Satan. And it was there to promote anger and fighting and misinformation, and it was very powerful. It was like a blob and it was black. And it didn't care that everybody died, it wanted them to die. And when it was finally destroyed, as it rose up out of that building and flew away, it was laughing. It was delighted! It's like when the army from the west gets inside of that building and puts an end to what they're doing, it's going to be a great relief. And then all kinds of evil are going to be uncovered and then people will realize they were fighting for the wrong reasons. They were lied to. A lot of people are believing a lot of wrong things and that's what's going to elevate the fighting and the aggravation."

Civil conflict was hardly all. Leth also claimed to have been shown a second conflict "that wasn't internal. It seemed like it was external, from the world, other countries."

Was this the Chinese and Russian incursion that Chauncey saw?

"I saw all kinds of storms and stuff hitting the East Coast of the country," said Leth, whose visions zig-zagged across multiple scenarios. He also saw "this huge tremendous explosion that looked like an atomic bomb because of the mushroom cloud. It looked like it was around the corner in Wyoming, perhaps Montana. So I'm thinking Yellowstone, because it's about where I saw the explosion take place.

"At the base I saw a ring of white like a pebble dropping in the water where it creates a wave that comes out from the drop. That's what it looked like and it was a ring of white that expanded across the entire continent. I believe in the middle of everything there could be a natural disaster like a serious earthquake because I saw flooding that looked like it was between Iowa and Nebraska, around the Omaha area, maybe a little bit north."

An appendix to the anonymous locution of 1990 had said, *"And so unless there is change, all of this—the constructs of men—will be destroyed. If men do not work together, men will destroy each other. If men do not work with nature, nature will destroy them. God's Creation will form a new earth. If men change, the transformation will be gradual. They will be a part of a new earth. The false societies of men will be dismantled without great harm. If not, it will occur drastically."* A further appendix had said, *"The angels have their instruction from east to west, and now a timetable has been set in motion. When the huge light is seen, I will act in a way I have not acted before."*

Chapter 33

DRAMATIC AND DRASTIC WERE COUNTLESS MODERN PROPHECIES. If something was too dire, that seemed a "bad fruit."

Or was it the case, as in Scripture, that admonitions from God, Jesus, and His evangelists, though often couched in a way that was transcendent, could be severe?

If one were walking in New York and again spotted that angelic "beggar"—the mysterious Gavreel, lanky in his thirties, perhaps early forties, let's say, whose brown beard and full head of long hair were far better coiffed than panhandlers or most of the normal passerby, for that matter, a very, very cleansed look, and skin somehow radiant—one would remember best that he wore an old but meticulously clean plaid jacket, probably wool, slightly dishabille, but in an appealing way.

Mostly, in the imagination, would be the hint of rose-lilac and gelid eyes, azure as a clear June sky.

"The grace of the Lord Jesus Christ, and the love of God, and the fellowship of the Holy Spirit be with you," he'd say.

One would study the lines of his face, sculpted into the authenticity of ageless sincerity. Though garden-fresh, his presence would transmit an age exceeding the age of the very rock underlying Manhattan.

Was he one of the angels with instruction?

Perhaps instead of the street attire he would be wearing a white robe, signaling the revelation of secrets—elucidating what Lucia had been given in 1944 as he led one to the Freedom Tower, where the elevator would rise at twenty miles an hour with panoramas displayed on the sides, illusions out the windows as if witnessing emergence from the bedrock five hundred years before, straight into undeveloped marshlands in the 1500s. As the elevator rose, it was a glimpse at the time of Indians who had been there by 7000 B.C. in thousands of encampments, before wildlife —beavers, plovers, flying squirrels, and snapping turtles—succumbed to what is suspected to have been a warming shift in climate (perhaps also overkill). A second wave of Native Americans came thousands of years later, mainly Lenape who farmed and greeted the first white settlers from Holland as the incredible port city drew foreign traders like a magnet.

The elevator windows were not merely panes of glass, no, but portals through time, witness to the very birth of the great metropolis from the bare bedrock. Time itself was unwinding, like an old pocket watch in reverse. It moved in tandem with the grand transformation, playing out on the sides of the elevator as it continued its swift journey, showing evolution of the skyline from the 1800s and to the first "skyscrapers:" the Empire State, Chrysler, and Woolworth, which at one time stood as the symbol of commerce. And then the massive Trade Center towers—their height always the focus, but their girth almost as awesome, perhaps the single greatest symbol on earth of the accomplishments and certainly wealth of Man.

"Do you know what they pay for the most expensive apartment on those new towers?" Gavreel asked as time unfolded to the current date—a quick but amazing journey to floor 102, where there was the observation floor overlooking the incredible mélange of multi-floor structures, crammed as tightly as subway commuters during the evening rush.

If asked that, I would have shaken my head.

"Two hundred and seventy million," would be the accurate reply. "For a single place to live. And yet those who live in the towers end up in the same sunken place as do those in Juarez who live in sheds. The poor reach the true heights faster." Suddenly I saw the image flash of a hole in the ground at a graveyard. "The more they reach skyward, the farther away they are from Heaven."

Upon arrival, the observation floor unfurled in its sprawling grandeur. It was a sight to behold - a vantage point that boasted an awe-inspiring view of the city's towering behemoths, each one a testament to human ambition and enterprise.

In this patchwork, in this aggregate, was the nerve center of modern society.

"There are forty-seven thousand, just in Manhattan," Gavreel might say as I look at what spanned in all directions.

"Forty-seven thousand?"

"Buildings," he said, reading my mind, answering what I was wondering. "And then there are the other boroughs and Long Island and New Jersey."

To the west stood the skyline of Newark as a little sister, and to the east, the ambitious towers of Brooklyn.

We went toward the edge and peered down at the riverine streets below, the meandering torrents of yellow cabs and delivery trucks and other cars that wove in and out of each other in no set pattern of logic or law, a remarkable chaos felt even way up in the clouds. Every time I wanted to see something closer, it's like my eyesight telescoped and I was able to zoom in as close as I cared to. Gavreel was watching the traffic along with me and finally said, "The Lord Christ will come as she has come, in light. Know this about the world: He would not appear on television, nor ride a car, nor travel in an airplane.

Michael H. Brown

Would He come in such a manner? Would He live in such a world? Your very conceptions of happiness and comforts are a great evil and falsity. How could this artifice last?"

"Look there," he would then say, suddenly pointing beyond the ocean, a bit northward.

And everything in front of me faded from view and was replaced by another city.

It was London.

It was in ruin. Through a swollen silence, the great city, once the heart-throb of Empire, in so many ways like New York, lay obliterated, swallowed and mangled and staggered by the nuclear voracity of mankind's self-destruction. It had been attacked. Once-proud fortresses were now cadavers of brick and mortar, toppled like fused tin soldiers, a knock-out by the fist of apocalypse.

Sprawled flat against the cracked, charcoal-blackened cement, where there was cement left, was the little that hadn't vaporized. Odd structures that still stood held grotesque resemblance to the skeletons of dinosaurs, joining them in extinction.

In the vision, this holograph that Gavreel had summoned, the palaces once embodying regal splendor remained only because they were far enough from ground zero.

Buckingham Palace. Windsor. Westminster. Their majesty was smeared under radioactive grime, resplendent domes and towering spires gone or badly effaced, leaving the skyline jagged. London Bridge, once standing proudly against the Thames, was now a procession of empty arches over a sullen debris-filled river. Facades no longer mirrored sunlight, mourning their reflections in the stagnant, toxic waters below. Glass had dissolved or melted. Big Ben was not there to record time. Nor was any person. The offices, the frenzied hives of adrenalin, stood vacant, their innards gutted. Once-thrum-

ming corridors echoed the deathly silence of oblivion, replaced by the relentless whistle of the nuclear wind, its dirge
an echo through shattered edifices. Streets once cobbled were
seared, carbonized, meandering like vagabonds.

This is what an angel might show; this is what ChatGPT
might project: an eternal pause, a long stare into the abyss.

"And this is but a limited attack," Gavreel would interject.
"Now look."

We turned to the south and I knew it was Florida. What I
saw was beyond what meteorologists project. Miami, a metropolis born of sunshine, of sea breeze, sandy dreams, had
been humbled by the raw, untempered wrath of a hyper-cat-
egory-five mega hurricane, its Art Deco and glass once reflecting sky and waves punctured and peeled back utterly by
the hurricane's uncompromising ferocity, the proud geom-
etry yielding to chaos, its glitzy high rises, the penthouses,
restaurants on A1A, entirely washed away or twisted into unnatural mournful pose in an aftermath of whitecaps.

A tsunami had swept over the region, under a parade of
tornadoes, and microbursts of explosive winds had crushed
or spun homes ringing the Everglades where no home was
meant to have been but where they had clustered, setting
them to whirl with palm fronds and rooftops and fence that
were shrapnel in neighborhoods devoid of a single standing
structure, testimony to sustained winds up of two hundred
and fifty miles per hour: velocity never seen by this state nor
any state, not with "Katrina," not with "Camille," "Sandy."
No: all barrier islands were washed over, scoured to original geology, the vegetation sheered as if by a cosmic lawn-
mower. Palm Beach, the seaside Garden of Eden, gilded with
the excesses of mammon: simply no longer. Mansions that
once shone with opulence—shiny as silver, glinting in proud
boast—now stripped to cement slabs and, in freak cases

where it still stood, skeletal timber. At Coconut Grove, quaint luxury had been reduced to shambles, the mangroves and tightly woven tapestry of cottages ripped asunder, as much by wind as floodwater—though the surge had turned lawns to whitecaps. Indian Creek was submerged too, its villas, bastion for the uber-wealthy, stomped into irrelevance, the intra-coastals stirred into dizzying eddies of flotsam, their illusions of permanence put unceremoniously to the lie. Millions had been trapped on Interstate 95, then 75, the storm taking a second hit Gulf side, cars buffeted or awash all the way to Tampa.

"This doesn't have to happen," was all Gavreel commented. "But it will."

He pivoted again to the east, this time eyes afar, thousands and thousands of miles. I knew it was Asia. I know now that it was Chongqing, and it was hit by an asteroid birthed in the cold, dark womb of the universe, a galactic fusillade eight times the speed of a bullet, charged with cosmic force and aimed with inhuman precision.

Its destination: the pulsating heart of Sichuan, the manic crossroads of the Yangtze and Jialing Rivers, a city that dallied with the edge of tomorrow, perpetually wrapped in the enigma of its own hyped urban heartbeat. On impact, the mighty celestial bolide strikes with raw energy never seen in recent millennia, splitting soundless heavens with a roar.

Once a city teeming with life, Chongqing is reduced to a topography of annihilation. The twin rivers boil and hiss, steaming under the heat, a monstrous vat bubbling with wroth. Structures that pierced Chongqing's smog just moments before: reduced to a crunched, scattered testament of humanity's impermanent hand. More than any other, the event would bear the stamp of an almighty, impartial power, indifferent to our mortal struggles because we had been indifferent to God.

Its impact would tell one tale: that—without the Lord's protection—we are subject to the roulette.

"And this would not be all," Gavreel would say, as I continued to gawk at the distant smoldering crater. "It will be a 'train' of bolides. Two smaller ones will hit the Atlantic. You can imagine the waves."

Actually, I couldn't. It was very hard to process. As we watched the scenes, tourists paid us no attention, not to our serious looks, our staring into thin air, at the horizon, nor Gavreel's white robe.

I wondered if they even saw us.

In a quick flash, there was the cerulean sky above a distant city in Africa. I later learned it was near Casablanca. We watched the hues of sundown surrender to an encroaching darkness.

Suddenly, a monstrous incandescent streak cleaved the atmosphere—the second bolide in the train—shattering, ruthless, unrelenting. As the towering monolith of the Hassan II Mosque met its gaze, its reflection would be distorted, mirrored back in fiery fragments, this hunk of cosmic rubble hitting the eastern Atlantic with a roar never before registered in human ears, shaking in the very fabric of sea, which had no choice but to yield walls of water as the fragment shot through water and blasted deep into ocean bottom. We would watch as a gargantuan plume of water and steam ascended towards the heavens while a third struck in the U.S. off Virginia Beach.

This chunk of rock might cut the sky at an angle, but with equal speed, birthing a horrific silence, as if nature had forgotten its script. Then water would suddenly wash back to sea, like a fantastic low tide, baring flapping fish on ocean floor for long minutes until the Atlantic rose and rose and rose, impossibly, a palisade of water rolling back with a grace that belied its cataclysmic intent.

The purpose was clear. It was a messenger of obliteration, a manifestation of justice borne from the belly of a twitching universe, dark matter and neutrinos and ghost particles reconfiguring and jiggering solar systems, touching each planetary axis, even those of stars, a cosmic flex that tipped everything just minutely from their routines and loosed fragments from the solar system, fragments no longer restrained as man's disorder was allowed to manifest. Cities, towns, and villages from Washington to the Carolinas could play no role but that of spectator, before assuming role as quarry, waiting to be consumed by this aquatic mountain, which had no real malice, no fiendish satisfaction, just cold, indifferent power that no longer knew bounds. Streets were drowned, monuments submerged, mansions leaving no trace. The face of the coast could be wiped clean—this vision would tell us.

Or was this Cape Cod; or Savannah?

In a flashback overseas—I "saw" thatched roofs swept away in agitated water in Ireland.

"It doesn't have to happen," Gavreel might repeat. "But it is no longer the final hour. Time is now in increments."

As the tidal wave receded, leaving a trail of devastation in its wake, a haunting stillness would descend on what had been gigantic naval facilities.

"Behold, they that see shall cry without: the angels of peace shall weep bitterly. The ways are made desolate; no one passeth by the road; the covenant is made void: he hath rejected the cities; he hath not regarded the men," says page 577 (*Isaiah* 33: 7-8).

"One of these will play out," said Gavreel. "And then another. One may come today, the next tomorrow, or a month apart, a year. But events will be beyond debate. Anyway," he said, looking into my eyes, "science will not be around to argue about it."

Perhaps I would remember what the seer Mirjana Dragicevi Soldo of Medjugorje told a priest, that the time between the first secret and the second will be of a certain period, between the second and third a different length. "For example," she had said, "and I stress, for example: the first secret may take place today and the second one already tomorrow." The first secret, she'd added, "will last for a little while." If people could see the secret, "all of them would most certainly be shaken enough to take a new and different look at themselves and everything around them."

Was it what the 1990 prophecy called "the initial event," and why it said God—quoting the Lord—would *act in a way I have not acted before.*

Gavreel might then turn—as would I—to the west. In the throbbing heart of America, the ground would rumble. It would not be a tremor, a mere grumble of discontentment, but a colossal convulsion that rips through the fabric of a continent. The great forces of earth will awaken from primordial slumber, their demonic temper as volatile as molten fury, earthen detonations sounded by the bass drums of occultism, tarot, voodoo, witchery, astrology, ghosthunters, channelers, crystals, amulets, pentagrams, malocchio, incantation, Santeria, kundalini, Ouija, kabala, fortunetellers.

The belly of the land would undulate, and then, a terrestrial convulsion, the pagan punch to the solar plexus of a nation whose very exploration of space had been a testimony to the pantheon—Apollo, Titan, Gemini, Mercury, Artemis—that had stamped paganism on the sky with rocketry: Now, far below, in the earth, energy would awaken. A finger on the axis will cause wobble. Missouri, Tennessee, Illinois, Wisconsin, Iowa—these weren't mere states but components of America's identity, the backbone, quintessential testaments to American stability. Yet they would shudder and twist and shake, their cities folding like paper maquettes under the grip of an overgrown capricious child while the Mississippi, that ancient river king, found itself usurped, its waters, which once coursed through the country's aorta, absorbed into an unfathomable lake birthed from chaos. The vast inland sea was not a simple body of water but a mirror reflecting the transformation, the anguish, the obliteration of land, linking the Great Lakes to the Gulf of Mexico, a watery gap through the busted cement of the nation.

"Remember that to reach the glory of Heaven, you must forgive every last matter," Gavreel advised in *non sequitur.* "You must love through all challenges, all conflict, all upheaval, all insult, all disappointment. You must know that life is a test and that no one escapes its trials, which will not stop until eternity. Yearn to do God's Will and purely His Will and attach yourself entirely to Jesus, not to any human, certainly not to a false light. Here you will find joy, and here you will find protection. May you always be protected. May God protect you," he might say, maintaining his stare to the west.

"Protect me?"

"You'll need it. Everyone will."

One would have only stared at him. "You have an important mission."

"A mission?"

He'd nod. "Everyone has a mission in life." After a pause, his eyes riant, his mouth dead-serious: "When more people in a region are headed for hell than not, the Lord acts."

I would follow his eyes. Beyond the horizon of the Midwest I might glimpse the Rockies and an old gold-mining town I now believe was Cripple Creek—a haunted ghoulish relic of the past, now casinos, still a stubborn symbol of man's hunger for the yellow metal of falsity. A sudden, pulsating tremor, the heartbeat of earth, a seismic growl simultaneous with what transpired in the Midwest, visceral, deeply primitive, would now haunt it, as a mountain stirred and suddenly swayed, releasing boulders in this instant of geological discontent: a deafening roar, a mountain's soul, spewing forth with massive dust clouds as the town buckled and bowed and soon was aflame or banished to widening crevices. That day, the mountain would speak, its thunderous voice reverberating through the bones of every living creature, a primal message: Even the "eternal" is vulnerable to change; even the mightiest can fall. I might see the same in the San Luis Valley where mountains in Colorado—occult-drenched Crestone— and Mount Blanca, home to UFOs—succumbed in the same fashion. The cosmic cards, the ghostly hand of geological time, would have reached to reshape the clay of creation.

Chapter 34

THIS WAS IN LINE WITH MILLIMAN, who saw the geologic cataclysm in several tsunamis and violent swerves in weather, swerves that would become all the more truculent and weaken the nation to its enemies.

"Russia's going to try to take over everywhere, and China is going to join them and become allies, work together," Milliman believed." She'd also seen profound coastal flooding from Florida up the East Coast with major intrusions of inland water, perhaps up to foothills: A "swelling of the waters" was the way she put it, reminding us of Lucia's emerging seas, as dense rain and melting ice rebelled against degradation of earth, the Ohio River perhaps ending up one day in her backyard, though she lived on a hill in Parkersburg, West Virginia.

She'd also foreseen the January 6 attack on the Capitol and in general a "black bloody cloud" hanging in the sky as throngs sought to overthrow governments in a number of nations.

In the midst of, or preceding, it all?

Milliman saw "little black boxes with cameras that were everywhere—on every street corner and building. We're being watched," she said. "Why, I don't know, but we are."

Chauncey envisioned Muslims allied with Russia and China invading from the south—Mexico—while actual jet fighters crossed the American continent.

Milliman saw the stars and stripes next to a red flag with the imprint of a black dragon.

In Iraq a seer named Dina Basher—in Mosul, which once was Nineveh—had seen Jesus "all in white with white rays around His Head and a Cross with light coming from it. He said that everyone must light a candle at home and in church and pray for others and for the churches, repenting for their sins because, He said, *'My arrival is very near.'*"

"Stay awake because you do not know when the time will come. I will give you an example of this," He said on January 14, 1992, to Dina—who has disappeared since the war there. *"A man traveling abroad leaves home and places his servants in charge, each with his work, and orders the gatekeeper to be on watch. Watch, therefore, you do not know when the lord of the house is coming, whether in the morning, in the evening, or at cock crow. I tell you a second time, stay awake, my dear ones."*

On that same day, Dina claimed, the Blessed Virgin Mary also appeared.

"Keep my words and keep my commandments and prayers and pray to me and my beloved Son," she'd said. *"Pray for your souls and fast for your souls. When you pray, meditate on the angelic salutations and meditate on the Apostle's Creed. My dear ones, I give you this message that you may do what I say. Sit in a church and examine your consciences and go to the priest and confess your sins. Come to the holy Eucharist because it brings you close to my beloved Son. Open the doors of the church and do not close them. Open your eyes and do not close them. Open your hearts and be wise like your heavenly Father. Be firm in these commandments, and I will stay with you forever. Do what I tell you and you will obtain graces from me. My beloved Son sacrificed Himself on the Cross for you. He shed His pure Blood for you because we love you. We come close to you and you run away from us. Why, my dear ones? Why this separation? You have covered your faces with a veil of darkness.*

"I beg of you that you may remove this veil. With a heavenly Light on your faces, I ask from each one of you to take this message to every church and every heart and to each person. My dear ones, I love you very much. My only question is, why do you close the doors to your hearts to me? Open them and you will see a white heavenly ray entering your homes and expelling the dark clouds from your hearts. Your faces will change to the faces of people with pure innocent hearts; they will turn to faces of angels and doves. The smile on your face will be a pure smile and not a false one. My last word is that you love one another so that my love remains in you."

This brought thundering to mind the 1990 Word in which Jesus told the anonymous recipient, *"I will come not as a man of flesh, but like My mother, who already nurses Me and holds Me in her arms, as a light and power. I will manifest Myself in a series of supernatural events similar to the apparitions but much more powerful. In other words, My second coming will be different than My first, and like My first, it will be spectacular to many but also unknown initially to many, or disbelieved. Yet truly I tell you, the arrogance of the world will have been broken, and so many more than normal will believe. I will come in towering light. My mother held me in her arms at Medjugorje, as an infant. I will come as she has come, in light."* Likewise had been the follow-up locution mentioning both east and west and the *"huge light,"* which took us to *Matthew* and how Jesus said He would arrive *"as the lightning cometh out of east, and appeareth even unto the west"* (24:27).

Would this series of His manifestations tower at multiple locales, Fátima, Medjugorje, perhaps the highlands of Ecuador, a peasant hinterland in Ukraine, Deep Africa, a mountain in Spain?

In spring of 2023, the locutionist Jennifer received a word

that said, *"My child, the great hour is approaching when many will be caught off guard! My Wounds are bleeding profusely and My only consolation is the prayers and acts of suffering My faithful offer to Me. The war that has been waged upon My Little ones has become a plague upon the innocent. I can no longer hold back My Father's just Hand. I can no longer restrain the justice of My Father upon His people who refuse the mercy of His Son, for I am Jesus.*

"This earth is going to begin to rock and tremble. On the day of the earthquake that will begin to ripple all across the world, many will come to see that their ways were not pleasing to Me. Satan has infiltrated every home, every family, and every church. He and his companions have infiltrated every nation and many hearts that no longer recognize the truth. He has infiltrated the minds of My children by using fear in order to bring false comfort, false hope, and false peace.

"The hour has come when those who have become the minions of his work will find themselves amongst those who have chosen the same path of darkness for all eternity."

The previous February she had quoted Him as saying, *"What side of the river will you be on when the earthquake comes; and the river rises and washes away its banks? Who will you call out to when darkness comes upon the earth and land that has been planted will yield no harvest because it is barren? Where will you run to when fire falls from the sky? My Children, you must begin to pray for greater discernment, for too many have taken up company with the devil and do not realize the darkness that is lingering around them. Mankind is provoking the just hand of My Father. I ask My Children to read My words of warning and realize what I have warned for quite some time is now upon your doorstep. Sin divides, but prayer and love multiply a bountiful harvest."*

"My children, the world is on the precipice of great change. Never surrender to the enemy that seeks to strip you of your

257

free will, to silence your voice that was created to proclaim the Gospel message."

"It is time to use your voice and no longer reason in fear, for fear does not come from Me, for I am Jesus. Time is short, for the world is on the precipice of great change. This world as you know it is passing away, and those who have not learned from history are soon to be standing in the midst of it. Take heed to the Gospel Message and live it; teach your brothers and sisters in humility how to pray; come to the fountain of My Mercy and do not have prideful hearts. I come to you in love and warning that prayer is the only vessel that will deter war. Prayer is the only vessel in which peace will come upon the world, for I am the Prince of Peace, for I am Jesus and My Mercy and Justice will prevail."

"Many are not prepared for the disruptions that are soon to come all around this world. Nation upon nation will feel the earth begin to tremble and many will fail to see that this warning is from Heaven. Do not listen to those who speak of science, for I Am the Creator of all the living. The days of darkness are no longer in the distance, for communication is soon to be extinguished."

Now too came to mind the final message from apparitions to an Ohio nun that came to be known as Our Lady of America, a message that said, *"There must be much more good than evil prevailing in order to prevent the holocaust that is so near approaching. Yet I tell you, My daughter, that even should such a destruction happen because there were not enough souls who took My warnings seriously, there will remain a remnant untouched by the chaos who, having been faithful in following Me and spreading My warnings, will gradually inhabit the earth again with their dedicated and holy lives. These souls will renew the earth in the power and light of the Holy Spirit, and these faithful children of Mine will be under My protection, and that of the Holy Angels, and they will partake of the life of the Divine Trinity in a most remarkable way. Let my dear children know this, precious daughter, so that they will have no excuse if they fail to heed my warnings."*

In 1988, in Nebraska, another anointed nun was approached by a radiant young stranger as she headed for a store to buy a new coffee pot. She felt compelled, though she really didn't need one. When she got there, the stranger handed her a twenty-three-page pamphlet with a tattered, inverted American flag on the cover, and when she looked up from it, he was simply gone.

The title of the pamphlet was "The Fall of America."

It had been published by a Christian group from Sacramento, with no indications of exactly who wrote it. What *was* known was that it bore three major predictions: That America will suddenly and almost totally be destroyed by the Soviet Union (which still was in existence); that Russia, however, would not occupy the U.S. after the battle ("possibly," it says, "because of nuclear contamination"); and that survivors of this holocaust would flee as refugees, form their own self-sufficient, protective refuges, or be taken as prisoners to other countries.

We were facing, it warned, the approach of "the ten-man world government."

"These (ten men)," it said, "will have one mind, and shall give their power and strength unto the Beast (*Revelation* 17:10, 10-13). A new world empire is about to arise. It is unique in that it will be run by a committee, after three nations are subdued by the eventual world dictator. This final empire is a conglomerate of the leopard, bear, and lion. But there's no mention of the eagle. The eagle has been so totally plucked that it ceases to exist. The U.S., like Sodom and Gomorrah, will be left uninhabitable when God's judgments are complete!

"When a number of worldwide catastrophes begin, the Beast blames them all on Christians, whom he slaughters by millions, while exalting himself as God," warned the booklet, so mysteriously circulated. "The catastrophes include plagues, poisoned oceans and lakes, earthquakes, tidal waves, worldwide forest fires, deadly hailstorms, a black-out of the sun, and changes in the earth's orbit, all of which may stem from a collision with a huge meteor and/or warheads launched (perhaps accidentally) from earth-orbiting satellites."

True Christians, it said further, would survive in the wilderness without dependence on the system.

In summary, it said: the United Nations will sign an agreement to rebuild the Temple; the Beast will be resurrected by the false prophet; there will be a global computer credit system (this stated years before the internet); two prophets would preach to the world; Christians would be forced to live by faith (no more lukewarmness); earth would be hit by a meteor or nuclear device; millions would die under the Beast; God's wrath will have been poured onto the world; Christ would return or manifest; His reign will begin.

Whatever the validity, it was in line with Saint Hildegard who, in her final prophecy ("The Five Beasts"), had labeled the last era as that of the "Grey Wolf" (*"Lupus Griseus"*).

"And the last is like a grey wolf," she wrote nearly a thousand years before. "For those times will have people who plunder each other, robbing the powerful and the fortunate; and in these conflicts they will show themselves to be neither black nor white, but grey in their cunning. And they will divide and conquer the ruler of those realms; and then the time will come when many will be ensnared, and the error of errors will rise from Hell to Heaven."

The notion that intense social unrest would lead up to manifestation of the Antichrist rang alarms at a time when America was so polarized it was almost at civil war. A narra-

tive unfurled, pregnant with consequences, that intense social unrest, not the genteel discomfort of academic debate or
the fevered pitch of electoral contest, but a profound convulsion of the social order, would be the herald of a dark birth.

The spirit of Babylon still lived, complained the pamphlet,
"in the form of capitalism and communism," concluding
that money "is just a symbol and now symbolizes our times,
which rightly belongs to God. Idolatry is valuing an object as
an end in itself. The U.S. has done this with money, by making it a crime even to destroy money. This kind of blind devotion to money destroys a person's (and a nation's) ability to
think rationally. Modern man has become so obsessed with
money that it now controls us rather than us controlling it.
Until we can again learn to live without money, we will never
be free to control it."

In her prophecy, Hildegard—who in the other eras had
not cited a specific sin—mentioned greed in the final one.

In sum, the saint saw a persecution of Christians after
natural disasters—just as did the pamphlet—but also, in the
midst of chaos, a revival of Christianity as the trial made it
purer and stronger and better ready to wage combat, to re-
act more quickly, when the Anti-Christ arrived with his own
persecution.

Were the events avoidable, were they set in stone?
They were avoidable.
If mankind maintained its current course, they were
however inevitable.
The pulse of prophecy gave us the extremes of what we
could face.
The Lord gave us an out. He gave us ways of peace.
Doing His Will brought protection and peace no matter
any circumstance. The closer we got to God, the more we
learned who we really are. We are not what society fashions.

We are not what our parents make. We are not what friends and relatives conceive or want or try to force us to be. We are who God created and find that essence only as we draw closer to Him.

It was urgent to do so. An angel would say this. An angel would instruct. An angel would indicate extremes—the evil that could and at this point will precipitate antichrist. The anti-Christian spirit would germinate. In the rubble, from the rubble, behind the rubble would step a personage of evil, a man of tremendous influence, forming the decisions of humankind by influencing those leaders still around in pockets of survival, in nations that had not been devastated, in the countries still intact. His power would be felt but unseen. Swiftly would he move, knowing his time was short, his ideas formulating the road to worldly "recovery" which was really the road of tyranny. Never, since Christ, had ideas been more powerful, than would be his. Like Jesus—mimicking Him—he would cause enormous effects without holding office, with no staff, devoid of ceremony, but rather by the power of spirit, the very black spirit that comes as a shining darkness—as light. The unknowing world after warfare—much combat—and the altered landscape would march in lockstep. As a new order of men was formed, he would influence them; he would be in the backdrop. He would be content with effects, not fame, in the societies of man; he would be revered by those who knew him, few in number but powerful. The populace would not know him until he had affected the new order of mankind in a diabolical way, all but eradicating Christianity. The persecution would exceed that of the Roman tyrants. In hidden places only, in quietest corners, in peasant closets, would the Cross be seen. Sacramentals of the church would be circulated with secrecy—one week in this house, the next across town, in place after place. The persecution would not be by the antichrist but at his implication. For a leader he will be, not. That is to say, he will not rule, control, or be at all obvious to the world at the peak of his influence. He will not be unlike a figure such as Marx, except his ideas will be more immediate. He will lead the leaders with force of spirit, not politics. Yet, his attempts at control will be only that: attempts. For his reign will end with the manifestation of Christ; his power will be broken by Jesus. In certain places, well-suited for devotion, made fully humble, will be the apparitions of Jesus in the splendor of columns of luminosity seen clearly by countless whose hearts are clean and open to God. His second coming is not like His first, no, but like His first, it will be spectacular to many but also unknown initially to many, or disbelieved. Yet truly, the arrogance of the world will have been broken, and so many more than normal will believe. Only with the breakdown of false society would this have been made possible, only with a peasant attitude, only with the newfound humility of humankind with his inventions scattered and broken and the Creation of God allowed again to flourish as the true landscape, trees poking through asphalt, highways turning to rocks, to pebbles, electrical poles now fallen wood in decay, cars and trucks and airplanes non-existent or on the way to banishment, electricity no longer more pervasive than the Holy Spirit: Only in a radically simplified world would return the Lord, in towers of light that beckon from places faraway. Like northern lights will His power and image form. The power of the devil and his forces of destruction will be defeated. It is a second coming for the present age. Where evil still tries to sprout anew will be Michael to suppress it, until the last dark vestiges are purged from an earth that in all its concepts of modernity had gone badly out of accordance with His Design.

Whose hearts are clean and open to God—a beam, a tower of light, will bear the person of His Son.

Chapter 35

"AND SO IT WILL GRIND ON," Gavreel would intone, as we continued to survey the landscape below. "Poles will shift. Melting ice will tip the balance. Do you want to see a sign of the times?"

He pointed to Europe.

I saw before me the chapel where Lucia received her apparitions of Mary and Jesus, the substructure supporting stone walls soggy and on the verge of collapse. Once a beacon of hallowed mystery and reverent awe, the tiny sanctuary now bore the weight of cruel time. I saw the timber holding up the roof, each fiber a silent testament to years of unattended decay: no longer the strong and steadfast pillars they once were, eaten away slowly, steadily, bearing the scars of neglect.

It had been here on December 10, 1925, where there was now rotting wood, that Lucia's cell illuminated and Our Lady materialized and "as if wanting to instill courage in me, gently puts her maternal hand on her right shoulder, showing me at the same time her Immaculate Heart that she holds in her other hand, surrounded by thorns," the visionary had related.

Gavreel would aim an austere steel-eyed burning gaze through the columns of the observatory, his expression, impervious as a monolith, granting no quarter to the sunbeams that played upon the edifice of the observatory, a glittering jewel of man's genius. The reflective shroud of the building, a tribute also to the human desire to mirror Heaven in earthly realms, couldn't subdue the solemnity etched on Gavreel's features. His countenance was hewn from granite, like an old-world sculptor's masterpiece, detached from the world and its transient gaieties, his eyes intense and unwavering, fixed again in a stare between the posts of our perch. Above us towered an antenna reaching the height of 1,776 feet for the year of Independence.

"This was not meant to be," he said brusquely. "A church—something dedicated to God, something acknowledging the true message of September 11—should have been planted here."

I continued to stare at a panorama that afforded views of fifty miles—the Liberty Statue, the Brooklyn Bridge, the expanse of Long Island. "This rises from fear, which lacks love," he continued about the tower. "Those who harbor disdain have lost their way. Those who stray follow themselves. Hatred has the energy of enticement in the name of good. True goodness follows the exact way of Jesus and puts no stock in the fantasies of men."

I would have questioned those words to the extent I could question them but in his presence the lips were forged shut. "Never before has mankind sought to bring all that was made by God under his own dominion. This arrogance will spell certain doom in a world that will change rapidly and with convulsions. No one can rise to the level of He Who with mere thought moves star systems or begins a new form of life, and yet, the attempts to do this are in progress. Therefore and soon will there be the destruction of a region in this world upon which many rely for sustenance. Its demise will be seen for what it means by those whose affinity is for the Divine and not for the temporal that so quickly passes. Put no stake in men who believe they can conquer nature but who in their arrogance show they can neither conquer darkness in themselves."

"And so—" I started to cut in.

"And so there is now going to be a disruption within the disruption around you because the lesson of Heaven has not been met. Remember that seeking God in earnest will provide the only sight in darkness. Otherwise the confusion sowed by the timeless nemesis will cloak all of reality with a false knowing. Never will those who follow the precepts of evil attain final victory, though it will now seem that way on this earth. Only praise God and light will come into any darkness."

"A 'disruption'?"

Gavreel would turn and send me a direct, kind look, his lineaments contoured somehow into the look both of brother and father, ancient and yet modern, with love but also grimness. "You know of the great sign of Fátima, the sign Lucia witnessed, from her lonely convent windows, the great aurora of 1938," he intoned.

He waited until I nodded.

"Before the events will be this sign."

With that he stretched his loose-sleeved right arm and pointed skyward from the top of the antenna and moved his hand in an arch northward, pointing toward Midtown, toward Rockefeller Center.

Thoughts of 1938 were again pertinent for auroras were sent by the sun which now was reaching a zenith in the activity of sunspots, as it had during the Middle Ages. It was a dynamo we hardly understood, we certainly could not fully grasp, not its size, the sun, not in deepest wells of energy, its play with the rest of the solar system and then the galaxy, the explosive powers such that in a moment flares could shoot to ten times the size of earth in a second with 3.8×10^{26} Joules of energy unleashed at each tick of the clock, the equivalent of a hundred billion nuclear bombs exploding every single relentless second.

During the summer of 2023, due at least in part to that cycle, the average temperature of earth reached the highest ever recorded and did so for three consecutive sweat-soaked skin-searing days.

This alone could tip things.

This would bear consequences.

It was not a matter of debate.

It was a matter of chastisement.

Not to mention what else is out there, an angel might interrupt, reading one's thoughts. Not to mention forces of dark matter and plasma.

I thought of the northern lights, and it caused me to think also of prophecies to do with other forms—supernatural forms—of unusual light. Sharon Milliman spoke of a supernatural light. "There is going to be a day of what they call the illumination of conscience," she told me. "I saw that in 2005, and the way it was shown to me was a giant angel that came to the earth and everybody, all over the world, could see this angel and everything stopped. People came out of their homes, off the battlefield, out of work, and could see this angel, who told everybody to hold their hands for one minute and everybody did and we took one step in the opposite direction of what the earth was spinning and time stopped, everything just stopped. There weren't any more wars, people weren't fighting with each other. Every single person came together for one minute and changed everything. Then the angel disappeared and that was it."

Could something so overt really occur—or might it be a metaphor for such an event?

"I do believe it's an event," insisted Milliman. "This is what I was shown. People were going to have like a mini-life review, see what they've done wrong in their lives, and change it. See what they've done right and choose to do that instead of what's wrong. We've already seen mysteries and wonders in the sky, crosses and pillars of fire, and people haven't changed. So what I took from what I saw is that during that one minute we'll have a chance to see how we've hurt others, and why we've gone to war, and all the division. We need everybody right now to get through what's coming. There needs to be forgiveness and learning from mistakes. We need to let go of pain. We need to see each other as one race."

This "illumination": Would people around the world actually see a celestial visitor, a messenger?

Milliman wasn't sure. What was coming would at the least be a great brightness—if not the form of an actual angel, seen everywhere, gigantic in the sky, she said, at least the angel's light—"so bright," she added, "I just know everybody just stopped."

I imagined the angel in New York at its highest summit pointing heavenward and murmuring, *"There is what your astronomers call the cosmic halo, and it is shifting. It is composed of stars and nebulae and stray planets, at the fringe of your galaxy. The forces within it will profoundly affect parts of the Milky Way—your galaxy—and alter its balance."*

The earth's axis would be unlatched: That could certainly cause it. It was one of endless possibilities, a shift in the cosmic halo. No one knew how many times fluctuations in space had caused disturbances on earth, but all it took was looking at the greatest forest conflagration in American history, the Peshtigo Fire in Wisconsin, and the most catastrophic urban conflagration, the Great Chicago Fire, for a notion, for both of those "unprecedented" events occurred not only the same year, but the same day (October 8, 1871).

That had been beyond coincidence—two entirely different events so linked. Besides unusually dry arid weather, besides inarguably strong winds, which granted earthly causes, might those historic blazes—and also in Michigan—have been sparked by a deteriorating comet called Biela, its pieces linked only with a "gaseous prolongation" through which earth may have passed around that time, some astronomers guess, vapors that impacted that particular part of the continent?

And might something similar loom in the future: an unexpected effect far beyond our telescopes that would cause a sudden disruption in our solar system—"touching" (and torching) the earth?

What if, in some sort of different cosmic perturbation, earth's axis shifted five degrees? That would be utterly and inarguably cataclysmic.

In one's mind materialized the Milky Way and a cluster of luminosity that might look to be stars or reflective cosmic clouds and an agitation in a segment of it: small but rippling outward.

The point: we had no idea what could occur in the deep reaches and recesses of space, and had no idea how many dimensions to it there were.

Gavreel's Bible would be missing page 611: "If that nation against which I have spoken shall repent of their evil, I also will repent of the evil that I have thought to do to them" (*Jeremiah* 28:8).

Might it be like the northern lights? Or was this not something truly out of human experience—unprecedented and bearing similarity to what other alleged mystics and seers (using the same term, "illumination") foresaw if mankind stayed his current course?

At Sievernich the seer Manuela received a message on February 25, 2023, about "lukewarmness," and was given the Scripture on page 211 (*Revelation* 3:15) and heard the Lord say, "Hold fast to the Word of the Eternal Father, to My Word, to the Scriptures. Everything else will go astray. Anything else means eternal death. The time of persecution has come. Therefore it is important that you pray, offer up, repent and live in sanctifying grace. This is the only way you can survive this time that is coming your way. If you listen to my word, you will be able to pass it well, because I will lead you through this time.

"Saint Michael will touch the earth with his sword. Look!'"

In the cloak of the King of Mercy, she saw Michael descend from Heaven to earth "and cut the earth with his sword," said Manuela. "This section is in the north of Russia and also affects the Arctic Circle."

"Russia is covered with green paint," said the seer. "Then all of a sudden the earth shook. Continents pass away. New continents emerge. I see big cracks on the globe. A big crack in Russia. A great rift in the eastern countries and in Africa. It looks to me like something is breaking away from Italy. In America and South America are also large cracks in the earth—America on land and in South America and even in the water.

"Fire and water work everywhere at the same time. Flood and fire. Mountains change too. This all happens at the time of a war. However, the King of Mercy holds His golden scepter over some people, and I see this is His protection. The Lord comes near to me and speaks in a soft voice: 'This has to happen. Have no fear!' Then He takes His scepter to His heart and it becomes the aspergill of His Sacred Heart, filled with His Precious Blood."

According to a journal called Geophysical Research Letters, geologists had confirmed that a new ocean was being created as the African continent—for now, with exquisite slowness—is split in half.

Besides Milliman, in West Virginia was a woman named Jennifer Morris who had a near-death experience on January 22, 2017, after spinal-fusion surgery and said that "all of a sudden I was floating and I'm in this light grayish-white space and there were two large golden orbs who I think may have been angels from God that were like radiating energy and I was given a vision of catastrophe because they are not happy with our creation and the state of the world."

Chapter 36

"REMEMBER," Gavreel might say, "the Power of the Most High can protect you from anything."

Finally I would ask the question. "Are you the angel who touches the earth? Are you the angel of announcement, of the secret?"

He wouldn't answer. There would be a tear in his eye. When he spoke, it would be only to say, "New Mexico has been ordained as a beacon of light, and also the place near the water where the cross stands."

That was to paraphrase an actual locution.

And with those words perhaps I would have seen a towering Cross next to an estuary near a plot of land with an ancient little chapel in Florida.

"The Church will be strengthened by trial," said the fictive but real, the contrived but authentic stranger, his eyes toward Saint Patrick's Cathedral, the spires visible from downtown supernormally. And with it might come an auricular hallucination—words heard from nowhere through the physical ear.

No longer would one hear tourists milling about on the observation deck.

Instead, it would be the distinct studied understated German accent of a Pope, Benedict XVI, giving a radio lecture as a professor, Dr. Joseph Aloisius Ratzinger, who'd taught at the

University of Regensburg, in 1969.

"From the crisis of today the Church of tomorrow will emerge—a Church that has lost much," he had actually said back then. "She will become small and will have to start afresh more or less from the beginning. She will no longer be able to inhabit many of the edifices she built in prosperity. As the number of her adherents diminishes, so it will lose many of her social privileges. In all of the upheaval, the Church will find her essence afresh—a more spiritual Church, not presuming upon a political mandate, flirting as little with the Left as with the Right.

"When the trial of this purification is past, a great power will flow from a more spiritualized and simplified Church.

"It is certain that the Church is facing very hard times," he said, almost quoting Hildegard. "The real crisis has scarcely begun. You will have to expect terrific upheavals. But in the end what will remain will not be the Church of the political cult but the Church of faith. It may well no longer be the dominant social power to the extent that she was until recently; but it will enjoy a fresh blossoming and be seen as man's home, where he will find life and hope beyond death."

On March 18, 2023—the day between Saint Pat's feast day and Saint Joseph's—was another "word" on a different aspect of the spiritual trial, the assault on the Church, to the anonymous 1990 recipient.

This one said, "The [UFO] phenomena are sent to direct mankind on errant ways," it claimed, for discernment. "They seek disorientation. They operate at both a spiritual and physical level in how they appear and also at both levels as far as the results they aim to achieve. They come from the source of evil that seeks to send religion and especially Judeo-Christian belief systems to the realm of fantasy, as strange creatures with no affinity for humans are now god. In this way will they seek to discard the works of Jesus. At a higher level, they will cause the same disorientation as gender consternation, but this time in the realms of science and spirituality—connecting them with a bond of falsity."

Gavreel would have a prediction of his own, reiterating another, earlier word from the anonymous locutionist.

"Before the initial event will be a sign. News of the disaster—the first warning—will be heard everywhere.

"And then, soon enough, will be events revealing God's Plan, amid the woes of purification."

Perhaps accompanying such words would be a holograph, another future chimera, the throbbing heart of South America and a cruel sun tracing a painful arc across the heavens, each day meting out hardship. No cloud would dare defy its fierce authority; no shade dare to obstruct its tyrannical searing mandate. Underneath this celestial force, the earth would moan.

So would emaciated children.

Or perhaps it would be a volcano. Suddenly, the earth juddered and groaned like an ancient giant stirred from slumber, releasing a seismic bellow that reverberated for thousands of miles, the primal roar sending soundscapes of terror. A colossal plume of ash, a monstrous monochrome pillar, twisted and raged upwards, as if it sought to claw its way to the very heavens. Chunks of earth, fragments of the mountain's very heart, were hurled into the stratosphere, hell's artillery in this spectacle of mayhem. Rivers of molten rock erupted from the wound, pouring down a mountainside like Niagara, the world bathed in a harsh, uncanny light, its atmosphere choked with the heavy scent of sulfur.

Drought. Famine.

Silty pits where the Amazon once flowed.

There would be war. Its winds were blowing.

"Your era is ending," said the 1990 locution. "Soon the world will not be the world you know. The Lord speaks not of a barren world, or one depopulated, but of the end of your technological era. Many inventions of mankind will be broken down and there will be a peasant way of life," Gavreel would add. "There is some time left before the great wonder, when in the sky will be written the dangers of the day and on earth will be fear, which is the ultimate plague."

I saw a map of Europe and the word 'PLAGUE" superimposed. Somewhere between the coffee shops of Paris and the cobblestones of Rome, where history crumbled beneath the weight of the present, the Black Death—or was it a new coronavirus?—resurfaced. As if chastising the arrogance of the human race, it poured out of its hibernation, devouring not just bodies, but the fabric of the present age.

Over Eurasia—and this was no surprise—was superimposed the word "WAR."

Here too: virus.

In North America: "CHAOS."

"After this breakdown of false society will come persecution of Christians and also a new world order," said the 1990 locution. *"The anti-christ will be on earth trying to affect the new world order. Hardly anyone will notice the extent of his influence until afterward. He will not be of tremendous visibility until he is accomplished. That is to say, he will not rule, control, or be at all obvious to the world at the peak of his influence. He will not be unlike a figure such as Marx, except his ideas will be more immediate."*

Now I "read" the words of President Woodrow Wilson more than a hundred years before, in 1913, in a book called *The New Freedom.* "Since I entered politics, I have chiefly had men's views confided to me privately," he actually had written. "Some of the biggest men in the United States, in the field of commerce and manufacture, are afraid of somebody, are afraid of something. They know that there is a power somewhere so organized, so subtle, so watchful, so interlocked, so complete, so pervasive, that they had better not speak above their breath when they speak in condemnation of it."

Part of the 1990 prophecy had said, "The seat of Satan in America is north of San Francisco."

I saw now row after sterile row of hyper-computers in cabinets at a laboratory for artificial intelligence. I saw the money behind it. I saw Bohemian Grove. I saw the huge statue of an owl overlooking a human effigy aflame as power-brokers from around the world toasted in what they said was only a mock ritual. I saw the gathering of an exclusive club of industrialists and scientists, meeting off the record and out of sight, in Rome. I saw bankers convened in Geneva. I saw meticulously attired attendees hobnobbing at a 19th-century architectural splendor in Lisbon, a castle in all but name, Pestana Palace Hotel, hosting the actual secretive meeting of Bilderbergs: royalty and corporate chieftains and secretaries of state, tech geniuses, media. I saw men manipulated at such conferences. I saw this chandeliered assemblage of Classical style—poetry writ in stone, aloof on a hill—a chapel, sacred and ironic, dedicated to Our Lady of Sorrows. "As for the anti-christ, remember Europe, and especially Central Europe," the 1990 prophecy said. Hungary? Belarus? I saw a laboratory. I'm not sure where it was. I saw a sprawling complex of cold steel and glass, an architectural marvel equal parts aesthetic and functional, as if someone had built a cathedral for science, which had become a great nemesis. I saw another chapel, this one entirely different, a non-denominational one serving the United Nations in New York and appointed with a cold six-ton magnetic "altar" that rested on a pillar below the floor that went into bedrock and—supposedly—tapped into the earth's hyper-dimensional energies, inducing a meditative state for its first caretakers, a group of occultists—this all was factual—based in Manhattan but with offices in London and Geneva, a group that considered Lucifer a "light-worker."

Perplexingly, the 1990 prophecy had also said, "Yet know too that God's Hand will be evident in South America."

I recalled the seer Pachi in Cuenca, Ecuador who had relayed a message from the Virgin on a mountain called El Cajas allegedly informing her that an antichrist was "already in the world. He's acting all over the world through various fields—not directly, but through such things as science," she told me "People don't know him. He is *going* to act directly and we're *going* to know him. He will get to people through television and all the ways of the world. But especially to youth in music and drugs. He is going to act directly in a terrible way after the punishment." Meanwhile Mary told her—what sequence no one knew—that *"at the end of the apparitions in the world, I will leave a great sign in this place and in all those where I have been."*

"Without obedience," an angel at the Freedom Tower might add, "the whole of hell will be unleashed, and the warring spirit of men unchained.

"In your heart, see God for Who He is and what good He brings. The joy that can be yours even in consternation. There is no health without connection to God. He has the life of all in His design.

"The devil has in his design plans of destruction."

"Only with humility is there holiness. Only with humility is there love. Lack of love is the actual root of all evil. It is a lack of love that leads to: mammon, greed, war, crime, lust, theft, idolatry, divorce, murder, and betrayal. Only when the fetters of lust, along with pride, are broken are we free to love. This can stop anything.

"If not, the ash of Sodom is in the eruptions to come."

We headed, in my imagining, for the elevator. I still don't think anyone noticed. Not a person swung a second look at his garb. This time, on the descent, instead of a panorama of the past, I "saw" the future. I again heard Gavreel's gentle but somber voice. "Not since times in history deep ago have men been so skewed in what they perceive with eyes that distort and minds that form reality in a way that has no true destiny."

As the elevator began its plunge, he might add, "Mankind has a choice. It is between this" –

Suddenly out the glass of the elevator was a vista I couldn't have imagined. There were buildings, but now they were beautiful, draped with robust green. Circular terraces with thick tall hedges spiraled around the tallest structures, which were made of some kind of material resembling rammed earth, sawdust, and burnt, compressed, cementitious clay. Rooftops were miniature forests. Bushes were everywhere, quivering with birds. I saw no streets. Perhaps transportation was underground. It was a preparation for Heaven. The air was crystal clear. People congregated on balconies, friendly and joyful, united in total spirit, some openly praying or laying hands on others, or on knees in supplication, praising God. This was key: thanks and praise.

I "saw" a group of men of all races, of all skin tones, in harmony, meeting with holy affection—farming in cooperation not competition with each other. I saw simple clean faces and attire like the tunics in ancient Palestine, nothing synthetic, no plastic, no oil, no polished brass. I saw women praying and noticed their words affected even the crops and weather. I saw lush gardens. I saw fish in erumpent abundance, in crystalline streams. Deer gathered at ponds. There were beaver, fox, otter. Doves roosted. There were many gardens. There were neighborhood farms. It was as if the very trees sang thanksgiving. I saw a convent in perfect repair filled with nuns working with hoes. I saw babies welcomed into the world.

"This is one future," continued Gavreel,

"Or you can choose this."

And in an instant what materialized on the sides of the elevator was a devastated cityscape of iron and bronze and cement, deeply scorched. There no longer was traffic. There was floodwater. I saw horrible panic in the city, marauding, looting, pillaging gangs. I watched them clash, even the elderly turned violent. I saw baleful tattooed spiked leather bikers waging guerilla warfare in a raw chaos that gorged itself on disorder, prowling the crumbling remains like hungry, feral creatures.

I saw a region that had survived. I saw men and women, a few well-coiffed but most waiting in bread lines along with the indigent, missing shoes or other articles of clothing, many with smudged jowls and gray-dusted hair. I saw them try to buy a better spot in line but their credit cards and cash, except for coins, useless. The gods of commerce, those insatiable deities that had once smiled on the city, had abandoned it—had abandoned Central Park South! I saw a crushed felled tangled statue—of Atlas, in Midtown. The currency of barter now was coffee, tea, canned food, batteries, toilet paper, and liquor miniatures. Nickels were coveted for their actual value in silver. I saw rations of Clorox to disinfect drinking water. I saw that only non-perishable food, seed, land, and wood were worth anything. I saw machines idle because people lacked the parts to repair them. I saw nothing electrical functioning. Solar was useless without replacement parts. I saw sewage in streets, and again hooligans—Huns—who had looted every store, targeting gun shops. I saw Chinese and Russians perched on the borders, eyeing the spoils until their nations too came under crushing duress.

Gavreel, if one were to meet him, or any messenger, would say softly, "When God decides something, it happens. The occurrences you have seen will occur over the course of fifteen years.

"During the purification, Michael will again rebuke the devil."

Now I might see into the supernatural. I might witness the havoc of demons through the streets of the city. I would glimpse massive, towering ones, these over entire regions. I would see hordes in various areas. Like horrid insects, some of them. Others, like gray aliens. Armies of the night. Still others, gargoyles perched on the skeletons, the busted ribs, of facades promising to collapse. A few would resemble dark knights. There was a man with chilling sheened eyes dressed in a meticulous suit that was deepest indigo orchestrating everything.

Angels—wanting to intercede—would look on.

As the elevator arrived back at the bottom, I would throw my glance to Gavreel.

He would no longer be there.

He would just be gone.

In this imagery were only chattering tourists, who I could now hear. They glanced at me.

Weeks, months, a few years would pass. Then one day would be a strange loud rumbling—first far off, but slowly drawing close.

The closer, the louder. A reverberation. Fading. Echoing. Stronger. Thunder underground. Or was it in the sky? Now, a high-pitched screech. Then, vibration like a string on a bass fiddle plucked in the bowels of the planet with no musical intent.

It would be haunting. An eerie banshee sound might accompany it. Then, perhaps, several booms. I would leave the city. "A crisis will come that will test the consciences of all," said the last addendum to the anonymous locution, dated July 23, at 5:41 a.m. "This is the enlightenment of the soul, its illumination in the stress of threat, in an era that will see too manifestations in splendor of the Lord."

On the way out I imagined driving in New Jersey along the turnpike looking back to Manhattan and the Statue of Liberty. Then the Freedom Tower. And then I would see it: what looked like a slightly illuminated arc in the sky, but growing, brightening.

It would be the aurora borealis, visible in New Jersey, an atmospheric phenomenon that in some ways would vaguely resemble a gigantic angel.

It would be between the Freedom Tower and 30 Rock.

But of course, it was overarching the entire hemisphere.

Two magnificent arcs of light rising in the east and west from which radiated pulsating beams like searchlights in dark red, greenish blue, and purple like the colors Lucia had seen from her lonely convent, hues that streamed and widened like wings and robe and what might look faintly like a trumpet.

Or was it a sword?

I don't know if there would be shock at such a sight, but I know time is short and that all protection comes with prayer and the Precious Blood and the Bible. I imagine reaching for one—the old Latin Vulgate handed down in my family—noticing it refurbished, with no torn pages, no more pages missing. I might open right to a passage that said, "After these things I looked, and behold, a door standing open in Heaven. And the first voice which I heard was like a trumpet speaking with me, saying, 'Come up here, and I will show you things that must take place after this.

"Hold fast what you have till I come."

At the very end of this, in the Book of Revelation, a missing page.

1375 in Chapter Two.

Looking it up, one would find: "And to the angel in Pergamos write, 'These things says He who has a sharp-edged sword: 'I know your works, and where you dwell, where Satan's throne is. And you hold fast to My Name, and did not deny My faith even in the days in which Antipas was my faithful martyr, who was killed among you, where Satan dwells.

"Hold fast what you have till I come."

Another missing page might be 467, in *Psalms*, torn right after 101:25.

I will never know what happened to that page. I don't even want to know yet. I know that one day soon, after tribulation, the page will reappear.

✝

Notes

CHAPTER 1: For a rundown of apparitions from 1830 on, see *The Final Hour* (Faith Publishing). For the Pope's vision see *Pope Leo XIII and the Prayer to St. Michael*, by Kevin Symonds. For Medjugorje messages, see *Words From Heaven*, issued by Caritas of Birmingham (eleventh edition). For the "mysterious stranger" and also the "word of knowledge," see the "1990 Prophecy," in the archives of Spirit Daily (www.spiritdaily.com). For the Ukrainian visionary, see *Witness*, by Josyp Terelya with Michael H. Brown (Faith Publishing). For the quote from Sister Lucia on the battle, see Frére Michel de la Sainte Trinité's *Third Secret* (Loreto Books).

CHAPTER 2: For the quotes on Sister Lucia's trials and tribulations, see *A Pathway Under the Gaze of Mary*, by the nuns at the Carmel of Coimbra and published by the World Apostolate of Fátima USA. The quote on the northern lights from Lucia is in *Fátima in Lucia's Own Words*, edited by Rev. Louis Kondo (Postulation Center, Fátima, Portugal), which I obtained during a 1989 visit to the site. For Lucia's quotes on the writing of the secret, see again the book published by the nuns in Coimbra. The text of the Third Secret is taken directly from the text released on May 13, 2000, by the Vatican, peculiar grammar and all. For Terelya, once more see *Witness*. For the Soviet naval disaster, see UPI, July 10, 1984, "The Soviet Union's Northern Fleet Has Been crippled."

CHAPTER 3: The report on John Paul II's comments comes from the German publication *Stimme des Glaubens*, which reported the exchange on May 13, 1981. For the Fátima secret, I used the Vatican's official release statement, commentary, and documents.

CHAPTER 4: For Sister Agnes Sasagawa, see *Akita: The Tears and Message of Mary*, by Teiji Yasuda (101 Foundation, New Jersey). Mélanie's secret is in the booklet *Apparition of the Blessed Virgin on the Mountain of LaSalette the 19th of September, 1846*, published by the Shepherdess of LaSalette, with an imprimatur (Monsignor Bishop of Lecce). Also, I visited the apparition site.

CHAPTER 5: For Ukraine, see again my book, *Witness: to Apparitions and Persecution in the U.S.S.R.*, Faith Publishing, 1991. I visited Kibeho in 2010 and also wrote the forward for a book about the apparitions, *Kibeho Rwanda—A Prophecy Fulfilled*, by Father Gabriel Maindro (Marian Spring Centre, Surrey, U.K. 1996). A thorough scholarly treatment of LaSalette and other major places of "secrets" is Sandra L. Zimdars-Swartz, *Encountering Mary of LaSalette to Medjugorje*.

CHAPTER 6: The Consecration of Russia and Ukraine by Pope Francis is taken from the Vatican's news site. For Mate Sego, see Sister Emmanuel's *The Hidden Child of Medjugorje, published by the Children of Medjugorje*. For Sister Lucia describing a "diabolic" trend, see Frére Michel de la Sainte Trinite's *The Whole Truth About Fátima*. The information on Jimmy Savile came from a Netflix documentary series, "Jimmy Savile: A British Horror Story," and Jeffrey Epstein from many news reports. For San Nicolás, see *Messages of Our Lady at San Nicolás*, Faith Publishing.

CHAPTER 7: For the number of undiscovered volcanoes, see *AGU Journal,* "Global Distribution and Morphology of Seamounts," April 6, 2023. For Padre Pio and fire, see Bernard Ruffin's definitive biography, *Padre Pio: The True Story.*

CHAPTERS 8 AND 9: The accounts of Eskimos can be found on YouTube. For events in nature, see my book, *Sent To Earth* (Queenship Publishing). The prophecy at the Vatican in 1976 was by Father Michael Scanlan of Franciscan University and reported by the *National Catholic Register* on June 25, 2020. For Cardinal Carlo Caffarra, see *Desde la Fe* (From the Faith), a weekly issued by the Archdiocese of Mexico in 2016. For various seers, including the one in Brazil, see Spirit Daily (www.spiritdaily.com).

CHAPTERS 10 AND 11: The information on Sievernich comes largely from a personal interview with the seer and also a scholar/translator close to her, Dr. Michael Hesemann. Russia's rate of abortion was derived from *Foreign Policy,* October 3, 2017. and church attendance there can be found in the *Moscow Times,* May 29, 2019. For the toxicity of dioxin, see among other sources my book *The Toxic Cloud.* The information on the cold snap came from CNN, December 25, 2020. For Pope Gregory, see my books, *The Last Secret* (Servant) and *Sent To Earth* (Queenship). For Garabandal, among many sources, see "Our Lady's Prophecies," on the website Garabandal.

CHAPTER 12: For the great aurora, see *The New York Times,* January 26, 1938, "Aurora Borealis Startles Europe; People Flee in Fear, Call Firemen." Lucia's observations were in *Fátima in Lucia's Own Words,* edited by Rev. Louis Kondor (Postulation Center, Fátima, Portugal). The aurora resembling a towering angel was photographed by Juha Kinnunen north of Jyväskylä, Finland, on September 23, 2001, and was posted on Space Weather. Gingrich's comments were in the forward for a book on an electromagnetic attack called *One Second After*, by John Matherson. Howard Storm's comments were in his book, *My Descent into Death*. The information on Rwanda came from a personal visit there as well as the booklet *Kibeho: Rwanda—A Prophecy Fulfilled*, by Father Gabriel Maindron.

CHAPTER 13: Pope Benedict's comments on gender theology came from Dr. John Haas, a former member of the Pontifical Academy for Life, who cited personal correspondence and a conversation at the Vatican in 2014, the year after Benedict relinquished his Petrine office, according to the Catholic *Herald*. For the quotes from Medjugorje, see *Words From Heaven*.

CHAPTER 14: For Crowley, see *The Final Hour* and *Prayer of the Warrior* [this author]. For UFOs and rock stars, see *Alien Rock: The Rock 'n' Roll Extraterrestrial Connection* by Michael Luckman.

CHAPTERS 15 AND 16: The information on Litmanová comes from a website dedicated to the apparitions as well as my personal interview. The information on Valentina Papagna also comes from her website and conversations with her. Sister Lucia's comments on other seers came during an interview with a group headed by Cardinal Ricardo Vidal of the Philippines on October 11, 1993. For Lipa, see *The Final Hour*. The Gallagher quotes came in part from the Facebook page of Archdiocesan Shrine of Santo Niño—Tondo Manila. The Esperanza information came from personal research, conversations, and observations.

CHAPTER 17: For the 1990 prophecies, see my books, *Tower of Light* and *Fear of Fire*. The quotes from the famous near-death experience come from an interview with her and also from her book, *The Ripple Effect*. I interviewed Kimberly Clark and also draw from her book, *After the Light*. The George Ritchie quotes come from websites and his book, *Return From Tomorrow*. (Highly recommended.) The Karen Thomas quotes are from a YouTube video. The quote from Saint Teresa of Avila is from her autobiography.

CHAPTERS 18 AND 19: James Chauncey's book was *Eyewitness To Heaven*. Sarah Menet's quotes are from her book, *There is No Death*. Quotes from Sondra Abrahams are from personal interviews and conversations. *The New Yorker* article was called "The Really Big One," July 13, 2015.

CHAPTERS 20 AND 21: For portals see the "Special Report," *Spirit Daily* July 2023 ("Portals To Other Dimensions?") See also the documentary series on Netflix, "Secrets of Skinwalker Ranch," and another "special report" on *Spirit Daily* about both Skinwalker Ranch and one near Phoenix called "Stardust." A book demonstrating the outbreak in bizarre phenomena, from orbs and UFOs to "bigfoot," werewolves, and other alleged "creatures," is *Creepy Cryptids and Strange UFO Encounters of Pennsylvania* by Stan Gordon, whom I interviewed. For *The Exorcist* and 666 Fifth Avenue, see *The New York Times*, April 14, 2018, "We Need An Exorcist!"

CHAPTERS 22, 23, AND 24: For Edison, see "Eight Famous People Who Believed in Communicating with the Dead," History Channel, October 5, 2021. For Tesla see the website, Super Weird Substance, "The Secular Shaman."

CHAPTERS 25, 26, AND 27: The Jogues quote I first saw upon visiting Auriesville in Upstate New York. For the Seredne prophecy, see *The Final Hour*, previously referenced. Some apparition messages come from the website, After the Warning. The quotes from Makandiwa came from YouTube videos of his sermons. I visited the site of the "Flatwoods Monster" in West Virginia. The Eskimos testimonies are available on YouTube.

CHAPTERS 28, 29, 30, 31: George Ritchie's book was *Return From Tomorrow*. For the bubonic plague and the spiritual backdrop, see *The Last Secret* (available at www.spiritdaily.com). For Raphael Minga Kwete of Kinshasa see www.michaeljournal.org. For Cora Evans, see her book, *Selected Writings*. For "Jennifer," I personally spoke with Father Joel Cycenas. Galuber's messages were on his website. I also reviewed the bishop's initial statement on him. I visited L.A. and extensively toured the neighborhoods cited. Also I interviewed local earthquake experts, as well as national and international ones, including a trip to the University of Tokyo and that city's seismic control center. Nearly a hundred meteorologists, climatologists, seismologists, volcanologists, and asteroid or comet experts were interviewed. For New York City I interviewed seismologists at the Lamont-Doherty Earth Observatory at Columbia University.

CHAPTERS 32, 33, 34: I visited the Hollywood signs area. I also visited various disaster sites, including those to do with hurricanes such as Andrew, Katrina, and Michael. I interviewed Sharon Milliman and also relied and quote from her book, *A Song In the Wind*. Much of the information on Dina Basher came from "The World Report," a newsletter issued by the Pittsburgh Center for Peace in McKees Rock, Pennsylvania, as well as from a video. See also my book *The Day Will Come*. The nun in Nebraska was Mother Nadine Brown of Intercessors of the Lamb. The Hildegard book is *The Five Beasts of St. Hildegard* by Reid J. Turner.

About the author

A former investigative journalist, **MICHAEL H. BROWN**, 71, is the author of thirty books, most of them Christian/Catholic. He has spoken in hundreds of churches, conducted retreats in more than a hundred cities, appeared on numerous TV and radio shows, including *Today, Nightline,* and Mother Angelica Live, and contributed to publications from *Reader's Digest* to *The Atlantic Monthly.* He is the author of bestsellers *The Final Hour, The Other Side,* and *Laying Waste: The Poisoning of America,* and *What You Take To Heaven.* His work uncovering the crisis at Love Canal in Niagara Falls was met with national acclaim. He has been director of the Christian/Catholic news and prophecy website, Spirit Daily (www.spiritdaily.com), since September 29, 2000.

Other Books
by Michael H. Brown

THE FINAL HOUR

TOWER OF LIGHT

AFTER LIFE

THE OTHER SIDE

SENT TO EARTH

THE GOD OF MIRACLES

THE GOD OF HEALING

WHAT YOU TAKE TO HEAVEN

SECRETS OF THE EUCHARIST

THE LAST SECRET

(available at www.spiritdaily.com)

www.ingramcontent.com/pod-product-compliance
Lightning Source LLC
Chambersburg PA
CBHW060903120626
46553CB00001B/186